Evolving World, Converging Man

BOOKS BY ROBERT FRANCOEUR

Perspectives in Evolution
Utopian Motherhood: New Trends in Human Reproduction

Evolving World, Converging Man

Robert Francoeur

HOLT, RINEHART AND WINSTON
New York   Chicago   San Francisco

SBN: 03-084517-3 Trade edition
SBN: 03-085623-X College edition
Printed in the United States of America

DEDICATED TO
MY PARENTS
WHO
STARTED ME ON THE QUEST
FOR MEANING.

contents

preface

Somewhere, perhaps two million years ago, the first men grappled with the inescapable human question of who they were and what their place was in their small but mysterious world. Today we face that same basic human question. Like the men of every era we must develop an image of ourselves which will support and nourish our lives. Yet, as with all past images of man, our image of ourselves is always the genetic and ever dependent offspring of our own unfinished picture of the world we inhabit.

The early Egyptians, Greeks and Chinese developed their unique images of man in religious, mythic and philosophic terms meaningful and satisfying to them by doing exactly what we must do today, by trying to situate the man they knew in their scientific image of the cosmos. The tiny flat earth of primitive man, capped by an eternal unchanging heavenly sphere, reduced him frequently to a helpless pawn of nature and the gods. With the dawn of the scientific western cultures and the birth of astronomy, man's earth mushroomed into a sphere, expanding to embrace unsuspected new lands and peoples. In the process man's religious image of himself expanded. But just as quickly, when Copernicus and Galileo set our earth spinning around the sun and our solar system roaming the reaches of galactic space, the philosophic and religious world of Dante's Divine Comedy and the high Middle Ages yielded to yet another image of man and his place in the world.

A hundred years ago, the revolutionary dimension of time, process and evolution spread from the heavens to our earth, bestowing first on life and then on man in particular an evolutionary history which continues even through today.

Ernst Mayr, the eminent biologist, has noted that *no greater revolution has occurred in the history of human thought than the radical shift from a fixed, stable cosmology to a dynamic, evolving ever-changing cosmogenesis.* That shift is far from complete. In fact, in some areas of our religious and philosophical thought we have hardly begun to explore the changes and modifications forced on us by the perspective of an evolving world.

This book traces the often startling and revolutionary interplay between our ever deepening scientific image of the world and our emerging religious-philosophic image of man. Against this historical backdrop we will sketch a tentative but very contemporary synthesis of the latest scientific views and the most contemporary religious and philosophic interpretations of man and his place in this universe. Drawing on the latest discoveries in paleontology and fossil men, we will explore man's origins and relate this scientific image with an evolutionary reinterpretation of the myths of Genesis and "the fall of man." In this task we will draw on the insights of Protestant, Catholic, Orthodox and Jewish theologians and biblical scholars, on some psychologists, existentialists and even a marxist philosopher. We will propose a complete scrapping of the classic body/soul image of man and the traditional distinction of matter/spirit which has been derived from a fixed, static, pre-Darwinian cosmology, and offer in its place some details of a new process view of man and his world along the lines of Teilhard de Chardin's evolutionary monism. This exploration will take us to a totally new depth in appreciating human nature and the meaning of death and the afterlife. Finally, on a more practical plane, we will raise serious questions about our role today as co-creators with God not merely of our world, but more important of our very own human nature and its future. We have already taken our first steps in the biological revolution. We already exercise some control of our genetic, biological and psychological evolution. We will expand that control drastically in the near future. But to do this with some sense of the rational and a modicum of wisdom, we must have a wholesome and integrated image of man and his world, consistent with our modern scientific image of the world and meaningful in terms of our philosophic and religious traditions.

The process view of man and our world which we propose here is far from complete. In many respects it is quite tentative and sketchy. But hopefully it will encourage and help the reader to explore further and think seriously of the radical impact the evolutionary dimension holds for our image of man and his world.

Evolving World, Converging Man

1

our changing picture
of the world

Modern man lives on a very tiny planet he calls "earth," hurtling through space at an unbelievable speed as it circles a third-class star we proudly label "our sun." These two specks of matter spin near the edge of the Milky Way, a galaxy swarming with some forty billion stars and a hundred billion comets, scattered through space like some monstrous pinwheel. Traveling at 186,000 miles a second, a flash of light takes only 100,-000 years to journey from one edge of this galaxy to the other, and 10,000 years to cross through its thickest region. For light reflected from the moon to reach earth takes but 1.3 seconds, from the sun a brief 8 minutes and from the nearest star 4.3 years.

On a clear moonless night over 2,000 stars can be seen with the naked eye alone. With field binoculars you can count more than 50,000 stars. A simple 2.5 inch telescope reaches out to embrace over a million stars while the giant 100 inch Mount Wilson telescope encompasses over a billion. Many of these stars are smaller than our sun but others make it look like a dwarf. The star Betelgeuse, for instance, is 400 times larger and 3,600 times brighter than our sun.

The 2,000 stars you can see with the naked eye all belong to our Milky Way, only one of several million galaxies cartwheeling through space. Light from the galaxy Andromeda, our nearest neighbor, travels for 1.7 million years to reach our earth, a short trip when one considers that most galaxies in the universe are more than 5 million light years apart.

If this picture of the universe stuns us with its immense, unimaginable dimensions, we should not be discouraged. Our own amazement, though, should help us understand and appreciate the reactions other men have experienced in ages past. Today's world of outer space is no more amazing to us than the discovery of a whole New World was to Columbus, or the first sight of Jupiter's moons was for Galileo. Each generation has had to face and ultimately accept the revolution created by the discovery of a "new world" beyond man's comprehension.— Beyond man's comprehension, perhaps, but after a while, men of every generation learn to live with their "new" world. Their patterns of thoughts, their everyday language, their theology and philosophy, soon learn to incorporate the amazing and startling new dimensions.

Modern astronomy has shown us the staggering smallness of man and his place in the universe: lost in unmeasureable reaches of space, a forlorn, lonely figure living a few brief years on an infinitesimal speck of matter adrift in an ocean of stars, comets, planets and empty space. Yet at the same time modern science has revealed the living cell, plant and animal as realities far more complex and highly organized in their activities than the most gigantic star or planet. Unlike the atom, molecule, cell, animal and man, the planets and stars are aggregates of jumbled matter, very much like unorganized piles of sand and gravel. We have only to examine the high degree of order and systems of energy, bonds of affinity, etc., which create the atom or molecule; we have only to examine the highly integrated and organized reality we call man's body, to appreciate the difference between an aggregate and a complexity. Even the interplanetary rockets with their over 138,000 working parts, or the electronic computers, both of which are creations of man, cannot compare in complexity with a tiny human baby whose body is composed of over 200 million cells all functioning together smoothly in an organism. This distinction between a true complex being and a mere aggregate is of vital importance, for many, like Teilhard de Chardin, are convinced that it is the key by which we can learn today man's important role in the universe.

There has always been something in man's nature telling him, so to speak, that no matter how large his world may become he will always have an important and even vital role to play in it. Centuries ago men had to find their place in the unknown and expanding "new" worlds of Marco Polo, Galileo and Columbus. Today, we face the same sort of task, perhaps on a larger scale, but still the same endless search for man's place in the universe. No matter what our picture of the world may be, whether it be the simple world of the Chosen People in the days of Abraham, the world of Dante and Aquinas, or the expanding universe of modern astronomy, man always faces the task of finding his role in the cosmic drama in which he is immersed.

Today the vast evolutionary tree of life is crowned by a creature capable of reflection and thought, a creature not only conscious and aware of the world outside himself and able to respond to that outer world, but also a creature conscious of his inner self and being. Darwin's finches may use cacti needles to probe for grubs and Jane Goodall's chimpanzees may fashion sponges of leaves or sticks into handy tools, but man is the only creature we know who fashions tools and machines to help him obtain a better picture of the universe in which he lives. Man is the only animal to forge instruments that make the invisible visible or that imitate and accelerate fantastically his mind's ability to compute and analyze.

In the past four centuries these instruments have helped man gain more and more control over his world, to delve deeper into the mysteries of the living cell and the atom, and to probe the realities of the heavens. Modern man can measure the astronomical distances of outer space and the infinitesimal distances within the atom. He can speak of light years or milliseconds. His computers answer in minutes mathematical problems that stagger the imagination, problems that would absorb all the energies of a team of scientists working over several generations. Telephones, radio and television, communication satellites, radio telescopes and electron microscopes expand man's senses into every corner of the world.

But it takes the unique self-conscious mind of man to turn these extensions of our senses into a meaningful pattern. All the sense impressions of telescope and microscope, of television camera and radio microphone come to focus in the human mind. In man something unique happens as the evolving universe becomes conscious of itself. In his art, science, work and play man forms a sounding board for the cosmos and in so doing he also continues and expands his search for meaning and a place in the cosmos.

To understand that search and our modern answer it is necessary to go back some million or more years when, after eons of slow, tedious evolution, man first appeared on this earth and began his perennial quest. The past is the key to both man's present place in the cosmos and to our preparation for the future. A decade or two ago the age of outer space and the computer dawned. Less than four hundred years ago the telescope and microscope caused a revolution in our picture of the world. Ten thousand years ago man learned to make tools of iron and bronze. And yet, man has been on this earth for more than a million years! During that time, man's picture of the world has changed drastically, growing with every new discovery and invention, sometimes maturing imperceptibly and at other times undergoing violent revolutions. New data and dimensions have been uncovered; new ways of looking at this data and organizing it have been discovered. We build on past world images, and yet we also at times create revolutions within this continuity of development.

Early man had only his senses and native intelligence with which to face the world. He had no written language and very little if any tradition or history to rely on in his attempts to understand the universe and his place in it. His knowledge of the world was limited to what he had seen for himself in his limited travels on foot and the lively, often exaggerated, tales of friendly nomads. His world was encircled by the nearest mountain range, forest, desert or sea. On every side, early man was surrounded by the unknown. He struggled with the world, wrestled with it, puzzled over its meaning, armed only with his senses and ability to reason.

From earliest times, man was forced to be a student of the world. His life depended on how well he managed to understand and master the elements that surrounded him. In the struggle to survive he relied on his skills as a hunter and his growing appreciation of the cycles evident in the seasons and changes of nature as well as his understanding of the habits of wild animals. His life was, if anything, a harsh and brutal struggle. More often than not it ended abruptly and violently when, in the constant search for food, he fell prey to marauding beasts. Few men ever lived to old age. Arthritis and rheumatism brought on by sleeping in damp caves or the open, parasite-infected, uncooked meat, and other problems of existence shortened man's life expectancy so that two or three decades was considered a ripe old age.

Though early man spent most of his waking hours fighting to survive in a hostile world, he still found time to think seriously about his place in the world. There were many things that made sense in the world he knew, certain experiences fitted naturally and easily into predictable and unpredictable patterns. Night always followed day, and the seasons had their regular cycles. Winter may have been the hardest season but it always gave way to the warmth renewal of spring. Nature was provident with food if one was an observant and wise hunter.

At the same time there were mysterious and quite unpredictable events. The sun meant warmth and food, but it could also bring a scorching drought with little warning. The cool spring rains usually meant new life for the forests and an abundance of food, but they could also bring a flash flood and disaster. Streams and lakes provided fish and an easy means of travel, yet sudden storms could turn their calm waters into a heaving, rolling monster capable of shattering man's puny vessels in death. Friendly cool breezes could become violent tornadoes and typhoons. The regular patterns of sun and moon could be interrupted by awesome eclipses. Stars and planets sometimes seemed to change into frightening comets or shooting stars. In many ways, the world was (and still is) quite unpredictable and uncontrollable.

Brute animals react instinctively to their surroundings generally without being able to modify or adapt their fixed behavior to new challenges and environments. Man, on the other hand, constantly strives to adapt himself not only to the obviously patterned events of his life but also to those experiences and realities which seem to fit no known pattern.

In the adaptation man constantly seeks general patterns into which he can fit new information and experiences. Confronted with a puzzling world, early man soon realized the necessity of a general pattern or overall picture. And when he found no visible or "natural" answer for certain unpredictable elements of the puzzle, he created his own answers. Myths (and some legends) were created in the attempt to show the real meaning behind the unexplained occurrences of life.

Today we are inclined to think of a myth as some sort of fable or fairy tale. Our first impression of the myths of ancient Rome and Greece, the stories of Zeus, Apollo, Venus and Mercury, is that these sacred myths have no historical basis or truth. But myths, whether primitive or modern, are serious attempts to account for and explain the unknown within an overall meaningful pattern or world vision. In the culture of primitive peoples, where the distinction between magic, religion and science is very blurred and undeveloped, sacred myths combine and interweave elements of all three approaches. Early man developed the sacred myth to explain elements of his experience which could not be explained in terms of concrete experience. Thus, the sacred myth is a very special form of history, as Mircea Eliade has clearly shown, aimed at explaining certain *cosmic* events in terms of a "supernatural" action. Early man had no scientific or experimental explanation for such ordinary events as storms, tornadoes, eclipses, or even the fire, wind and life itself. Likewise his science told him nothing about the creation or origins of his earth and the universe. The sacred myth was his answer. It enabled him to fit these unexplained phenomena into a total and understandable image of the world.

Modern man faces similar problems with phenomena unexplainable in terms of today's scientific knowledge, and in our own inimitable sophistication, we too resort to the myth as an answer. But today, with the development of experimental science and a more critical theological mind, we are very careful about limiting the scope of our myths to a single plane, either of science or of religion. If you listen carefully to a good scientific explanation of the phenomenon of heredity and life contained in the alpha helix of DNA, the chromosome chain of life, or to the various astrophysical explanations about the origins of our earth, it is easy to detect a mythic element, shorn however of any "supernatural intervention." Our knowledge of heredity, life and the origins of the universe are far more extensive and profound today than they were in the days of Ptolemy, Galileo, or Darwin. But whether we speak of Darwin's "pangens" or the Watson and Crick DNA code, Laplace's cosmogenic theory of planetary collisions or the modern pulsation theory, we are still trying to explain what today still escapes man's full grasp. An important difference, and one we should note, between the primitive "sacred myth" and our modern scientific myths is the fact that modern scientists prefer to look upon their myths as "working hypotheses" which stimulate and challenge man's efforts to find a more complete answer rather than rest on his laurels in the belief that his myth contains the whole answer.

The sacred or religious myth of the primitive is, in its own way, *true history*. As Mircea Eliade has shown, it is sacred because it deals with the ultimate realities of man's life in terms of the supernatural actions of the gods in some primordial, timeless heaven. Such myths are also cosmic since they attempt to explain the origins of our earth, the sun, moon or stars, or the origins of some human custom. The sacred myth, however, is not simply an imaginary explanation. It has even today a very practical function for primitive man, a use which highlights the very close relationship between magic, religion and science in the early days of mankind. Primitive man believed that if he knew how something in his world actually came into existence, he could control or manipulate it to his advantage.

This is the function of magic, and the man who knows one of the sacred cosmic myths in some way shares in the sacred action of creation it relates.

We have only the slightest traces today of these religious myths created thousands of years ago at a time when man had only an oral tradition. The myths of Greece and Rome represent highly developed and sophisticated forms of these early myths, divested of their magical function. It is, in fact, almost impossible to see in them anything of the original form of the sacred cosmic myths. Fortunately, there are a few primitive societies still extant today, in Australia, South America and Africa, where the sacred myth can be studied in its near original form. Like his ancestor thousands of years ago, the Australian aborigine is convinced that the wise man, the tribal medicine man, possesses power over the forces of nature simply because he knows the sacred myths of creation. Because the medicine man knows how the gods created rain in the timeless golden age, he can teach others the rain dance which not only repeats in dramatic form that creation but also, by appeasing the gods, induces them to send rain to a parched earth. The sand paintings of the North American Indian are always designed by the ancients of the tribe, the men of wisdom who learned the myths of creation from their ancestors long ago. By repeating the story of man's creation in a sand painting, the medicine man can almost force the gods to cure a sick Indian. Such is the practical side of the sacred myth.

This functional aspect of the primitive sacred myth leads us to consider the closely related origins of science. The sacred myth tried to explain nature in terms of the actions of the gods. The early cosmogonies were attempts to explain the world and its creation in terms of science and experimental knowledge. But as is evident in the studies of Eliade and others, these two approaches to reality often mingle and interweave in primitive cultures.

Science was born of man's attempt to understand his world and control it. In this effort, science, magic and religion have often collaborated. Science was, in fact, born with its roots in the magic and religious practices of primitive societies centuries past. Ethnologists have shown how our more advanced civilizations were formed from the fusion, in varying amounts, of three primary cultures: that of the hunters, the herdsmen and the farmers or peasants. Each of these primary cultures had its own system of magic and religious beliefs, some of which have persisted even into our modern life.*

The totemistic magic of the hunters, the first of these three primary cultures, is based on the belief that some animal or natural object is related by blood to a certain family or tribe. The family or tribe then takes the animal or object as its magical totem, a symbol of power over certain forces in the world. The North American Indian and Eskimo offer beautiful examples of this practice. Over the centuries the totemistic magic of the hunters has contributed more to the rise of art than to the advance of science. It seems, in fact, that our modern science has developed more from a combination of the other two primary cultures, those of the herdsmen and farmers.

Man, as we have noted, experiences some unexplained compulsion to control and dominate the world around him. This control can be achieved through a study of the so-called laws of nature which are actually deductions and generalizations made by man rather than *unchangeable* principles of behavior written in the heart of nature. Man can deduce a general pattern, which we call a law, from his varied experiences and this pattern can be very useful in his daily life. But man can also learn to control his world by social contacts wherein he sets up certain rules of behavior governing those social contacts. The first approach to mastery of the world entails a study and con-

---

* The "primary societies" discussed here should not be taken in the sense of a literal history of culture. The distinction serves rather to set up conceptual typologies which have some relation to ecological and economic patterns of life. As trends they do not refer to historically identifiable peoples, but to a very broad development sequence in the evolution of human culture. For example, strictly speaking, there never has been a truly matriarchal society in which women have had all the power. There are, of course, communities and cultures where the relationship is determined chiefly through the mother's lineage. In these matrilineal cultures the males still hold the main authority since the mother's brother, rather than her husband, is responsible for what we in our patriarchal pattern term "fatherly duties."

trol of matter, while the second requires a mastery of words and the ability to communicate.

In general, primitive people do not distinguish clearly between animate and inanimate matter. (And in this they may be more modern than we think, a point we will discuss later.) The control of nature, both animate and inanimate, then, assumes two basic forms, depending on whether one is concerned more about the mastery of the laws of nature, or the mastery of words. The primary cultures of the herdsmen and the farmers place different emphasis on these two approaches.

In the patriarchal herdsman society the emphasis rests on a mastery of the word. The tribe of Abraham in the Old Testament is a typical example of this approach with its shamanistic magic. The story of Abraham and his family offer many examples of man's attempt to control nature by incantations and magical formulae. If the chosen people were ever to learn the true name of Elohim they would then hold a magical power over God. They would own him, much as Adam gained control over the animals of the world simply by naming them.

The matriarchal societies of the early farmers, on the other hand, placed more emphasis on magical practices aimed at achieving mastery over matter as such. In this approach models rather than names are crucial. Thus the Voodoo magician makes a man sick by sticking needles into a model he has made of that person.

Another aspect of man's control of nature is the foretelling of future or unknown events. Methods of divination or prophecy in the two primary cultures parallel their emphasis on words or models. Among the patriarchal societies, divination is based on living organic systems: the flight of birds, the cracks in an oracle bone or the entrails of a sacrificial animal. In such divinations the sage who interprets the patterns is all important. His success as a prophet depends on how well he can read the signs of nature. The link between the unknown event and the seer is a psychological type of causality. When someone tells a person to do something and he immediately does it, the man who gave the order may very well think he is the cause of the second person's action. And in a way he is. Psychological causality applies to the interaction of two living systems, one acting and the other reacting or responding. Prophecy and divination based on psychological causality remains always a probable forecast at best, since the person giving the order is never quite sure that the other party will respond as desired.

In the matriarchal system of the farmer, success in the harvest of crops is directly determined by the smooth change of seasons which in turn is due to the immutable course of the stars. The belief that the stars are active causes, controlling the fate of everything on this earth implies a concept of causality, as Professor Taschdjian suggests in the Introduction to his book on *Organic Communications*, in which a heavenly force acts on a completely passive body. In this culture the outside cause *produces* the effect rather than *induces* it. Since an outside force actually causes an inert body to move and since spatial movements are reversible, this approach to magic tries to explain phenomena by reducing them to reversible identities. The Voodoo magician maintains that the cause, his sticking pins in a doll, is identical with the effect, the man getting sick or dying. This is a logical rather than a psychological approach to magic, infallible in its context.

Modern science can be traced back to these earliest and most primitive attempts to master and control the world around us. Today the scientist pursues the mastery of the world. For some this mastery is linked with an attempt to make a working model of something in nature; for others it seems to depend more on coming up with the proper descriptive name for some process, structure, organism or system. But whether they emphasize the creation of working models or the determination of proper scientific names, the result eventually is *a cosmogony, a theory or explanation of how this universe came into being and how it continues to operate.*

The sacred myths and scientific cosmogonies of primitive peoples are instructive because they represent man's earliest attempts to understand, appreciate and thus control the universe. Our understanding of the modern scientific image of the world and its relationship to our religious picture can only deepen and crystallize when we come to appreciate the relationship of early sacred myths and cosmogonies. Early man did not know how to separate the scientific from the religious, and one wonders whether modern man, despite his protestations to the contrary, has done much better in this regard.

In this context certain characteristics show up repeatedly in the sacred myths and early cosmogonies. First, both are serious attempts to explain the origin and beginning of things. They weave together in a single overall pattern concepts drawn from early man's daily life, from his science as well as from his religious and magical practices and beliefs. Second, these myths and cosmogonies invariably tell of man's attempt to gain the upper hand in a seemingly hopeless struggle against the overwhelming "eternal" forces of nature. Man lives and dies, passing unnoticed like the ashes of autumn leaves, yet the world and the heavens remain eternally unchanged, or so it seems. A third and final characteristic, and a crucial one for our future discussion, is the fact that both the sacred myth and the early cosmogonies present a changeless world, created perfect and complete in its essence from the very first moment of time. Only man's perversion and weakness turned a paradise into a place of tribulation and trial. These three characteristics should be kept in mind as we pursue the modern scientific and religious aspects of man's changing world image.

Among the earliest myths and cosmogonies known today is one from ancient India, perhaps five thousand years old. This primitive account pictures the world as a flat piece of land completely surrounded by sea, both of which were spread over a huge tray or platform resting on the backs of three gigantic elephants which stood on the back of an even more monstrous tortoise.

The early Egyptians also believed that our world was flat. Mixing religious beliefs with early scientific observations, their image of the world relates its birth from the mating of the earth god, Keb, and the sky goddess, Nut. For the Egyptians, the sky was a heavenly river, the Nile, along which their sun god, Ra, sailed from east to west each day. During the night Ra stole beneath the surface of the earth, through the abode of the dead, to return to his starting point in the east before the next dawn. Occasionally on these trips, a giant serpent would attack the sun god's boat. And though Ra always routed the dragon, the sun would be darkened in an eclipse during the struggle.

Many similar myths dealing with the creation and nature of our world could be detailed but one particular world image is central for our concern here: that developed by the Babylonians some 2,500 years before Christ. This image dominated most of western man's attempts to understand the world until a few centuries ago when Copernicus and Galileo introduced a new approach. The Babylonian image has not only influenced our scientific cosmogonies, but also our religious understanding of the world. When the authors of Genesis set about explaining the context in which God made a covenant with the sons of Abraham they eventually traced this covenant back to the beginning of the cosmos, but they had to do this in terms of a cosmology intelligible to the Hebrews of that day. In portraying the origins of the world and mankind the men who composed the book of Genesis with its several accounts of creation based their story on the Babylonian cosmogony.

Like most early cosmogonies, the Babylonian image of the world weaves together both mythical and scientific elements. *Enuma Elish* tells of the hero Marduk who slays the dragon-goddess Tiamat and carves up her corpse to fashion the heavens and the earth. The earth was pictured as an immense mountain surrounded by and floating on a vast ocean. Above the earth was the solid vault of the heavens, the firmament, which rested like an inverted bowl on the waters of the great deep. Above the land the firmament provided support for the sun, moon, stars and planets as well as occasional portals for the rain which originated in the waters above the firmament.

To see the relationship between the Babylonian concept of the world and the story of creation recorded in Genesis we must go back eighteen centuries before Christ when the family of Abraham lived outside the city of Harran on the Euphrates River in northern Mesopotamia. Abraham and his family were herdsmen, semi-nomads who worshiped the many gods of their pagan culture, especially the moon god Sin and his queen Nin-gal. Over the years, prompted by the Spirit, Abraham and his family grew in their trust of the one God, El Shaddai, the God of Harran. Prompted no doubt by the Hurrian invasion, Abraham left the city of Harran and plunged into the wilderness, a pilgrim. Out of this experience emerged the Chosen People, the descendants of Abraham. Abraham's only accomplishment, but a major one nevertheless, was his gradual acceptance and growing belief in the supremacy of God, El Shaddai, whom Genesis calls Elohim or Yahweh. Looking back on this legendary history the authors of Genesis, a thousand years later, saw in Abraham's survival and subsequent prosperity a sign to the chosen people that Elohim is indeed the one true supreme God. Into Abraham's prilgrimage the authors of Genesis read a faith in God and the theme of a Promised Land. "Go out from your country and from your kindred and from your father's house and come into a land which I will show you. It is Yahweh who speaks."

As a nomadic tribe wandering through the harsh deserts of the Persian peninsula, the early Hebrews had little time or inclination for science, astronomy or philosophy. The little they knew of the world was borrowed from their neighbors, particularly the Babylonians. The Hebrew people were in frequent contact with the Babylonian and other pagan city-states flourishing in the Near East from the days of Abraham to the time of the great king, Nebuchadnezzar. In 597 Nebuchadnezzar conquered the Hebrews, deporting most of them to serve as slaves in his capital. These influences come to surface in the expression the Hebrew people gave their religious beliefs, first in oral traditions handed down by word of mouth and then after centuries in the written accounts that finally were compiled into the book we now know as Genesis.

Whereas the Babylonians blended the mythical elements of polytheism with the scientific in their myth of creation, the Hebrews radically modified the picture by inserting a monotheistic heart into the cosmogonic details they borrowed from the Babylonians.

For many centuries afterwards, in fact, down almost to the end of the 16th century after Christ, the world image common in western civilization was very much the same image held by the early Babylonians and Hebrews. Even the vast communications network and explorations that accompanied the building of the Roman Empire added little to this world image. A Greek geographer named Strabo, for instance, traveled a good deal during the first century of Christianity. His maps picture a very small world, a flat irregular island traversed by a long chain of mountains and surrounded by a vast ocean.

Not everyone at that time, of course, agreed with this picture of the world. Anaxagoras, a Greek philosopher and mathematician teaching in Athens 500 B.C., was banished from his homeland and threatened with death for suggesting that the sun was a ball of fire almost as large as Greece. Yet the Pythagoreans and other Greek thinkers accepted the assumption that the earth was spherical instead of flat.

One hundred years later Aristotle, a very capable scientist as well as a leading western philosopher, wrote numerous books dealing with such varied topics as physics, mathematics, politics, botany, zoology and philosophy. In his book on astronomy, *About the Heavens*, Aristotle made some common-sense observations which today might seem trivial and self-evident, even though they were far from obvious to the men of Greece 350 B.C. In support of his belief that the earth is round rather than flat, Aristotle pointed out that only a spherical earth could explain why the hulls of ships sailing out to sea disappear before their sails do. He also argued that eclipses of the moon are due to the shadow of our earth passing across the lunar surface. Since that shadow is round, our earth must be round.

Though Aristotle was well respected as a learned teacher, the ordinary man in the street paid little attention to his suggestion. They found it hard to imagine a round earth where people and boats at the antipodes would not be upside down or fall off into space. Naturally, people in those days did not understand the forces of gravity which "pull" everything on our earth's surface towards its center.

Two hundred years before Christ, a famous scientist named Eratosthenes lived in the Greek colony of Alexandria in Egypt. He had heard from friends in Cyene, a city further up the Nile near today's Aswan Dam, that during the summer solstice the noon sun was directly overhead and vertical objects in the city cast no shadow. From his own experience Eratosthenes knew that on the same day the noon sun cast a fair shadow from vertical buildings in Alexandria. This he explained by suggesting that the earth was spherical. Since the angle of shadow in Alexandria was seven degrees and a circle has 360 degrees, he calculated that the total circumference of our earth should be fifty times the distance between the two cities which was about 500 miles. This early estimate, 25,000 miles, comes very close to our best modern estimates.

For early man to imagine a world several hundred times larger than the world he knew, and a world which was almost totally unexplored and unknown, was perhaps asking too much. Eratosthenes and his fellow astronomers were ignored, and men went on believing in a flat earth.

One of the most important steps leading to our modern world image was the gradual realization that Aristotle and Eratosthenes were right about the earth being round. Exactly when this realization became dominant in western thought is unknown, but by the second century after Christ, geographers were drawing maps of a spherical world. Ptolemy, an Egyptian geographer, was one of the most influential astronomers and mathematicians of that era. His maps show fairly accurate details of Europe, Asia and North Africa, but beyond this was only "terra incognita" and the Sea of Darkness.

Once man learned that his earth was round, he quite naturally had to rework his image of the universe in terms of this new scientific knowledge. It was taken for granted that the earth was the immobile center of the universe and that all the heavenly bodies revolved around it each day. This was only a common-sense, everyday observation. There were no telescopes as yet and no reason to suspect that the earth was not the immobile center of the universe, just as it had been in the earlier Babylonian and Hebrew world image.

The great Italian poet of the Middle Ages, Dante Alighieri (1265–1321) based the whole geography of his *Divine Comedy* on Ptolemy's image of the universe. In this beautiful allegory of man's sojourn on this earth, Dante pictures the earth as a sphere at the very center of the universe with the stars, planets and sun arranged around it in ten concentric spheres. Dante placed all mankind and the whole then known world on one side of the earth with Jerusalem and Golgotha at the very center of the inhabited world. Descending into the bowels of the earth, Dante pictured it as hollowed out in seven, funnel-shaped layers. On the uppermost and broadest level, near the surface of our world, were the souls of those who died without baptism and the virtuous pagans who died before Christ. The lower levels were peopled with the damned of hell. Satan had his throne at the bottom of this subterranean cavity, at the center of the earth.

As Dante continued his allegorical journey past Satan and along the tortuous path leading through the hemisphere of water, the Sea of Darkness, he reached the other side of the world. Here he found a lone mountain in the center of the Sea of Darkness, its craggy peak divided into seven layers, one for each of the seven capital vices. On the seven levels of Purgatory, sinners worked out their sinful actions until proper atonement was made and they were ready for Paradise. Climbing the mountain of Purgatory, Dante finally arrived at the gates of Eden, from which Adam and Eve had long ago been exiled. His allegorical sojourn then took him on a tour of the ten celestial spheres, domain of the angels and saints. God's throne was located in the tenth and outermost sphere where, according to the astronomer Ptolemy, perfect calm and peace reigned. The celestial spheres were eternal, changeless and without blemish, an ideal setting for the Paradise Christians hoped to attain after death.

The medieval image of the universe, so picturesquely portrayed by Dante, is a harmonious blending of concepts drawn from the physical sciences, philosophy and theology of the day. It presents a sophisticated theological explanation of man and his place in the universe, a definite advance over the more primitive image drawn by the earlier Babylonians, Egyptians and Hebrews. One of the key factors leading to this more sophisticated theological view was the important shift brought about by the acceptance of a spherical earth instead of the simple flat saucer image.

The next major change in our image of the universe came during the Renaissance when men began to explore the unknown lands that populated Dante's Sea of Darkness. Again, since theological explanations are always intimately interwoven and based on our scientific image of the world, certain modifications were forced on the theologians.

For many centuries Christians had looked on the Bible as literally true in every detail. Quite naturally and without question they accepted the belief that God created the world in six days and rested on the seventh. They likewise accepted as literally true the ages of the great biblical patriarchs. Word for word, they accepted the account of the great flood of Noah which according to Genesis covered the whole earth and wiped out every living creature save those in the ark. When the known world consisted only of the Roman Empire, it was easy for people to believe these accounts as true historical records of actual events. Still, questions raised by Aristotle, Eratosthenes and others did create some doubts for those versed in both the physical and theological sciences.

If the deluge covered the whole earth, then scholars would have to explain how animals and plants spread again over the earth after the waters receded from Mount Ararat where the ark supposedly came to rest. In the fifth century, Augustine, the famous bishop of Hippo in North Africa, suggested that God used a number of means to redistribute the animals after the flood. Frogs and snakes and the like were no problem since they could be spontaneously produced from the mud left by the flood. Gnats, fleas, mosquitoes and flies also could come from the mud just as mice and rats were produced spontaneously by dirt in dark corners. Domesticated animals reached distant and new lands when early, unknown explorers took them along on their migrations. But the migration of the wild animals was another problem. For islands close to shore, one might conjecture that wolves and other beasts of the wild swam or floated out to them. When the distance from shore seemed to rule out this explanation, Augustine proposed that some early, unknown explorer might have taken wild animals along with him to provide sport for hunting. Apparently the logic of a small raft crowded by wild beasts and the navigator did not trouble Augustine. Finally, when all other explanations failed, the angels could always be called upon for assistance.

Augustine's explanation of the flood appeared very sensible in terms of the scientific knowledge of his day, and Christians generally accepted it as the best explanation until the Crusades began to expand man's image of the world. The voyages of Marco Polo, Magellan, Vasco da Gama and Columbus placed increasing strain on the belief that the deluge had covered the whole surface of the earth. But before this problem could be solved by the theologians, another perhaps more pressing problem came into focus.

In 1632 Galileo Galilei published his *Dialogue Concerning the Two Great Systems of the World.* This controversial work discussed two quite different images of the universe: the classic earth-centered image of Ptolemy accepted by Christians everywhere, and the new heliocentric system proposed by the Polish priest and astronomer, Copernicus, a century earlier. Plato had, according to tradition, told the astronomers of his day that they must explain the motions of heavenly bodies in terms of uniform circular movements or orbits. For the stars this was a simple matter since one could assume, as Ptolemy and Dante had, that all the stars were fixed on spheres revolving around the earth once a day. To account for the irregular movements of the seven "wanderers," the sun, the moon and the five then known planets, Aristotle proposed fifty-five spheres. Later astronomers reduced the number of spheres by working with eccentric circles and epicycles in a complicated system that Galileo and Johannes Kepler found quite unacceptable. The revolt against the classic geocentric universe gained further momentum when Galileo's thirty power telescope led to the discovery of Jupiter's satellites and spots on the sun which, in the Ptolemaic universe, was supposed to be spotless, eternal and perfect.

The image of the universe proposed by Copernicus, Galileo and Kepler was a new world, its movements no longer centered on man and this earth. The perfect spherical orbits of the heavenly bodies disappeared as the telescope reached further into space and, in the process, certain theological explanations began to appear irrelevant and meaningless.

In 1675 Olaus Roemer added to the discontent with the old world image and the theological explanations based on it when he discovered that there is a slight delay in the reappearance of one of Jupiter's satellite moons after an eclipse. Until this discovery the accepted belief was that light travels instantaneously. The lag observed by Roemer indicated that light from the moons of Jupiter, which are spread out in space, take different lengths of time to reach the earth. On this evidence Roemer concluded that light travels at a definite, finite speed. The dimension of time, a crucial element in our modern world image, thus began to work its way into man's thinking.

The temporal dimension exposed by Roemer ultimately prepared the way for an acceptance of cosmic evolution, the temporal development of the universe.

The new science of astronomy added many details to a new image of the universe as a changing and evolving system. Slowly *cosmogenesis replaced a fixed, static cosmos.* Isaac Newton (1642–1727) and Johannes Kepler (1571–1630) pictured the heavens as a sort of celestial machine operated by gravity. They kept God in their image of the universe by casting him in the role of creator of this vast cosmic machine long ago at the beginning of time. Once established or constructed in the beginning the machine simply ticked on like some gigantic clock. But slowly pieces began to fall into place in a way that suggested an evolutionary image for the universe. In 1717 Edmund Halley calculated that our whole solar system is drifting through space towards some distant goal. Emmanuel Kant (1724–1804) and the astronomer Pierre Laplace (1749–1827) proposed for the first time the scientific concept of a cosmic evolution, *a gradual development and growth of our solar system and the whole universe in time.* Thus, time as a dimension of thought slowly began to take on definite features. The concept of extremely slow changes occurring with the passage of time, the concept of evolution, was first applied to the heavens. Only gradually and after many struggles among both scientists and theologians was this perspective applied to the geological history of our earth, to living organisms, and finally, within the last hundred years, to man himself. By 1750 most scientists had accepted the idea of an evolution of the heavens. But the idea that our earth might also be changing or evolving had been suggested by only a few daring thinkers, who, quite naturally, were ignored as wild, perhaps insane dreamers. The idea that living organisms, or man, might evolve was almost unthinkable for even the most venturesome minds of the eighteenth century.

Shortly before the astronomers discovered the changing temporal dimension of the heavens, the Reverend John Lightfoot, an eminent biblical scholar and former vice-chancellor of Cambridge University, announced that he had made a careful analysis of the ages of the patriarchs and other Old Testament personages. From this study he concluded that man had been created by the Trinity on September 17, 3928 B.C., at nine o'clock in the morning. Archbishop Ussher, Primate of Ireland, carried this calculation another step, setting the date for the great deluge at 2348 B.C. and October 23, 4004 B.C. for the first day of creation. Thus, while the heavens might be evolving, most Christians in the eighteenth century were convinced that the earth was then just as it had always been.

Towards the end of the eighteenth century, all Europe was fascinated with James Watt's steam engine. The age of the machine had dawned and everything was pictured in terms of mechanics. Men even pictured the earth as some gigantic clock wound up at the moment of creation and ticking away ever since, always the same and never really changing.

The first hints that the dimension of time and evolution might also apply to the earth came when James Hutton (1726–1797), a Scottish geologist, stated that he could find "no vestige of a beginning, no prospect of an end" for the earth. If this was true, if the layers of our earth gave no indication of a beginning, then what of the biblical chronologies and dates worked out by Lightfoot and Ussher?

Very quickly the questions raised by the new science of geology piled up, throwing a growing doubt on the *continued* validity of classic theological explanations about creation and the origin of our universe. The classic explanations were useful and valid for past ages, but might not Christians of the eighteenth century require new theological explanations in keeping with their changing scientific world image?

For many centuries men had been intrigued and puzzled by curious rocks we now call fossils. Aristotle was among the first to discuss these imitations of the living world. While the scientists puzzled over their real significance, ordinary people collected fossils as amulets, good luck charms, or trinkets. Some scholars thought they were working models discarded by the Creator as he laid out plans for the world; others thought they might be models for some future creation. The superstitious viewed them as sports and freaks of nature, formed by the action of some supernatural principle within the rocks which originally came from the stars. For others, fossils were instruments of the devil, deceptive temptations intended to mislead man into proud curiosity about the mysteries of the earth which were none of his business. "Porous bodies petrified by a lapidifying juice, or produced by the tumultuous movements of terrestrial exaltations!"

For people who insisted on taking the biblical account of creation as literally true in every detail, fossils were indeed a puzzlement. The learned Cotton Mather (1663–1728) offered an ingenious solution after carefully examining a gigantic fossil thigh bone uncovered near Albany, New York. This seventeen foot relic and the four pound tooth found with it were definite evidence of the giants that roamed the earth in the days just before the great deluge. Had not the author of Genesis spoken of the "giants (who) lived on the earth in those days, when first the sons of God mated with the daughters of men, and by them had children"? With understandable logic for the day, some of these fossils were venerated in the churches of Europe as relics of the age of Adam. One reputable scholar, in fact, suggested that on the basis of fossil evidence Adam had stood one hundred and twenty-three feet, nine inches tall, and Eve a scant five feet shorter.

"Afflicted skeleton of old, doomed to damnation, Soften, thou stone, the hearts of a wicked generation." With this invocation worthy of an Old Testament prophet, Hansjakob Scheuchzer called on a fossil human skeleton to rise in judgment of anyone brash enough to question the reality of the Great Deluge. Scheuchzer's "old sinner" was uncovered in a limestone quarry in upper Baden in the early eighteenth century. The public fought for copies of Scheuchzer's treatise, *A Most Rare Memorial of that Accursed Generation of Men of the First World, the Skeleton of a Man Drowned in the Flood.*

Eventually Cotton Mather's relic of an antediluvian giant proved to be the remains of an extinct member of the elephant family, a mastodon thigh bone and tooth, and Scheuchzer's "old sinner" only a marine dinosaur. But most people in the seventeenth and eighteenth century were quite unwilling and indeed unable to see how death could have existed in the world prior to the fall of Adam. They were convinced that after God created the universe perfect and complete in six days all nature was at peace. Before Adam's sinful rebellion there was neither death nor suffering. Hence the possibility of dinosaurs and other animals living and dying before the appearance of man was simply inconceivable.

Two centuries earlier Leonardo da Vinci had offered a very sensible solution to the problem of fossils when he noted that "They say these shells were formed in the hills by the influence of the stars. But I would ask them where in the hills today are the stars now forming shells of distinct ages and species? And how can the influence of the stars explain the origin of gravel which occurs at different heights in the hills and is composed of pebbles rounded as if by the motion of running water? Or how can such a cause account for the petrification of various leaves, sea-weeds and marine crabs in the same places?" Tramping through the hills around Rome in search of marble for his sculpturing, Leonardo da Vinci had solved the mystery of fossils, but few people heeded his ideas for the simple reason that they entailed an acceptance of an evolutionary history and development of our earth along with a rejection of the literal interpretation of Genesis and the story of creation. As the scientists piled up more and more fossils in their museums, it became increasingly more difficult to explain them as insignificant accidents or rejected models of creation. The precise data for creation and the flood likewise became less probable. Yet as always, man was very reluctant to change his way of thinking, even when the evidence against his beliefs became overwhelming.

To preserve the common Christian explanation of creation, some scholars, led by the great comparative anatomist, Baron Cuvier (1769–1832), suggested a theory and explanation of creation known as "catastrophism." Fossils could be easily explained, Cuvier claimed, by admitting that there were actually six great floods, one at the end of each day of creation, when God wiped out every form of life on earth before starting a fresh new creation the next morning. Each new day God reproduced those earlier forms of life which he liked and added some new experimental forms. Finally on the sixth day God created man and placed him in a garden filled with those animals and plants he had decided would be useful for man. After a few generations, when mankind became engrossed in sin, God sent the final and greatest deluge.

Cuvier's theory of catastrophism met with real opposition from the budding science of geology. Earlier, James Hutton had suggested that catastrophes such as earthquakes, volcanic eruptions and massive floods have been far less important in the formation of our earth than the ceaseless, almost imperceptible erosion and remolding of the earth by raindrops, frost, ice and wind. Charles Lyell (1797–1875), an English geologist, expanded Hutton's suggestion and exposed its tremendous implications for our changing world image. Lyell pointed out that universal catastrophes simply do not exist in nature. Instead, the crust of our earth is victim of slow, imperceptible processes of change; mountains, rivers, valleys, lakes, deserts, marshes and coastlines are all slowly molded and reformed by the natural forces of erosion and geological activity. As our earth slowly cooled from its initial state as a molten, flaming mass, a crust formed on the surface. Then, like any cooling body, the earth contracted ever so gradually, its "skin" wrinkling to produce the vast mountain ranges. The soft caress of the wind, the icy fingers of frost, and the quiet erosion of streams then whittle away the granite peaks even as new mountain ranges rise elsewhere. The "uniformist theory" pictures a world with a relatively stable or uniform history in which "supernatural" catastrophes have no place, and where the chronologies of Lightfoot and Ussher have no foundation.

The geologists brought the dimension of evolutionary time into our changing image of the universe, just as Galileo and Copernicus introduced it into our image of the heavens a few centuries earlier.

The picture of the world common to western Europeans two hundred years ago, however, was still based on a conception of creation drawn from the ancient Greek and Roman philosophers. This was (and is) a belief that every species of animal and plant was established by God in the beginning as complete and perfect. Each species of plant and animal was thought to be eternally unchangeable, occupying its own proper niche in the "Great Chain of Being." This concept viewed the elements in the world around us as spread out, so to speak, in a hierarchy, like some cosmic ladder whose rungs account for the lowest form of creation, the inanimate rocks and minerals, the various species of plants and animals, and finally man, the angels and God. This hierarchy of being, fixed and stable, was very important in the world image of Dante and Aquinas. It is a concept of creation rooted in the fixity of natural species.

Even so, the man of the late eighteenth century was beginning to feel the growing impact of the evolutionary perspective in his understanding of the world of living beings. Carl Linnaeus (1707–1778), the botanist responsible for classifying scientifically much of the world of life, was a great advocate of the fixity or unchangableness of natural species and their direct creation by God. Yet towards the end of his life, as he studied certain animals and plants which seemed intermediate between the natural species he knew, Linnaeus began to wonder if perhaps species might not change and evolve.

A few years later, in 1809, Jean Baptiste Lamarck (1744–1829) proposed the first scientific explanation of an evolutionary development of plants and animals. His efforts were vital in preparing the ground for Charles Darwin. Drawing on the geological insights of Hutton and Lyell, the evolutionary concepts of Lamarck so vehemently denounced by Cuvier, the views of the English political economist Thomas Malthus, Adam Smith, David Hume and his own grandfather, Erasmus Darwin, Charles Darwin applied the dimension of time, change and evolution to the history of life on this planet in his famous *Origin of Species*, published in 1859.

Twenty years later Darwin made the final step in revolutionizing our image of the world from something fixed and static to a dynamic, evolutionary image when he published the *Descent of Man*. Here for the first time in the history of human thought, the dimension of time, the evolutionary perspective, was applied to man himself. Instead of holding a fixed position at the heart of a geocentric universe, man now took his place as the leading shoot of a long tedious evolutionary process involving the whole universe.

Today man has *an entirely new image* of the world and of his place in it, far different from that of Thomas Aquinas, Dante or Ptolemy. The revolutionary change came first in scientific circles, with the theologians and philosophers often lagging far behind in their attempts to present religious explanations in keeping with this new image. From a *cosmos* to a *cosmogenesis* is a radical step. And while it is clear that man can never return to a fixed, geocentric world image, we are still adding many details to our overall scientific picture. The task of educating people to accept the new scientific image of an evolving universe is difficult enough, considering the need for careful popularization and the communication of technological knowledge to the masses for whom scientific jargon is only confusion. But even more difficult is the task of educating people today to rethink their religious explanations and beliefs in the framework of an evolving universe. Quite frequently strong emotional attachments are involved in this shift and many people of varied religious persuasions are unwilling to accept such rethinking. Often they would prefer to live in a dichotomous world where their scientific convictions reside in one pigeonhole and their religious beliefs exist in a parallel but completely isolated compartment. Despite the overwhelming evidence of modern science to the contrary, many people still believe that man was created in 4004 B.C. or that he evolved from an ape; that individual species cannot evolve and were directly created by God.

It is quite easy and common for people to forget the basic element involved in the task of incorporating the evolutionary dimension into our religious image of the world. It is not a question of changing our religious beliefs, but rather the task is to work out *new explanations* of those beliefs. A Christian may state that he believes in one God, but how he explains and understands the reality of that God varies from age to age, from culture to culture. For the early Christians a picture of God carried many overtones of the Old Testament concept of judge along with the image of "our Father." For the Victorians God was the creator of all things who set this universe in motion like some gigantic clock and then retired, so to speak, into outer space, the heavens above. Our modern image of God again has changed. There is *an essential distinction between unchangeable religious beliefs and our ever changing explanations of those beliefs.* Our religious beliefs never change in their essence—for this is basic to Christianity—yet each generation of theologians and philosophers must work out *new explanations* of these truths in keeping with our ever changing world image.

A failure to recognize this elementary distinction made the Scopes "Monkey Trial" not only possible in 1925 but also a sensation that rocked the whole United States. John Scopes, a high school biology teacher at Dayton, Tennessee, violated the state law by teaching that "heretical and atheistic" theory of evolution. Practically the whole Christian world rose to denounce him in a circus trial. William Jennings Bryan, three times candidate for President of the United States, and Clarence Darrow, a famous criminal lawyer, were respectively prosecutor and defense attorney in a trial marked by antics beyond imagination. The trial ended with a suspended fine, but the debate continues even today for people who cannot or will not accept the fact that an evolutionary world image changes not our basic Christian beliefs but only the frail human attempts each generation must make to explain better and with more penetration those basic truths.

In 1966 three American states and one Canadian province still outlawed the teaching of evolution on the basis that it contradicts the Christian bible and tradition. In May of 1966, the kingdom of Saudi Arabia was shaken by Sheik Abdelaziz bin Baz, vice-president of the Islamic University of Medina. In an article for two Arabic newspapers, the Sheik expressed his dismay at man's changing world image: "Much publicity has been given . . . to the theory that the earth rotates and the sun is fixed. I believe it is my duty to write a brief essay to guide the reader to the proofs of the falsity of this theory and a realisation of the truth. Hence, I say the Holy Koran, the Prophet's teaching, the majority of Islamic scientists and the actual facts all prove that the sun is running in its orbit as Almighty God ordained, and that the earth is fixed and stable, spread out by God for his mankind and made a bed and cradle for them, fixed down firmly by mountains lest it shake." Of much the same mind is a British society dedicated to defending the belief that our earth is flat and not spherical. This group issues denunciations of every astronaut who claims to have seen and photographed the round earth far beneath his orbiting capsule.

Again in 1966 a leading Protestant group warned its members that it "will not tolerate any teaching of evolution as dogmatic fact." Yet in the very same month, a leading Protestant journal urged its readers to consider seriously the creative challenge posed by an evolutionary world image. The editorial wisely compared our present situation with the rejection of Galileo's new heliocentric world image in the sixteenth century. "In that era theology and the Ptolemaic theory were identical for the Church. Instead of repudiating the (scientific) theory which Galileo had proven false and adjusting its theology accordingly, the Church compelled the scientist to deny demonstrable truth and to cease his search for more truth." After a long battle, which continues in some areas even today, many Christians learned to distinguish between unchangeable religious truths and theological explanations formulated in the context of an ever changing scientific world image. The practical acceptance of this distinction and the constant challenge it offers the theologian has, as the editors of the Protestant journal pointed out, permitted a new and deeper understanding of many basic truths of our Christian tradition.

2

a seed is planted

If the Empire State Building were reduced to the size of a bacterium and used as a point for comparison, the earth would be roughly the size of a pea and our sun the size of a pumpkin. The millions of galaxies that make up our universe could then be represented by clustered pumpkins scattered about within the orbit of Jupiter. Or to take another tack, we could picture the universe by reducing it to the scale of the earth, in which case one would find 10,000 suns squeezed into every cubic inch of the earth's volume. From this it is obviously quite impossible for us to grasp the true dimensions of the universe. Billions and billions of stars, planets and galaxies! Even when reduced to the scale of every day realities we know so well, the image remains unwieldy and beyond our full grasp.

Length, breadth and depth: geometric Euclidean space. But the universe has a fourth dimension which adds to our problem. The vast reaches of outer space, the infinitesimal dimensions of the atom, both are complemented by the third infinity of time and duration. The universe began some six billion years ago, perhaps even as far back as fourteen billion years.

Einstein once remarked that the most unintelligible thing about the world is that it remains intelligible despite these unimaginable infinities. Science has always worked on an assumption, an act of faith, in the ability of man to find logic and understand the world outside his self-consciousness. In ages past, scientists and scholars, philosophers and theologians as well, have tried with great success to find a *cosmos* in the data that constantly bombarded their senses. Webster has defined "cosmos" as: "1. the universe considered as a harmonious and

orderly system: opposed to *chaos.* 2. harmony; order; organization. 3. any complete and orderly system." The implication is
obvious: men of every generation create their own *cosmos* by
integrating the varied phenomena of their known world into a
"harmonious and orderly system." In the past, this has been the
geocentric, fixed world image. But as we have seen, that image
has gradually shifted to incorporate the new dimension of time
and evolution. Of cosmologies we have many, but we have yet
to work out a full image of cosmogenesis. Today, science and
theology face *the task of building a new world image.* But as
before in man's search for a cosmos, our search today is based
on the assumption that our universe is logical and intelligible,
that we can discern in its many varied revelations general patterns and "universal laws" which we can then piece together
into a meaningful and relevant cosmogenesis. The search for
order and harmony and hence meaning continues, but on a
new and deeper plane.

For many people the word "evolution" means that man came
from an ape, that various forms of life have changed over the
centuries, or perhaps that living organisms came from dead
matter. Evolution has about as many meanings as there are
people who use the term. Realizing this confusion and hoping
perhaps to offer a simple, concise solution, the scientists, gathered at the University of Chicago to celebrate the hundredth
anniversary of Charles Darwin's *Origin of Species,* tried to
squeeze into a short definition all that modern science understands when it speaks of evolution. "Evolution," they wrote, "is
definable in general terms as a one-way irreversible process in
time, which during its course generates novelty, diversity, and
higher levels of organization. It operates in all sectors of the
phenomenal universe but has been most fully described and
analyzed in the biological sector."

While not the happiest of definitions, the above two sen-
tences represent the closest point scientists have come as a
group to distilling the essence of the modern evolutionary world
image. It emphasizes, quite properly, that evolution is not
limited to the development of life and man on this earth, but
rather embraces the whole universe. The universe is *a process*

in time, a process which in its main trends is irreversible, constantly leading to new forms of life, ever more complex and conscious. Evolution is an accepted scientific fact today, *our modern image of the universe.*

In this and the remaining chapters of this book we hope to present an outline for a new cosmos, or better, a cosmogenesis touching on key issues of science, philosophy and theology in the Christian tradition. As a basis for this exploration we would like to sketch briefly but in essence, the present knowledge of science regarding our evolving universe. For convenience we will break this survey into four distinct but related areas of scientific investigation. Since the days of Galileo, astronomers and physicists have been examining the vast history of the stars and planets. More recently the physicists have focused their attention on the atom and inorganic matter. The infinitely large and the infinitely small: an evolutionary cosmogony, a veritable *cosmogenesis.* A second aspect of the modern scientific image deals with the evolution of the earth itself and its crust: *geogenesis.* The most fascinating and best known phase of evolution is that of *biogenesis*, the evolutionary history of plant and animal life on this earth and the study of its causal factors. Finally, the scientists speak of the culmination and extension of organic evolution in the emergence of man, *anthropogenesis.*

In these various phases of cosmic evolution the scientists must search an encyclopedic pile of facts and details, trying to find general patterns and trends, the so-called "laws" of "nature." To find these general patterns, the individual scientist must link his own specialized findings with those of men in other fields. Piece by piece, the patterns emerge as science seeks some hypothesis which will relate and include all known phenomena. Today that pattern is the dimension of evolution, the only explanation which can make sense out of a mountain of seemingly unrelated minutiae and data.

Throughout the history of evolution as scientists know it today, we can observe a groping towards greater complexity from the subatomic particles, atoms and molecules, on through the organic compounds, the one- and many-celled animals, to man, the most complex creature we know. A true complex, in terms of modern science, integrates and unites many different forms or levels of being to a harmonious whole or system. Thus a variety of subatomic particles is organized together to form the more complex reality we call the atom. The same synthesis and integration occurs on the level of atoms which join to form molecules, on the molecular plane where the basis for the living cell slowly emerges, on the level of cells where many individual cells unite and specialize to perform the many diverse functions required of a complex organic system found in the plants and animals, and finally, in man and mankind. In this view, the planets and stars do not qualify as true complex systems. They are rather like mounds of gravel, simple aggregates or junk piles thrown together by gravity and chance without order or specific arrangement. Neither is the crystal, strictly speaking, a complex in terms of evolution. Its component atoms and molecules have a certain complexity of their own, but as such the crystal is only an ordered, repetitive arrangement of those atoms and molecules. The crystal does not integrate a variety of elements, nor does it unite them into a totally new level of being as subatomic particles are organized in an atom or cells in the human body.

Parallel with this general trend in evolution towards greater complexity is the gradual evolution of that inner aspect we observe so clearly in the human phenomenon: a gradual, halting development of spontaneity, freedom and consciousness or the ability to react and respond to the environment outside. There is in the dynamics of the atom and the molecule a certain very limited spontaneity or ability to react with the environment and elements outside itself, but it is really only among living organisms and especially man that we can observe this trend clearly. From the one-celled paramecium or amoeba, on to the corals of the tropic seas, the starfish and sea urchin, the fish, amphibians, reptiles, mammals and man, we can easily observe how, as the central nervous system increases in complexity, new degrees of freedom appear. As we mount the scale of evolutionary history and the tree of life, animals become freer of the limitations imposed by their surroundings, freer in their ability to move around in search of food and a suitable environment, less dependent on specific living conditions and more spontaneous and conscious in their behavior.

The general pattern or *law of increasing complexity-consciousness*, as Teilhard de Chardin termed it, is evident on each of the four phases of evolution, and, as we shall also see in our survey here, it represents an ascending spiral of smaller repeating patterns or stages.

Whenever we observe the appearance of a new level of existence, such as the atom, molecule, cell or man, we find an initial phase of scattering or *divergence* during which the new species of reality develops all sorts of modifications and specializations, exploring all possible forms that species might take. Once this new species has entered all the niches open to it, once it has established and adapted itself to its environment, certain branches of the group will inevitably begin to *converge*, concentrating and focusing their evolutionary energies and creative instabilities. In this way, certain branches of a species will reach a "boiling point." The evolutionary pressure continues to build until, at a certain critical point, the convergence brings about the *emergence* of a new form of reality. An instance of this, which we will touch on in dealing with biogenesis, is the convergence of molecules around chains of carbon atoms which eventually led to the emergence of organic molecules, the building blocks of life.

With this general pattern of increasing complexity/consciousness in mind as a broad trend binding together the various laws of thermodynamics, gravity, relativity, genetics, physiology, and others in a meaningful overall image, and with the dialectics of divergence/convergence/emergence to shed light on the individual levels of evolution we can pursue our sketch of a cosmos in genesis.

COSMOGENESIS

Modern theories about the evolutionary origins of our solar system have added considerable detail to this relatively unexplored area. The problem has absorbed the interest of astronomers since the days of Copernicus, but recent advances in technology have opened up whole new avenues.

In 1840, the first photographs, daguerreotypes, were made of the moon; ten years later astronomers made the first photographs of a star. Today telescopes are often constructed specifically for such photographic studies. An important parallel development came in 1859 when Gustav Kirchhoff (1824–1887) found that the spectrum of light emitted by any burning object is characteristic of the density, chemical constitution and temperature of that object. Burning table salt, sodium chloride crystals, observed through a prism offers a simple demonstration of this phenomenon. When color photography was developed in recent decades and adapted to telescopes, astronomers had an important tool in their search of space. They could then study the density, chemical make-up and temperature of the stars from their spectra. A bright-line or emission spectrum is produced by hot gases of low density while the dark-line, absorption spectrum, produced by a cool gas, reveals the nature of stars in the characteristic patterns of black bands indicating the absorption of certain wave lengths of light by the burning star.

The human eye has a very limited range, and the photographic plate is only slightly more sensitive. In 1932, when Karl Jansky of the Bell Telephone Laboratories observed radio waves coming from bodies in outer space, he uncovered an even more sensitive "eye" by which man could sharpen his "gaze" in the heavens: the radio telescope which maps the heavenly bodies by recording the radio waves they produce. The 200-inch Mount Palomar light telescope enlarges objects in space about 1000 times. The VLA, or Very Large Array Radio Telescopes, now in the planning stage, will bring these objects another 1000 times closer. Among the larger radio telescopes already analyzing high frequency waves emitted by galaxies, stars and planets are the giant single disk antennae of Jodrell Bank, England, and Goobang, Australia. Squadrons of smaller movable antennae can now plot minute phase differences in the reception of radio waves from a particular source, and, with the aid of computers, convert these minute differences into quite accurate distances. The squadron at Canberra, Australia, has arms one mile long; the Green Bank, West Virginia, squadron has three eighty-five foot antennae, two mounted on tracks and capable of moving 1.7 miles with an accuracy of two-tenths of a millimeter. Among the fixed VLA telescopes, the Australian complex is outstanding, composed as it is of ninety-six dish antennae arranged in a two mile circle. A giant VLA telescope has been proposed, consisting of thirty-six dishes, each eighty-five feet in diameter, strung out in a Y formation each arm of which will be thirteen miles long!

The universe we know today contains millions of galaxies, expanding and moving away from each other much like dots painted on a balloon as it is blown up. This simple fact has revealed some very important information to the scientists. The spectra emitted by some galaxies and stars is more in the red range than it is for others which appear to be quite similar in other characteristics. This shift of spectra to the lower red frequencies recalls a similar phenomenon in the world of sound where a train speeding past us seems to lower the pitch of its whistle as it moves away. It has been suggested that some galaxies and stars are moving away from us faster than others, and that their light therefore appears lower in frequency.

This and other information has permitted scientists to combine the most valid insights of two earlier astronomical theories, the "big bang" and "pulsation" theories, into a new explanation of the origin of the universe. This new theory pictures the beginning of the universe as a gigantic explosion of incredibly compressed matter-energy, followed by eons of steady expansion. This "primitive atom," first suggested by Abbé Lamaitre, packed all the substance of our universe within a space roughly the size of Mars' orbit. In this incredibly condensed state, a single cubic centimeter of matter, less than a thimbleful, would weigh almost two hundred million tons! Billions of years ago this "primitive atom" exploded and within the brief span of less than an hour some scientists believe all the natural atoms and isotopes were created. Almost as quickly the scattering and rapidly developing galaxies slowed down to the steady rate of expansion we observe today.

With the information available today we cannot answer two important questions. We cannot, for instance, tell whether the universe actually began with a creation out of nothing. The universe might have begun with the explosion of a newly created mass of matter-energy, but this explosion could just as easily have been the most recent in an endless series of pulsations. Many scientists today believe that while the universe is still expanding it is also slowing down imperceptibly. The mutual gravitational pull of the galaxies will then eventually reverse its movement and begin a phase of contraction that will return the universe to its primitive state. Once the universe reaches that point, it will again explode to form a new universe. In this view of a pulsating universe, matter-energy is neither created nor destroyed; it is only rearranged. It is interesting to note that long before the discoveries of modern astronomy, Thomas Aquinas contended that there is no intrinsic contradiction in speaking about the eternity of matter.

Astronomers have long puzzled over what they have called the "quasi-stellar blue objects," quasars for short, and the "blue galaxies" or quasi-quasars. While over half a million of these bodies are known to exist, scientists have been hard put to explain just what they are and what their importance and place in the universe is. Only recently the "blue galaxies" have yielded an important clue about the birth of the universe. Calculations now indicate that the time-span for a single expansion of the universe is approximately eighty-two billion years, with the date of the most recent cosmic explosion, marking the birth of our universe, being some fourteen billion years ago. These observations lend serious weight to a combination of the "pulsation" and "big bang" theories in our ever changing image of the universe.

Despite the evidence in favor of the "big bang" theory and the fact that it is the only theory of the origin of the universe now supported by evidence, scientists face a major problem in accepting it. Cosmology and particle physics study matter at the two extremes of the size scale; the former deals with the largest possible aggregation of matter, the whole universe, while the latter examines its smallest distinguishable fragments. Yet both sciences deal with matter as such and their theories should be compatible.

The world of subatomic particles is marvelously symmetrical and balanced between matter and antimatter. For every particle there is an antiparticle. The cosmologist, for his part, has found no room for antimatter in his picture of the universe and its origins. In fact, his observations seem to exclude its presence. If both matter and antimatter were present in the "primitive atom" from which our universe evolved, the "big bang" would have been instead an instantaneous annihilation of all matter for when a proton and an antiproton meet they annihilate each other in a burst of gamma ray energy.

The world of antimatter came to light some forty years ago when Dr. P. A. M. Dirac tried to apply the principles of Einstein's special relativity theory to the behavior of subatomic particles. The theory can apply only if the world of ordinary matter is reflected by a mirror-image world of antimatter in which the electrical charge is reversed, left becomes right and objects are capable of moving backward in time. The idea of antimatter was soon supported by considerable and growing evidence from experiments in the creation and annihilation of various subatomic particles.

Today very few physicists explicitly claim that the universe is asymmetrical and contains no antimatter, but the question remains whether the amount of matter in that mirror world equals that in our world, and where it can be located without causing the annihilation of the universe now or at its birth eons ago. One possibility has been offered by Drs. Hannes Alfen and Aina Elvius of Sweden's Royal Institute of Technology and the Stockholm Observatory. They suggest that at the time of its birth each galaxy is a highly compacted core of matter and antimatter. The annihilation of matter naturally occurs in this situation at a very high rate, producing the vast amounts of energy which characterize today's incipient galaxies, the quasars. As a galaxy ages, matter and antimatter separate, possibly urged in opposite directions by magnetic fields. Outside the core which slowly burns out, regions of matter and antimatter begin to build up and both stars and antistars, planets and antiplanets form on the galaxy's outer edges.

Sketchy and tentative as is this picture of the universe's origins it offers us sufficient backdrop for our moving on to the origins of our solar system, the earth and life itself on our planet.

One of the earliest astronomical theories offered to explain our own solar system's origins was proposed by George Louis Comte de Buffon (1707–1788), a French scientist. He suggested that fragments broke off our sun and remained whirling around it, forming the nine planets and their satellites.

In 1796 another French scientist, Laplace, suggested that our solar system began as a vast saucer-shaped cloud of hot gases revolving in space. As this cloud cooled and shrank, its spinning increased until eddies or rings formed. These rings gradually swept up more and more matter until they formed our present planetary system. While serious objections have been lodged against Laplace's theory it is still the basis for the most widely accepted explanation today. With many modifications in Laplace's original proposal, we can picture the birth of our sun as a star formed from a vast cloud of dust and gases slowly rotating in space. In time this immense rotating disk, the sun at its center, developed huge whirlpools scattered throughout the system. These whirlpools eventually formed into smaller globes of dust and gas, each gradually cooling to form a new planet. Those planets nearest the sun would be solid and compact, because of the gravitational forces of the sun and its heat. Their gaseous atmospheres would be dissipated by the sun's heat. More distant planets would remain less compact, with their gaseous coverings remaining to this day.

Recently, an English astronomer, Fred Hoyle, has proposed another view of our solar system and its origins. He suggests that our sun once had a companion star which exploded several billion years ago. Most of the exploding matter from this star would have been hurled deep into outer space, but enough gaseous matter remained within the sun's gravitational field to form eventually the planets of our solar system. Hoyle's suggestion is quite compatible with the high frequency of twin stars in our galaxy. Along these lines it is interesting to recall that our own earth once had two moons, one of which plunged into northern Argentina some 6,000 years ago.

Keeping in mind this image of cosmogenesis, it might be profitable to apply the general law of increasing complexity/ consciousness and the dialectics this involves to the various levels of reality that evolved during this early period of cosmic evolution. In the first hour or so of our universe's history, a very rapid evolution occurred. The thirty-two or more subatomic particles known today are very short-lived. Some of them exist in free space for no more than a ten billionth of a second, while certain subatomic combinations called resonances have a life span of only a hundred thousandth of a billion billionth of a second. With such short life-spans, it is easy to picture the rapid divergence of matter-energy into the more than two hundred forms of subatomic particles, ranging from the familiar electron, neutron and position to the more exotic photons, neutrino, Mu† and Mu*. This divergence was quickly followed by convergence and the formation of the first atoms.

On the atomic plane, evolution again took a very rapid pace as the newly formed universe underwent a stage of divergence, producing the ninety-two natural elements which form the basis of our somewhat stable universe and earth. Divergence on the atomic level also included several hundred natural isotopes of the ninety-two elements. But again, as on the subatomic plane, the possibilities of divergence were limited and once all the possible forms of atoms, stable and radioactive, had evolved, a phase of convergence led to the formation of new unions, joining different kinds of atoms to form molecules.

GEOGENESIS AND BIOGENESIS

Anyone who has stood on the edge of the Grand Canyon, driven through Bryce and Zion National Parks, or along the highways that cut through the Appalachian or Rocky Mountains has seen the fingerprints of geogenesis, the evolution of our earth's crust. The geologist is a professional student of that history. Though he is primarily concerned with the sedimentary effects of primeval seas, the wrinkling and folding of the earth's crust, the activities of volcanos, glaciers and the erosive sea and wind, the geologist is also very conscious that within the layers of the earth is buried the history of life. In the flaky sedimentary rock, the compressed dust of long extinct volcanos, the mineralized remains of petrified wood (agate) and the golden transparency of amber are nestled the delicate traces of life past. Biogenesis is intimately interwoven with geogenesis, and for this reason we will treat the two histories as one.

In the early days of geology, the only way to determine the age of a particular fossil was to count the sedimentary layers of a particular deposit and then match these up with such clear records as those of Grand Canyon. This procedure is not unlike that of the forestry expert who counts the rings of a tree's cross section to ascertain its age. Like the tree, many sedimentary deposits show definite annual "rings" called varves. Examination of these highly compressed layers indicate that it takes anywhere from four to ten thousand years to form a one foot thick layer of sedimentary rock.

Today geologists and paleontologists have more precise and reliable methods of dating fossil remains of life. These methods make use of the natural atomic decay of certain radioactive elements. A basic example of this is the use of carbon. A certain percentage of all the carbon in the earth and atmosphere is radioactively unstable: the isotope carbon 14. During its lifetime, every animal and plant incorporates some of this unstable carbon isotope into its tissues along with the more common stable carbon. After death, the radioactive carbon continues to decay at a steady determined rate to the stable nitrogen 14. Since no new carbon 14 is taken in by the dead organism, the percentage of carbon 14 decreases at a regular rate, one half of it decaying every 5,568 years. By measuring the amount of carbon 14 present in a fossil and comparing this with the total amount of carbon in the fossil scientists can determine how long ago a certain fossilized animal lived. This method is very accurate for fossils up to twenty-five thousand years old. With less accuracy it can be applied to fossils dating back forty thousand years.

When Dr. L. S. B. Leakey discovered the first fossils of the "Nutcracker Man" in 1960 in the Olduvai Gorge of Tanzania the crucial question was the age of this fossil man. Since it was found in association with volcanic ash, scientists at the University of California in Berkeley made very precise measurements of the radioactive decay of potassium 40 to the inert gas argon within the volcanic rock. After many tests, the scientists made an announcement that startled the whole world. Man, they said, was not just three-quarters of a million years old, the age of Java and Peking Man, but one and three-quarter million years old—more than twice as long as had been thought.

In outlining the history of geogenesis and biogenesis it is easy to become lost in the billions and millions of years this evolution took. Thus we might find a simple comparison or scheme helpful. Rather than speak about enormous numbers which have little real meaning for us, we can draw a scale between the history of the earth and a hypothetical year in which fourteen million years equals one "day" and half a million years equals "one hour."

January 1 to November 16: The Pre-Cambrian Era

Roughly five billion years ago, as the earth's crust slowly congealed, and the steaming vapors of the atmosphere condensed on the still hot granite, life was born in the primeval oceans. The growing weight of evidence now indicates that originally the earth's crust was composed on two supercontinents: *Laurasia*, which later split up to form North America, Europe and Asia, and *Gondwanaland*, named for a region of India, which some two hundred million years ago fragmented into what is now Africa, the Persian peninsula, South America, southern India, Australia, New Guinea, New Zealand and Antarctica. Impossible as this idea of supercontinents splitting and drifting slowly apart may seem, scientists were first led to propose the idea because of very similar fossil plants found in both

India and Africa dating back some 250 million years. But ferns
and plants can spread their seeds by winds and ocean currents,
so the improbable theory was not seriously considered.

But geologists soon found strong similarities in the rather
unique geological layers of South America's eastern coast and
Africa's western coast. Then in December of 1967 scientists
found a small piece of a jaw bone embedded in a rock ridge
some hundred miles east of the famous Beardmore Glacier
which British explorers used as a guide in their first attempts
to reach the South Pole. Two million years earlier it had belonged to a five-foot salamander-like amphibian, inhabiting the
tropic swamps of Antarctica along with giant ferns. This fresh
water Labyrinthodont was very similar to other fossils found
in Australia and South Africa in parallel geological deposits.
Two years later, in December of 1969, a large bed of fossil
amphibians and reptiles was uncovered in the Alexandra Mountain Range flanking the Beardmore Glacier on the west. Crucial
among these finds were the remains of more Labyrinthodonts
and the land dwelling thecodonts, a varied group of reptiles
from which eventually evolved the dinosaurs and birds. *Lystro-
saurus*, a key fossil uncovered at the time, was a reptilian
counterpart of the modern hippopotamus. The discovery of
this land reptile, already known to have inhabited wide regions
of South Africa, India, China and Russia, has been described
by leading paleontologists as "the first really convincing biological evidence of continental drift."

Whatever may have been the situation of the early land
masses, their condition was relatively unimportant for the early
stages of the evolution of life. Life originated in the primeval
oceans and there the interaction was between the atmosphere
and a relatively small number of chemical building blocks in
the seas. We do not yet know, and perhaps may never know for
certain, just what were the conditions which prevailed on the
surface of our earth when living organisms first came into being.
Today our atmosphere is composed of oxygen, nitrogen, carbon dioxide, water vapor and traces of other gases. In the Pre-
Cambrian era the atmosphere was quite different. High temperatures common at that time would have made it impossible

for certain gases to remain free in the atmosphere. Thus, oxygen would combine with hydrogen to form methane and water. Nitrogen would combine with hydrogen to form ammonia. And these compounds would then enter into combination with other elements in the newly formed crust.

Until the mid nineteen sixties most scientists believed that the primeval atmosphere was a combination of methane (CH_4), ammonia (NH_3), water vapor and gaseous nitrogen. Many experiments were carried out simulating in the laboratory these supposed conditions. By subjecting these components to basic natural forces such as ultraviolet light and electrical charges, scientists were able to produce artificially many of the building blocks of life.

More recently some geologists have pointed out serious problems in the methane-ammonia theory. They suggest that the atmosphere and oceans originated from gases seeping through the newly formed crust or spewed forth in volcanic eruptions from the earth's molten core. This theory claims that volatile compounds in these erupting gases would have reacted with chemicals in the earth's crust to form an alkaline ocean and an atmosphere of carbon monoxide, carbon dioxide, nitrogen and hydrogen. With the atmosphere only beginning to form, the earth was not shielded as it is today from solar radiation. This energy alone, bombarding the new atmosphere, could have catalyzed the production of hydrogen cyanide. In the laboratory, under simulated conditions, P. H. Abelson has found that hydrogen cyanide yields amino acids and other substances important to the origin of life.

It really does not matter for our purposes here which theory finally proves acceptable. We have in these laboratory experiments several different ways of simulating the primeval conditions and creating from inorganic, non-living raw materials the very building blocks of life.

We have no real evidence, either direct or indirect, of the earliest forms of life that emerged from the thin hot "soup" of amino acids, sugars, phosphates and other compounds within the primeval oceans.

Among the inorganic molecules divergent evolution has been

very limited since the most common elements composing these molecules, oxygen and silicon, have only one or two open chemical bonds. The carbon atom, on the other hand, is unique in possessing a valence of four, making it possible for a single carbon atom to bind four other atoms as in methane (CH_4), or to form long chains such as found in polypeptids, amino acids and proteinoids. Convergence around carbon atoms leads to the emergence of megamolecules, the organic compounds, and eventually, to life.

Divergence among the organic compounds is practically without bounds, and yet certain forms appear to have had some advantage in the evolution of life. Only the left-handed amino acids can form the polypeptid and protein chains we observe in living creatures today. Those amino acids which coil to the right are either toxic or cannot be incorporated into a living organism. Besides these stereochemical patterns, another important limitation is imposed on organic molecules by both chemical affinities and the physical crowding of molecules on a spherical globe. The latter limitation played a major role in the slow, tedious emergence of living organisms, after many false starts and misadventures.

Progress in the evolution of early forms of life was, as our comparison with a calendar year shows, excruciatingly slow, covering ten and a half months in our "year." There were, however, some very important advances achieved during this period. There was the development of the abilities to replicate or reproduce structures, to maintain organization in a complicated system of feedback information, and to produce or use "food." Most likely subcellular organelles, similar to the mitochondria and plastids of today's cells, appeared first as a necessary preparation for the evolution of one-celled life. Another distinct advance was the appearance of cells with distinct nuclei and heredity controlled by chromosomes. All of this tedious evolution began some three and a half billion years ago according to the most recent estimates.

As the earth's surface slowly cooled from its earlier molten state and formed barren stretches of rock, oceans appeared. In these primeval waters was sheltered and fostered the evolution of minute bacteria, fungi and algae, some of which could produce their own food by photosynthesis. For the most part, the bacteria and blue-green algae ended up in an evolutionary sidebranch, remaining unchanged down to the present, perhaps because they failed to develop an organized nucleus. Another type of microscopic organism, the flagellates, was not so stymied. Blessed with a nucleus and enzyme systems capable of manufacturing food by photosynthesis, these minute animals are the ancestral stock from which has evolved the whole gamut of higher life forms. Across the bridge of colonial flagellates, another step in convergence, the evolutionary stream passed on to develop the primitive sponges with their loose association of one-celled animals, the earliest jellyfish and polyps (the first animals to possess mouths and stomachs), and on to the gutless flatworms, the proud possessors of the first real nervous systems.

After some rather exotic experiments, nature settled on the efficient bisexual mode of reproduction, the mating of male and female. Such simplicity, complicated as it is in man, nevertheless has distinct advantages over the problems created by the twenty-eight mating types found in the one-celled paramecium!

From January to mid-November evolution continued its groping, tedious course, meandering through the true flatworms and eventually giving rise to the segmented worms and mollusks with true body cavities, and then the very successful insects. The primitive echinoderms, ancestor of the modern starfish, scientists believe form the original stock from which has evolved all the vertebrates and higher animals.

Toward the end of the Pre-Cambrian or Proterozoic era, the climate cooled enough to permit the formation of glaciers which over eons chiseled, gouged, ground and cracked the barren rock to produce gravel, sand and finally soil. Tediously the earth was etched: its land pulverized and readied for terrestrial life.

With the appearance of one-celled life, evolution wrought a new covering for the earth, the biosphere, rooted in the earth's crust and atmosphere, yet transcending that plane of existence.

Biologists have classified some twenty thousand species of one-celled plants and animals, most of them quite ancient. Their diversity gives vivid testimony to the prolific divergence of primitive life prior to the evolution of the colonial flagellates and metazoons (many-celled animals). While most of the animals in the Pre-Cambrian seas were microscopic or quite small, some plants like the giant sea kelps reached a length of five or six hundred feet.

Among the metazoons, patterns of evolution are very complicated as the birth of each new species is immediately followed by its divergence into many forms, the chance development of new varieties by gene mutation and natural selection. Each new species undergoes this phase of exploration before one or a few branches respond to the forces of natural selection and begin to concentrate their creative instability and lack of complete adaptation to meet the challenge of a changing environment. Such convergence often leads to the slow emergence of new species.

As the animal kingdom continues to evolve, we can recognize a very gradual shift in emphasis from the exterior aspect of things to the interior, from simple physical complexity to psychological awareness and spontaneity. As the animal kingdom evolves, newer species are more complex, true, but more important they are more conscious and more responsive to their surroundings, more open in their instinctual behavior, and freer of the limitations imposed on them by their environment. Evolution is a single process involving the whole organism, both its outer complexity and its inner consciousness, but particularly in the animal world a shift in emphasis occurs from the primacy of the organic and biological to that of the psychological and social.

Throughout the whole animal kingdom, consciousness seems to be proportional to an animal's power of choice. Between mobility and consciousness there is an obvious relationship. An animal that can move around freely in its own territory is more conscious and freer to choose than a sessile animal like the barnacle. In the higher animals a certain necessary connection appears evident between consciousness and the complexity of the brain and central nervous system. The more the nervous system develops, the more numerous and precise are the choices the animal can make. In those animals which have degenerated into helpless parasites one could almost say that consciousness has become dormant. Among the plants, consciousness seems to awaken in just the degree to which a plant regains the liberty of movement. Thus, to find the best examples of consciousness in the plant kingdom we must descend almost to its evolutionary origins, to the motile zoospores of algae and the one-celled organisms that hesitate between plant and animal. In the animal world we must ascend to the highest and most recently evolved forms to find our best examples of consciousness and spontaneity.

What precisely do we mean, though, when we say that the fish is freer or more conscious than the coral or starfish, or that the mammal is freer than the reptile? From top to bottom the animal kingdom is, without exception, slave to its physiological functions and endocrine secretions. The animal can never liberate itself from this imposed control any more than it can escape its blind innate instincts. Physiological functions, endocrine secretions and instincts are the direct and inescapable consequence of an animal's evolutionary history, part and parcel of its nature. Yet, at the same time, there is a real difference in consciousness among the various animals, if we view this in terms of freedom and choice. From the one-celled protista to man there is a gradual advance in freedom of movement, liberation from a strict dependence on specific environments, liberation from the necessity of using the forelimbs for walking or digging, liberation from the imperatives of a closed instinctual behavior and the development of a more flexible, open, instinctual behavior. The latter allows for adaptation and liberation from the time-consuming task of transmitting acquired characteristics and experience through the development of speech and cultural traditions.

But this is taking us far ahead to the climax of our study of life, to man. Before we reach that point I think it would be helpful to present a broad outline of the evolution that prepared the way for man. From January 1st to mid-November may be a very slow, tedious beginning for life and man. Nevertheless it is basic to both. An appreciation of it is quite essential to our understanding of man's place in an evolutionary world and our later discussion of theological thought in a cosmogenic context.

THE PALEOZOIC ERA

November 16 to November 25: The Cambrian Period

Most scientists today place the beginning of the Cambrian period at roughly six hundred million years ago. Rocks from this period contain a rich variety of fossil algae, bacteria and even the first spore-bearing plants. The earth's newly formed land surface was still barren, but as the seas warmed, the wide variety of marine plants and invertebrate animals increased by geometric leaps and bounds. Shrimp-like arthropods abounded among the representatives of every major animal phylum except the chordates. During the one hundred million years of this period evolution quickened its pace noticeably.

Onc arthropod of this period, the trilobite, was so successful that it accounted for sixty percent of the animal population. Similar in many ways to the modern horseshoe crab, some were a foot long, and their descendants can be found in the fossil deposits of the next three hundred million years.

November 25 to December 1, 6 a.m.: The Ordovician Period

When the Ordovician period began some five hundred million years ago, the seas along our continental shores swarmed with marine algae and the United States was fragmented into a cluster of large islands surrounded by coral reefs. The climate was much warmer, almost tropical. Fresh water streams harbored the first fish, small primitive creatures without jaws that eventually found their way to the sea to feed on a variety of marine life, the first clams, starfish, and nautiloid mollusks—ancestors of today's octopus and squid. With seventy per cent of the United States under water, volcanic activity and heaving of the earth's crust slowly lifted the New England mountains from Maine to Alabama.

December 1, 6 a.m. to December 3: The Silurian Period.

A cooling of the world's climate 425 million years ago marked the beginning of the Silurian period. Volcanic activity in New England and Eastern Canada continued as much of the eastern coast slipped again into salty marshes and seas. Only the mountains of Vermont broke the flatness of the low land masses and the salt basin that covered a hundred thousand square miles of the midwest. Many of the salt mines now underlying New York, Pennsylvania and Michigan were formed in this era. A few primitive plants, mainly club mosses, etched a foothold on the barren land along with the first scorpions and millipedes.

December 3 to noon of December 7: The Devonian Period.

After twenty million years the Silurian period gave way to the Devonian, named for the Devonshire region of England, where rich fossil deposits of this period have been found. Broad tidal marshlands were common, their shores lined with giant cone-bearing trees and exotic spidery plants, the first liverworts, horsetails, and ferns. The climate was warmer and more varied than before.

Among the teeming population of spiders, insects and fish a very important animal made its appearance. The main line of fish would eventually evolve into our modern bony fish, the teleosts. But during the Devonian period, a minor side branch of the primitive fishes became the first vertebrate group to have an internal nasal passage which permitted breathing air without the mouth being opened. The Dipnoi, or lungfish, also possessed paired fins with prominent fleshy lobes. These fins, scientists believe, were an important step in the evolution of paired limbs with an internal skeleton. Three species of lungfish have survived the ages and still live in the mud flats of central Australia, the Nile Valley and western Paraguay where they breathe through a pair of lungs that eventually evolved as sacs off the pharynx.

The main line of lung fish, however, has changed little since Devonian times, and it was an almost insignificant sub-branch of the dipnoi that made the first crucial step onto land. This "cousin" of the dipnoi goes by the rather esoteric name of Crossopterygian. It had a much more progressive skeleton and much more developed paired fins. The bony skeleton in its paired lobed fins is quite similar to the limb structure of the first amphibians. This characteristic, plus an internal nasal passage and primitive lungs, makes the typical crossopterygian an ideal source from which all land animals could have evolved.

Often in speaking of evolution the man in the street jokes about so-called "missing links," those hypothetical bridges between one species or form and another. In the past the fact that these transitional forms were more often hypothetical led many critics to argue against the validity of evolution. Today many "missing links" are no longer hypothetical. Fossil evidence has been unearthed which testifies clearly to certain transitions critical to an evolutionary scheme of life. Occasionally the scientist is even more fortunate, as when a fish closely related to the primitive crossopterygians everyone considered long extinct unexpectedly turned up in a fisherman's net off the coast of Madagascar in 1939. This massive deep-bodied fish, almost five feet long and covered with large bluish scales, created some excitement in the fish market of East London, South Africa, but since then several specimens of *Latimeria* have been caught and examined in detail.

In our scheme the Devonian period consumes only four and a half days, from 405 to 345 million years ago, yet this was a turning point for evolution.

Noon of December 7 to December 12: The Carboniferous Period.

The next sixty-five million years would have delighted any devotee of Florida and California, as a tropic climate extended from Iceland and Greenland to the tip of South America. Tropical seas, everglades and warm marshes were everywhere. On shore appeared the first known mosses, seed ferns and conifers, the cone-bearing ancestors of the modern pines. Insects were all over. Giant dragonflies glided on wings two and a half feet wide through forests of club mosses a hundred feet tall. Cockroaches on the same monstrous scale scurried about the lush vegetation which slowly sank into the marshland muck. Century after century, layer upon layer, this decaying vegetation was gradually transformed into peat, then soft and hard coal, petroleum and oil.

Fish flourished in an inland ocean two thousand miles wide and covering the western two-thirds of the United States. In the first half of the Carboniferous period, the Mississippian era, the first true reptiles evolved. Amphibians, however, were still the dominant form even into the second half of this period, the Pennsylvanian era.

December 12 to December 15, noon: The Permian Period

In a few million years geological turmoil and upheavals of the land wreaked havoc with the tropical paradise of the Carboniferous period. Mountain ranges replaced marshes and shallow seas. A vast salt desert stretched from New Mexico to Kansas and another covered large areas of Russia and Germany. Glaciers blanketed much of Africa, Australia and South America. The giant tropical forests disappeared and the great seed ferns, club mosses and tree ferns became extinct.

The geological turmoil of this period was probably climaxed by the initial breaking up of the supercontinents, Laurasia and Gondwanaland. With Texas-sized fragments somehow disappearing in the process, the embryonic continents of relatively light granite tediously drifted apart at the rate of a few inches a year, floating like monstrous islands on the earth's dense mantle of molten basalt.

Turmoil and chaos marked another milestone in animal evolution. In the struggle for supremacy on the land, the Achilles' heel of the amphibian's life cycle came to light: water is essential in amphibian reproduction as they must lay their eggs in it. Thus as ponds, lakes and streams yielded to deserts and mountains during this period, early reptiles like *Seymouria* gained a distinct advantage by producing eggs with shells that prevented desiccation of the delicate embryo and eliminated the need for the cool shelter of water. By the end of the Permian period, after some fifty million years, the reptiles had replaced the amphibians as the dominant land animal.

THE MESOZOIC ERA

December 15, noon, to December 19: The Triassic Period

The third of the four great eras of biogenesis, the Mesozoic, is subdivided into only three periods, the first lasting about fifty million years, from 230 to 180 million years ago. After the tumultuous Permian period, the earth settled back into another era of tropic and subtropic climates. During the Triassic period land areas continued to increase, and the Appalachian mountains reached their peak development. The forests slowly lost their exotic character as the early pines and firs became more common. The first cycads appeared, stately trees with unprotected seeds similar to the pines but with some traits of the earlier tree ferns and palms. The only member of this family to survive to the present is the feathery oriental ginkgo or maidenhair tree which until the last century was found only in the imperial courts of Japan and China.

The reptiles continued to extend their domain, some of them returning to the seas where they evolved into true monsters of the deep. Somewhat later, others took to the air. But the important step in this era was made by much smaller animals, almost lost among the monstrous egg-laying reptiles, tiny premammalian reptiles that would eventually evolve into the true mammals, our ancestors.

December 19 to December 22: The Jurassic Period

The age of the dinosaurs began some 180 million years ago. The first half of that age, the Jurassic, lasted forty-five million years. Worldwide the climate was quite temperate with forests of cycads and conifers flourishing along with the dinosaurs. As happens repeatedly in evolution, new and important forms of life appeared almost unnoticed among the more successful, better adapted and hence dominant, at least for a while. Among Jurassic fossils we find the first evidence of flowering plants and of mammals. Of immediate concern for us are the tiny shrew-like mammals that led a precarious life underfoot the monstrous dinosaurs. For the next hundred million years they would remain just as inconspicuous, yet already they possessed certain newly evolved characteristics which would eventually allow them to replace the dinosaurs. Besides important modifications in their skeleton, the early mammals had the advantage of giving birth to live young sheltered in the maternal womb until mature enough to care for themselves. Of course, their young had to be nursed, but they were far less vulnerable to predatory animals than were the abandoned, unprotected eggs of the reptiles. In the newly evolved mammals a coat of body hair and internal mechanisms maintained a constant body temperature, while the reptiles, with little control over the body temperature, were often at the mercy of changing climates.

Fossil deposits of the late Jurassic Period contain remains of many classic dinosaurs: the Brontosaurus, a long-necked and equally long-tailed vegetarian goliath tipping the scale at between thirty and fifty tons and stretching some eighty feet from head to tail, his brain weighing about two pounds; Stegosaurus, only twenty feet long but nicely armoured with heavy bony plates and a tail tipped with three massive spikes to fend off attackers.

Supremacy in the air was contested by two distinct branches of the animal world: the pterosaurs, small dinosaurs whose forelimbs had evolved to the point where they could soar over the shallow Jurassic lagoons snatching up fish in their long beaks, and Archeopteryx, the ancestor of all birds. Several fossils of Archeopteryx have been uncovered, complete to the smallest feather. A small bird, about the size of a modern crow, it retained many characteristics of its reptilian ancestors along with its newly evolved feathers.

How did animals ever evolve wings and develop the ability to fly? Two possible solutions have been suggested by scientists. Some think that forelimbs evolved into wings as a result of reptiles running along the ground and using their forelimbs to add speed. Gradually through natural selection and further adaptation, this practice could produce animals capable of flying. Another possibility is that climbing reptiles which originally jumped from tree to tree or to the ground may gradually have mutated to forms capable of gliding and then flying. Both changes would have been rooted in genetic mutations and obviously took many centuries and countless generations of groping, zig-zagging evolution.

December 22 to December 27: The Cretaceous Period

With this period the age of dinosaurs came to an end.

From 135 to 63 million years ago the climates were quite varied, mainly because of many new mountain chains which interrupted the old patterns of air currents: the Sierra Nevada, Andes, Himalayan and Rocky mountains all came into being during this period. A shallow sea now covered all the central states, reaching up into Canada and down over all Mexico and Florida. Between the surging Rockies and the California coast another narrow sea stretched north and south. Many new varieties of flowering trees and plants had evolved, dominating the older conifers. In the lagoons and shallow seas, the first teleosts, or bony fish, appeared.

The dinosaurs reached their peak and then suddenly disappeared, much to the puzzlement of scientists who now suspect that a massive radiation explosion on the sun may have been the cause for the sudden demise. Despite all the advantages of size and strength, the dinosaurs fell victim to a complex of enemies: the much smaller, more agile mammals, ferocious insectivores that no doubt preyed on the dinosaurs unprotected eggs; changes in vegetation patterns and food supplies as a result of the new mountain ranges, and a dramatic though slow shift in the climates. In the end, the sixty-foot sea serpent,

Elasmosaur and the invincible Tyrannosaurus rex yielded to the tiny mammals, and ultimately to man.

THE CENOZOIC ERA

The fourth and last of the great geological eras, the Cenozoic, covers roughly the last sixty-three million years, in our comparison, from about noon of December 27 to New Year's Eve. For convenience sake, it has been divided into two main periods, the Tertiary and Quaternary, with several subdivision or epochs as follows:

Period	Epoch	Began	Beginning in our "Hypothetical year"
	Recent	Recorded history	A few minutes
Quaternary	Pleistocene	3 million	c. Dec. 31, 6:30 p.m.
	Pliocene	13 million	c. Dec. 31, 1:30 a.m.
	Miocene	25 million	c. Dec. 30, 5:30 a.m.
	Oligocene	36 million	c. Dec. 29, 4:00 a.m.
	Eocene	58 million	c. Dec. 27, 8:00 p.m.
Tertiary	Paleocene	63 million	c. Dec. 27, noon
Cretaceous		135 million	c. Dec. 22

To go into detail about the extensive fossil records of this period would take us astray of our purposes here. It would also run the risk of losing the reader along the way with little accomplished other than an exposure to volumes of data. During this era practically all the higher mammals and many other specialized and now familiar animals evolved. Among these, the evolution of the horse and elephant are especially well documented. A few words on their history may give the reader an outline of this period which immediately precedes the appearance of man.

In the early Eocene epoch, some sixty million years ago, a small four-footed animal browsed among the shrubs and grassy plains of North America. The size of a fox terrier, Eohippus is considered the first member of the horse family. Besides his size Eohippus was distinguished by having three toes on his hind feet and four on his forefeet. Two major groups developed from this early equine form, one of which invaded the Old World through Siberia before it died out. The second group continued to evolve, for some thirty million years, until it had doubled its size by the Miocene epoch. Miohippus was a browser, like his ancestor, but he had lost the fourth toe. Several different branches arose from the Miohippus complex twenty-five million years ago. Among these were the first grazers which later became extinct. By the end of the Miocene the horse had again doubled its size as indicated by fossils of Merychippus. In the Pliocene, shortly before the appearance of man, several distinct groups of horses grazed the North American plains. Some again followed the land bridge connecting Alaska with Siberia to reach Asia and finally Europe, but as before the Old World species died out. About this same time another group found its way into South America only to suffer extinction. Finally, about five million years ago, a fairly modern-type horse appeared, Pliohippus, with a single toe on each foot. Eventually, the descendants of Pliohippus invaded every continent except Australia and Antarctica. This time, however, extinction occurred in North America so that the horses brought by the colonists were entirely new to the Indians.

The evolution of the elephant begins somewhat later than that of the horse, during the late Eocene. Moeritherium of northern Egypt, the first member of the elephant family, stood about two feet tall and had only the slightest hint of a trunk. His descendant, Palaeomastodon, had a fair trunk complete with small tusks. This primitive mastodon invaded India and later most of Europe and Asia. Finally, during the Miocene, he reached North America. In the New World, Triophodon attained a height of almost seven feet, though his teeth and jaws indicate he was not the ancestor of the modern elephant. This title seems to belong to Gomphotherium, a widespread species living during the Miocene and Pliocene. Among the many extinct elephant forms, Gomphotherium probably evolved into the Ice Age mastodons, mammoths and modern elephants.

During the Pleistocene, when man first appeared, four elephant species lived in the United States, and both elephants and mastodons were to be found in South America. Some thirty thousand years ago, when man first came to North America he found the nine and a half foot mastodon worthy prey for his spear. While the harsh Ice Ages posed no problem for the giant mastodons or the slightly smaller wooly mammoths that ranged from Canada to Europe, man, the hunter, apparently did raise the question of survival not only for the elephant and mastodon but also for many other animals.

Early in the Pleistocene, some two million years ago, man entered the cosmic drama, slowly to assume control of this earth, as Yahweh commanded in Genesis. Two million years ago man began to create his cosmos and in so doing he took into hand the hopes for the future.

3

man, the late-comer

"What is man?" Buckminster Fuller gave an intriguing answer back in 1938 when he proposed the following definition: "A self-balancing, twenty-eight-jointed adaptor-base biped; an electrochemical reduction plant, integral with segregated stowages of special energy extracts in storage batteries for subsequent actuation of thousands of hydraulic and pneumatic pumps with motors attached; 62,000 miles of capillaries . . . the whole, extraordinary complex mechanism guided with exquisite precision from a turret in which are located telescopic and microscopic self-registering and recording rangefinders, a spectroscope, etc.; the turret control being closely allied with an air-conditioning intake-and-exhaust and a main fuel intake. . . ."*

This scientific image of man carries little of the vision of the future or of the challenging role played by man as the apex of evolution's arrow, so beautifully expressed by Teilhard de Chardin on countless occasions. Buckminster Fuller's definition may strike us as humorous or irritating, but it is hardly challenging or provocative of man's commitment to extending the process of cosmic evolution. Yet there is a certain amount of truth in it that cannot be ignored. This truth, *partial* as it is, has been emphasized by other scientific writers, by Desmond Morris' cheeky juxtaposition of man and ape in *The Naked Ape*, by Robert Ardrey's emphasis on man's violent origins in *African Genesis* and his instinctual bonds with the animal world in *The Territorial Imperative*, and by Konrad Lorenz' study of man's hostile heredity in the controversial book *On*

* Buckminster Fuller, *Nine Chains to the Moon*, J. P. Lippincott.

Aggression. Incomplete as these views of man may be, we cannot dispute the value of their basic insights into man's roots in the animal world and in the cosmos.

The French atomic scientist, Louis de Broglie, once suggested that "the great marvel in the progress of science is that it reveals to us a certain concordance between our thoughts and things as they are, a certain possibility of grasping, by means of the resources of our intellect and the rules of logic, *the profound relations existing among phenomena.*"

Intellectually and in perfect accord with the rules of logic we can explain the profound relations and similarities existing between animals of every level, from the amoeba to the coral polyp to the insect, vertebrate, mammal and man by repeating in an up-to-date language the belief that in the beginning, God created each individual species perfect and completely formed. The consistency we observe in protein formation, in general structural patterns, in metabolic processes, in homologies of the skeletal and organic systems, in sera, in chromosomal and genetic patterns, all this can be explained if we assume that in the vast course of history God has continually intervened in the course of nature to create new species and finally man. But a Victorian God of the Gaps is hardly palatable to modern man and especially the modern scientist who resents any gratuitous invocation of a "deus ex machina" to explain something which science at the moment finds unexplainable. A theology based on a God of the Gaps hardly encourages man to pursue his scientific search for concrete answers. Furthermore, it has always been enveloped in a defensive cloud that views science and its quest as somehow inimical to religious beliefs and destructive of man's inner dimensions and goal.

This is probably true if we try to maintain the impossible mugwumpian position of accepting an evolutionary scientific image of the world while hanging on for dear life to an anachronistic, fixed religious interpretation of creation, cosmos and man.

Without destroying or weakening, man's religious perspective we can interpret the profound relations and similarities existing between man and the animal and cosmic worlds in a perspective other than that of the Ptolemaic and Thomistic view. We can view these profound similarities and relations as arising from the sequential roles played by the various levels of being in a common evolutionary process. As we will see in subsequent chapters, this shift in our theological perspective far from weakening or destroying man's commitment to the future actually strengthens and feeds that challenge with a dynamism that no fixed theological explanation could ever hope to match.

But before we plunge into that shift in theological perspective, imposing and attractive as that task is, we must first explore an evolutionary image of man as modern science sees it in terms of the paleontological record.

Fossils are quite scarce both because of the combination of circumstances required for their formation and also the limited possibilities of man finding them in an undisturbed setting where they can be properly identified and dated. When we reach the area of pre-human and human evolution fossils become even more rare. As the immediate ancestors of man became more proficient in the use of primitive tools and in hunting, competition among the closely related species naturally increased. Individuals and populations in the line leading to man simply decimated their less progressive cousins. In that line we have evidence not only of the deadliness of the struggle for survival in the near complete extinction of all parahuman forms, but also of the distinct advantages of those in the line leading to man. Even before the human level was reached, our ancestors were more skilled in the use of tools than their neighbors. Their fingers and hands were more supple; their eyes more adapted to binocular vision. These two traits coupled with the predatory nature of these higher primates would have been of crucial advantage when the food supply ran low and competition rose. Small wonder that our evidence for human evolution is at times sketchy.

The student of comparative anatomy places the human species in the broad biological group of mammals. This animal group first came on the scene some seventy to a hundred million years ago when the therapsids, the transitional form of mammal-like reptiles, left their aquatic home during the Triassic and Jurassic periods. In the transition, these animals developed more mammal-like teeth, skull and jaws as well as a more advanced mode of walking. The newly evolved mammals of the Jurassic world were small, the size of mice and rats in most cases, though at least one species had already attained the size of a domestic cat. Size, however, was not crucial to survival or success in this case as these primitive mammals possessed a creative instability and other advantages that allowed them to specialize very quickly along many different lines.

From this varied group eventually evolved the primates, the monkeys, apes, chimpanzees, orangoutang and man as well as lesser known members like the primitive and tiny goblin-like tarsier of Malaysia. Its fossil ancestors were most likely the stem from which the whole primate group came. During the late Oligocene era, fossil ancestors of the Ceylonese Langur apparently gave rise to a side branch from which descended all the monkeys of the Old World.

About the same time a small gibbon-like creature, *Propliopithecus*, populated the Fayum region of Egypt. Millions of years ago this region, near the present Aswan Dam, was the shoreline of a vast tropical jungle that sheltered a primate population far more varied and extensive than has existed anywhere since. *Propliopithecus*, along with *Parapithecus* from the early Oligocene and *Pliopithecus* from the Miocene, indicate the course of gibbon evolution.

Between *Propliopithecus*, some thirty million years ago, and our next known ancestor, the Dryopithecines, is a gap of some ten million years for which we have no fossil evidence.

The Dryopithecines were a very cosmopolitan group both in their time span, which extended roughly from twenty to nine million years ago, and in their range, which extended over Africa, Europe and Asia. In this span of eleven million years many forms of the Dryopithecines evolved, most of which died out after some unsuccessful adaptations. One family, the Proconsul type, however, was quite successful. Members of this group ranged through a variety of sizes and forms from that of a large monkey to one the size of a gorilla. The skulls of Proconsul generally resemble that of an ape, though without the heavy eye-brow ridge and the shelflike reinforcement behind the front teeth of the lower jaw, both characteristic of the modern gorilla. His limbs indicate that he lived pretty much on the ground, using his forearms for support like the modern ape, but also on occasion walking somewhat erect. Yet certain characteristics of the forearm foreshadow those of the human line. After considerable and quite heated debate over where Proconsul belongs in the evolutionary schema, most scientists today place him somewhere among the early stages of the ape family, rather than at the dividing point of the two branches leading to man and the ape as first thought.

In January of 1967, Dr. L.S.B. Leakey announced the discovery of the remains of eight adults and one child, the oldest known members of the Dryopithecine complex as well as the oldest known members of the family of man, the *Hominidae*. Leakey has given the group the genus name of *Kenyapithecus* and divided it into two species, *africanus* and *wickeri*. Whether this splintering into new species and genera will stand the test of time is not known, but these ancestors of man once roamed the forests around Lake Victoria, South Africa, and their importance in outlining human evolution is great. Of their life and habits we know next to nothing except that they were omnivorous, living off small animals, berries, nuts and roots some nineteen to twenty million years ago.

Recently scientists at the University of California, Berkeley, have tried to work out an evolutionary timetable for the primates by comparing the serum albumin, a common protein constituent of the blood, taken from all the modern primates. In analyzing the albumins of man and the other primates, these scientists suggest that the human line and African apes shared a common ancestor as recently as the Pliocene period and began their separate paths about five million years ago. They also suggest that the orangoutang separated from the line leading to the African apes about eight million years ago, with the gibbons breaking off from the mainstream some ten million years ago. This timetable, based on theories of the rate of albumin evolutionary changes which closely reflect genetic mutations, could lead to a revision of the commonly accepted timetable given above which dates man's divergence from the apes back some twenty or thirty million years. For the present, we can show only the main lines of human evolution and accept the question marks, both in the dating and the evaluation of fossils.

Even when first announced, Leakey's 1967 discovery created quite a fury among the paleontologists. It would have required a major revision in the date commonly accepted for the separation of the primate line into a pongid or ape branch and the hominid or prehuman man line, shoving this back some six million years from fourteen to twenty million years ago. Important new evidence, however, came in the summer of 1969 when Simons and Pilbeam, two Yale University scientists, reevaluated some Dryopithecine remains uncovered in India in the late 1920s. The two fossil jaws, which had lain on museum shelves for years, were dated at between eight and fifteen million years old. But far more important was their reassignment to the Ramapithecine group which had until then been included under the broad Dryopithecine grouping. The Yale scientists argued from details of the teeth and jaws that these two fossils were definitely prehuman men, along the line leading to the Australopithecines and eventually man, but also that they were very early representatives of the hominid line. Most scientists accepted this evidence and have now returned to the earlier conjecture of roughly fourteen million years ago for the splintering of the primate line to man and ape. Leakey's twenty million year old "hominid" has been reassigned to the ape line.

In tracing man's ancestry we should recall that we are not dealing with straight lines of evolutionary descent. Our ancestral lineage resembles much more a tangled bush than the clearly delineated branches of an elm or oak tree. And even in the tangled bush we have only a few scattered reference points, many of which are hard to situate properly and without question in the overall picture.

Between the most recent Ramapithecines, some nine million years old, and the next known fossils in the line leading to man is another gap of some five million years for which we have no evidence of proto- or prehuman men. This gap is particularly disturbing since it was the era during which the prehuman primates apparently migrated from a center in India to a more congenial setting in South Africa. It also makes most likely the emergence of tool-making and critical changes in life style for our ancestors.

Another important 1969 discovery was made by a team headed under the direction of Professor F. Clark Howell from the University of Chicago. In an ancient swamp and delta of the Omo River of southern Ethiopia Howell recovered forty hominid teeth and two jaws. The jaws clearly appeared to be related to the robust forms of the Australopithecines or southern apes while the teeth appeared to be related to the gracile or light-boned Australopithecines which many consider to be either human or immediately prehuman.

What happened between nine and four million years ago? Despite our lack of direct evidence, a relative wealth of material on both ends has made it possible for scientists to picture with some detail the probable missing links.

Paleontologists picture these missing transitional forms as slightly larger than our modern gibbons, hairy and tailless, with no forehead but well developed facial muscles. Their large canine teeth interlocked so that they could only chew up and down. Living in small bands of from ten to thirty, their social groups likely consisted of a few adult males and several females with their offspring. Each band seems to have had its own roughly defined territory with a home base in the trees nearby where they nested. Expert climbers, they could also run for short distances on two legs, though striding or walking was impossible for them. As for tools, it is quite likely that they used sticks and stones, perhaps even reshaping these with their hands or teeth to suit their purposes better. Their diet was mainly vegetarian, supplemented by worms, grubs, and small sick or injured animals that were easy to capture.

Studies in primate psychology indicate that relations between neighboring bands were probably hostile, or at best, neutral. Even so, there was enough contact to allow for intermating and the exchange of genes. Communications were quite limited as all indications point to an absence of the power of verbal speech.

Four million years ago, or perhaps a little earlier, our earth's climate changed enough to turn thick forests into broad grassy plains with scattered clusters of trees. In this new environment the hominids were forced to leave their arboreal homes. Adaptations came slowly in some cases and not at all in others. Some of these hominids gradually developed the ability to run and even to walk erect. These eventually evolved into the higher primates and man, while those bands that remained in the dwindling forests gradually gave rise through a Langur-type to the modern gibbons. In all these primitive groups, the strongest males dominated. As more progressive forms appeared with expanded powers of communication through a simple verbal language, leadership of the bands must have shifted slowly to the older males. In a society bound by verbal communication the premium is placed not on brute strength, but on age, since a longer life allows an individual time to learn more.

As the Pliocene period gave way to the early Pleistocene, roughly two and a half million years ago, our fossil record picks up again. For primate evolution this era marks a turning point and the probable appearance of the first human beings. Long droughts had brought the primate population almost to a standstill when suddenly conditions became much more favorable and an explosively rapid evolution occurred within the primate groups.

This turning point is marked in time by an interesting phenomenon. Some two and a half million years ago our earth's magnetic axis silently shifted. A tell-tale record of this shift has been left in the volcanic rocks that spewed forth in South Africa at that time. This molten lava contained tiny metallic fragments which oriented themselves like the needle of a magnetic compass only to be frozen in position as the rock congealed. Over the centuries a whole series of such frozen compasses marks the perigrinations of our magnetic poles. Today they offer a very precise means of dating fossils found within the same rocks. Coupled with the now standard potassium-argon analysis (see p. 42), these minute frozen compasses supply scientists additional clues to the actual age of the earliest known member of man's family, the Kanapoi hominid. Only the lower part of an upper arm managed to escape the rapacious jaws of the crocodiles that infested an ancient lake in Kenya some two and a half million years ago, but this elbow is enough to tell scientists that it once belonged to a direct and immediate ancestor of man. Preliminary analysis of this recent find indicates that it belongs somewhere between the Ramapithecine group of Dryopithecines and the more recent Australopithecines, of which it may have been the first known representative.

By the beginning of the Pleistocene, two million years ago, the primate stock leading to man was represented by two, possibly three types, though some scientists prefer to clump these under a single label of Australopithecines. The famous "Nutcracker Man," *Zinjanthropus bosei*, and other heavy-boned, robust forms like *Paranthropus* and the Australopithecines of Kromdrai, Peninj and Swartkrans might be clustered together, either as near-men contemporary with true man or as members of the human family that specialized and later died out. With giant molar teeth, massive jaws and equally massive facial muscles, these robust forms were well equipped to survive on a vegetarian diet. Their skulls were equally heavy-boned to support the jaws and associated muscles, a factor that left little room for brain development. Zinjanthropus is a classic example of this for his skull is almost flat with no forehead at all. This limitation of the possible development of the brain may have been one of the factors that led eventually to the extinction of the robust Australopithecines some 250,000 years ago.

A second type or race of the Australopithecines is characterized by much lighter bones and a diet of meat. The classic Australopithecines of Taung, Sterkfontein, Makapansgat and Garusi, all in southern Africa, are good examples of this general grouping. When first discovered in the 1930s, these Australopithecines were a real mystery. For one thing, most scientists had assumed that the crucial turning point in human evolution came with the development of a large brain which was then followed by the ability to communicate in a language and to make tools. The Australopithecines had quite small brains but according to Doctors Broom and Dart, their discoverers, they used crude natural tools. For the scientists this posed a dilemma. If these fossils represented only pre- or near-men, then how could their use of tools be explained, disputed as that claim might have been? And if they were actually human, then how explain their small brains?

In the 1930s and 1940s the dispute raged furiously among the specialists and without light being shed on the real issue because certain key pieces were missing. Three of these missing pieces in the puzzle have come to light since 1960, primarily through the tireless efforts and extraordinary "luck" of L.S.B. Leakey in his diggings at the Olduvai Gorge in Tanzania.

The first clue came with the discovery of the "Nutcracker Man," a perfect example of the robust vegetarian Australopithecines. When first discovered, Leakey cautiously dated it at about three-quarters of a million years ago. The new fossil raised some interesting side questions, one of which was the circle of artificially rounded stones carefully arranged on the living floor close to where the fossil bones of the Nutcracker Man were found. They might have been the foundation for a dwelling, but in any event they seemed to indicate a certain amount of intelligence on the part of the individual who laid them out originally.

Then there was the so-called "pre-Zinj child," the skeleton of a young child apparently predating the Nutcracker Man. Again crude pebble tools were uncovered in the deposits, seemingly from the same age, and again indicating some rational intelligence.

These two pieces began to make sense in terms of the overall picture when, after several years of research, Leakey and scientists at the University of California announced a revision of the Nutcracker Man's age. Dating him at one and three-quarter million years by the potassium-argon method, the origins of man were pushed back more than a million years earlier than previously thought. Man's age on earth was more than doubled in one stroke.

In 1965 Leakey announced details and a clarification of the "pre-Zinjanthropus child." With the potassium-argon technique the stone circle, remnant of an ancient shelter, was dated at about 1,800,000 years ago and the remains of the child along with the foot and collar-bone of a woman found in the same deposit, slightly more recent in age. The scientific world was shocked at this doubling of mankind's age, but subsequent finds have only confirmed the dating. To indicate their definite position within man's ancestry and family, the pre-Zinj child and woman were given the scientific designation of *Homo habilis*. More recently, Dr. Leakey announced the discovery of an almost perfect complete skull of *Homo habilis*, giving us some valuable information about this manlike creature, smaller than the modern pygmy, which lived over two million years ago.

In 1966 Leakey announced the discovery of a third crucial piece in the puzzle, another member of the habiline family. The skull and jaw of a woman, this fossil was given the popular name of "Cinderella." Dated some 800,000 years ago, a million years after the pre-Zinj child and woman, this fossil may be an important link in the possible direct line of modern-type man from the pre-Zinj forms to "Cinderella," on through the very controversial and fragmentary Kanam jaw and Kanjera skull to Cromagnon and modern man. Though Leakey maintains that the robust Australopithecines form a separate side branch of para-humans, most scientists view them as a race or subdivision within the human line that died out some 250,000 years ago. The more gracile, classic Australopithecines died out somewhat earlier during the Lower Pleistocene, 500,000 years ago.

Exactly when true man appeared on the scene is a question no scientist, philosopher, or theologian can answer. The prime reason for this inability is the fact that no one can set up a definite list of criteria characteristic of man which can then be applied *without dispute* to all fossil remains. To speak of man as a tool maker and user, for instance, in the sense that only man can make and use tools is to ignore the important discoveries of Jane Goodall's work with the chimpanzees in the wilds of Africa. Miss Goodall has photographed the chimps, on occasion, chewing leaves just enough to convert them into a handy sponge for water in tree cavities that cannot be reached with the tongue. The chimps also fashion tools from branches, trimming and shortening them to suit their purposes. Likewise, the social bond of a family cannot be the sole criterion of human existence since many studies of chimpanzees, baboons and other primates indicate the presence of a well developed and quite "human" social structure. Symbolic language is another criterion often suggested, though Miss Goodall's studies indicate that abstract communication exists among the chimpanzees and anthropologists tell us that primitive man existed some time before verbal communication developed. In addition, the criterion of speech faces an impossible hurdle in the fact that scientists often cannot tell whether a particular fossil skeleton possessed the ability to talk when alive. Even if the scientists decide that a particular fossil possessed the facial and tongue muscles along with the hard palate necessary for speech as we know it today, no one can say for certain that he used this capacity. And besides, some animals like the parrot and Myna bird can articulate words without the hard palate and facial muscle so necessary in human speech. An upright stance and gait, binocular vision, the opposable thumbs, each of these is hardly an exclusive characteristic of man, and even if taken in combination—arbitrary as our combination may be—human evolution still occurred as a process involving gradual transitions in *physical* characteristics. All in all, the question of dating man's first appearance on this earth remains a mystery, though it seems safe enough to say that mankind probably evolved from the primate stock somewhere in southeastern Africa between two and two and a half million years ago.

The real problem of terminology should by now be apparent to those not trained in science and paleontology. In dealing with modern man and the living primates it is easy to make a distinction between human and non-human. In picturing the early stages of human evolution we are often tempted to combine these two modern terminal forms with a hyphen and say that the early forms were "ape-men" or "man-apes." Such a practice forces the present into the past and is completely invalid as it contradicts the facts of evolutionary development. Even when we speak of a fossil being "near-man," "pre-hominoid," or "para-hominoid," we must be careful not to picture this fossil in terms of our modern experience of man. Modern type man, *Homo sapiens sapiens*, is a far cry from *Homo habilis*. Man as we know him today emerged very gradually, and the physical distinction between his earliest form and the para-human primates that shared the earth with him is often blurred or indistinct. But those early forms, both human and non-human, are quite primitive and quite removed from our modern primate forms. Even so, only two million years of evolution separate us from *Homo habilis* while our common ancestry with the ape extends back at least five million years and probably twenty million years.

The great Ice Ages, four in all, began during the days of *Homo habilis* and the Australopithecines and lasted until some forty thousand years ago. In this time immense sheets of ice, often more than a mile thick, advanced and retreated four times over northern Europe, Asia and North America. At present we have no evidence that *Homo habilis* ever migrated from southeast Africa, but it seems certain that somewhere around 700,000 years ago this creature, scarcely four feet tall, did leave Africa for Eurasia. Even before this, perhaps, the habiline or Australopithecine group gave rise to the first *Homo erectus*. "George" of Maiko Gully, Olduvai, appears to be the first in this very important stage of human evolution which includes the well known fossil men of Java and Peking. "George" dates back a million years, about 300,000 years before the *Homo erectus* of Peking and Java. Recently Leakey uncovered a contemporary cousin of the Java and Peking fossils at Olduvai, so that the sequence from the Maiko Gully fossil appears as the beginning of a side branch within the human family that eventually became extinct, with the main stream passing through the habiline, "Cinderella" and other less specialized forms.

The story of *Homo erectus* dates back to the stormy days of Charles Darwin. When his *Descent of Man* appeared in 1871 discussions of the missing link between man and the ape set European circles spinning in debates. A Dutch doctor came to the conclusion that the only way to settle the debate would be to find the missing "ape-man," which Darwin and Haeckel set up as the hypothetical ancestor of man and the ape. This, of course, was long before the discovery of the Australopithecines, and at the time, only two fossil remains of early man had been uncovered. These though were not really understood or appreciated since most people still assumed that man had appeared on the scene at most some fifty thousand years ago.

While the debate raged on, Dr. Dubois decided that the most likely place to find the missing link would be the fossil-bearing areas of Trinil, Java, close to the Solo River. In 1889 he resigned his post in the Netherlands and persuaded the government to give him an assignment near his chosen site. After two seasons of digging near the Solo River, Dubois unearthed a piece of a human jaw, part of a skull and a few teeth. These were indeed the missing link or, better, one of several important missing links, the first of many subsequent finds belonging to the group popularly known as the Java man. Originally scientists referred to this fossil as *Pithecanthropus javenensis*; today they include it in the broader group of *Homo erectus*.

Dubois' discovery did not settle the debate about man's evolution. Actually it added to the furor, so unusual was this fossil and so unwilling were many scientists and laymen to accept man's evolution from a subhuman species. For many years the Java man was refused a position within the human family and relegated to the ape group. Today there is no doubt that *Homo erectus* of Java and his near cousin, *Homo erectus* of Peking (discovered in 1928) represent a definite stage of evolution within the family of man, either in the direct line to modern man or as a side branch that eventually became isolated and extinct. The controverted Chellean man of Maiko Gorge and Olduvai, *Atlanthropus* from Aleria, and the Mauer man of Germany may also fit into this early *Homo erectus* phase.

Early pictures of the "cave man" from Java and Peking portray a rather brutish, hairy individual, stooped and bow-legged. It is always difficult to reconstruct the perishable facial features from the bare bones of a skull which tell us nothing about the texture or color of the skin, or about its supposed hairiness. In the early days of evolutionary thought scientists were often prejudiced by preconceived notions of what early man "ought to be like." Today scientists and artists are much more careful about their reconstructions of fossil man.

A more valid picture of the Peking and Java men shows a man, perhaps five feet tall, with a low sloping forehead, protruding mouth and receding chin. His brain capacity was smaller than modern man's but considerably larger than that of the Australopithecines. Above the eyes, a very heavy bony brow seems to place him somewhat off the direct line of our ancestors, though certainly within the family of man. In many other ways, *Homo erectus* seems to have been a highly specialized group which because of geographic isolation eventually became cut off from a less specialized central group from which modern man has descended. Of this central, unspecialized group we have very little concrete evidence, though "George" of Maiko Gully and "Cinderella" of Olduvai may have belonged to it. Of the more specialized *Homo erectus* we have many fossil remains scattered over Africa, Asia and Europe and dating from 600,000 to about 350,000 years ago.

When the early forms of Neanderthal man evolved either from a central *Homo erectus* group or from the later representatives of the habiline group, human evolution entered a new phase. First uncovered in the Neander Valley of Germany and since unearthed all over northern Africa, Europe, western Asia and the Near East, Neanderthal man forms a true complex of many different forms. Living in the tundra areas along the edge of the great glaciers that covered much of northern Germany, England and south-central Russia, he was a skilled hunter and the first human to use animal hides for clothing. His tools were rough shaped stones, greatly advanced over the simple hand ax of Peking and Java man and the pebble tools of the habilines. In brain capacity Neanderthal man matched, and in some cases, exceeded that of modern man.

Neanderthal man has been plagued by the same derogatory stereotype of the "cave man" that afflicted our early images of the Java man. There is however some substance in the picture of a massive, heavy-bodied, barrel-chested, bull-necked brute with bulging low forehead and slightly bowed legs, since this aptly describes one of the many Neanderthal types. This very specialized form lived some forty thousand years ago just before the last great glacial period. But there were other less "primitive" forms of Neanderthal man, such as those found in the caves of Mount Carmel. These fossil men represent an earlier stage in the Neanderthal complex and it is probably from them rather than from the much later and more specialized forms of the typical "cave man" that modern man eventually evolved. It seems likely that the classic Neanderthal "cave man" represents a side branch that became isolated, highly specialized and finally extinct.

Of the earliest forms of modern-type man, we have only fragmentary records in the fossil remains of Mount Carmel, Kanam and Kanjera, Heidelberg, Ternafine in Algeria, Swanscombe in England, Steinheim in Germany, and Fontechevade in France. They may have derived directly from the habiline state through an early unspecialized *Homo erectus* or through a transitional phase of an unspecialized *Homo erectus neanderthalensis*, but in either event the early *Homo sapiens* forms quickly replaced the more specialized *Homo erectus* and Neanderthal men. Whether this came about through intermarriage and absorption, by conquest, or because the more specialized forms were decimated by disease we may never know for certain.

Cromagnon man was in almost every way a typical modern-type man in his skeleton. Unlike the shorter Neanderthal men, males in the Cromagnon population averaged six feet in height, with the women averaging about five and a half feet. With a jutting lower jaw (orthognathic), Cromagnon's skull was typically modern, with no heavy eye-brow ridges, a high forehead and rounder brain case. The earliest of the Cromagnon people possessed a rather high type of Old Stone Age culture known as Aurignacian. Besides some rather sophisticated stone tools they used bone, particularly for making awls, needles and skin-working tools. The beauty of their cave paintings still are marvels of art in the caves of southern France and Spain, while the care with which they buried their dead is but another indication of their well developed culture.

Cromagnon man probably came to Europe as an invader from Asia around 27,000 years ago. Eventually the Aurignacian culture was replaced by another, that of the Magdalenian people who lived in Europe some 15,000 years ago. They in turn were replaced by a succession of Mesolithic or Middle Stone Age cultures which brought the advent of agriculture and the domestication of animals.

Eight to ten thousand years ago the world's climate again changed drastically. For the large mammals this meant disaster, the extinction of the wooly mammoths and rhinoceros, the cave bears, giant wolves, as well as of the reindeer and horses of North America. Confronted with this radical change in environment and new waves of invaders from Asia, mankind in Europe took a major step forward. Further advances in tool making were introduced but more important were the shifts observable in man's social structures. Communal living became more common and extensive in its patterns. By the beginning of the New Stone Age, the Neolithic, some 10,000 years ago man had reached most of the out-of-the-way regions of the earth, including Australia. Several waves of immigration across the Bering Straits connecting Siberia and Alaska, starting some 40,000 years ago, populated the New World.

This survey of human evolution covers some thirty million years of preparation and some two million years of mankind's development. Again it is difficult to grasp in a concrete way the immense reaches of time. To shed some light on the task of visualizing human evolution we can adapt the schema we used in dealing with the evolution of life. To set the scale in terms of man's appearance between two and two and a half million years ago, we can reduce this span, in terms of a calendar year, so that one "day" equals six thousand years and one "hour" equals 250 years.

Thus man evolves from a common, still unknown ancestor, in the Australopithecines or habiline group on January first. The robust forms of *Australopithecus*, represented by *Paran-*

thropus and *Zinjanthropus,* managed to survive well into the fall, dying out in late October and early November, while the more classic, gracile Australopithecines seem to have survived only to the end of summer. In the beginning *Homo habilis* could run on two legs and even walk for short distances. As time passed man developed the ability to walk or stride for longer periods. Hunting in small bands and craftsman of simple pebble tools, he communicated both culture and embryonic art, though an extensive language was unlikely and communications may have been limited to a non-verbal language. The use of fire likewise underwent a gradual development, first as a defense against wild animals of the night and for warmth, and only much later in Neanderthal times for cooking meat.

In its early stages human evolution was extremely slow and tedious, just as the evolution of life was in its infancy. Thousands of years and hundreds of centuries were spent in the almost imperceptible improvement of stone tools and hunting skills. During this span, man's brain increased both in size and complexity, doubling in size.

The Peking and Java men would be situated in early October of our schema with Neanderthal man appearing somewhere in mid-November. The first clear indications of a religious belief would be found somewhere around December 20th in the burial sites of the later Neanderthaloids. By December 28th all the primitive, non-sapiens forms of man had died out or been absorbed by the more advanced Cromagnon invaders. Agriculture and the beginnings of an urban culture began during the evening of December 29th. Greece reached its zenith about 2:30 P.M. of December 31st and the Christian era began an hour and a half later, at 4 P.M. When Columbus discovered America a few minutes after 10 P.M. New Year's Eve, he found not only a new world but also the Indians who had migrated there sometime on Christmas Day. The Mayflower Pact was signed about 10:35 P.M. New Year's Eve, while the American colonies gained their independence at the battles of Lexington, Concord and Yorktown about 11:15 the same evening.

When man emerged from his animal origins over two million years ago, a new era began in cosmic evolution. As in all the earlier phases of that evolution, mankind immediately began to diverge and spread out over the face of the land. New races, subspecies and cultures emerged and developed as small groups became geographically isolated. Yet because of a nomadic ability to live most anywhere by creating his own environment, individual groups of men never became so isolated that their divergence reached to the point of species formation. To form a new species a particular group must be isolated from the main stock for many centuries so that random mutations in both groups can accumulate to the point where the two groups are no longer genetically compatible. Geographic isolation must eventually build into reproductive isolation, the inability of the two groups to mate and produce fertile offspring, for this is the biological basis of species. Mankind indeed has diverged but never to the point of splitting up into isolated species.

A second important aspect of the emergence of man is the fact that mankind has taken into its hands the thread of cosmic history. Rather than simply adapting and responding to the environment as the brute animals still do, man creates his own environment. Increasingly, and especially with the recent technological explosion, mankind is more and more immersed in a controlled environment, an environment which he himself controls. This, perhaps, is man's most challenging task today and tomorrow—the task of directing and extending human (and cosmic) evolution along paths that will permit the fuller expansion of his humanity and the completion of his fullest potentials.

Finally, the emergence of man turns the cosmos in upon itself. In man, as Teilhard de Chardin so often said so well, evolution becomes conscious of itself. In man, the emphasis of evolution shifts gradually from the biological and the organic to the psychological and social. In man, evolution focuses and concentrates all its energies on the expansion of consciousness. For cosmic evolution this is a crucial turn of affairs since it means that convergence on the human level will focus on man's intellectual, social and moral evolution more than on an increase in his biological complexity. To put it another way, in man, evolution will concentrate on increasing both complexity and consciousness in man's inner dimensions and leave the increase of complexity/consciousness of man's biological and organic aspect to trail along in the wake.

All of which brings us to man's present situation, and the task of confronting a new scientific image of man and the universe with a theological image still for the most part rooted in and restricted by the dimensions of a pre-Darwinian fixed world vision. The task we will set ourselves to in the following chapters is simply that of outlining a new theological perspective, of sketching an overall evolutionary explanation of creation, the nature of man and the universe, man's fall or rise, and finally a scientific prognosis of man's future.

4

creation, man, and the world in process

We began this exploration of man's place in evolution with an examination of some early images of the world and their gradual metamorphosis over the centuries. More often than not, these transformations took shape first in the scientific realm and only much later made their way or, better, forced their entrance into the reluctant world of the theologian. New scientific discoveries have repeatedly brought new insights into the theological explanations worked out by succeeding generations. Thus a constant process of renovation, evolution and revolution occurs within theological thought as man tries to keep the expression and explanation of his religious beliefs in accord with his ever changing world-image drawn from science and experience.

Since the days of Moses, Christ and the medieval theologians, some rather drastic, even radical, changes have been incorporated into our Christian perspective. And this very fact forces us to reevaluate our conception of just what it means to be a Christian and what we imply when we speak of the Christian *faith*. Do we mean the acceptance of a certain list of defined revealed dogmas which can never change or be modified, or do we rather indicate a living and on-going revelation of God in and through Christ, the Word of God, along with man's living response to that revelation? To reduce our Christian faith to a list of dogmas is not only simplistic but also in a real sense heretical and idolatrous. The Christian who recites the Apostles' Creed and believes that the whole of his faith is encapsulated

in that finite list is actually guilty of creating an idol out of some
very human constructs.

Every attempt on the part of man to express in words the
mystery of our Christian faith is doomed to partial failure. It
was this very inability of man to grasp fully the mystery of God
and of man's relationship with his Creator that made Thomas
Aquinas a "Christian agnostic." In his work *On Truth*,
Aquinas reminded us that "What God really is will always be
hidden from us, and this is the supreme knowledge which we
can have of God in this life—that we know that he transcends
every idea we can ever form of him." Yet how often in a
simplistic, logical and legalistic view of our faith do we forget
this wisdom and try to erect our human formulas, even those
infallibly defined by the magisterium, into unchangeable idols.
Very much like Linus clutching his blanket, we seek psychological and emotional security in verbalisms to which we attribute divine (salvific) attributes.

The supposed conflict between science and religion more
often than not results from a confusion between religious faith
and belief. Theologian Mary Daly has clearly underscored this
vital distinction in an article for *Commonweal*. She wrote:
"One of the most prevalent distortions is the notion of faith as
an act of knowledge with a low degree of evidence. Actually,
this is a description of belief, rather than faith, and it leads to
the idea that an 'act of the will' is necessary to make up for the
lack of evidence for what one affirms as true. Thus, one wills or
decides to believe certain propositions proposed by the Church
as being 'divinely revealed.' It is precisely this notion which
underlies the indoctrination from which Catholics have suffered. What it means is that one unquestioningly accepts as
true certain formulae, on the assumption that if they are ques-
tioned or doubted, faith is lost and serious sin is committed. It
means that the 'believer' gives assent to his own brainwashing,
to spiritual mutilation. It is the very opposite of that 'faith
which seeks understanding' which has driven the saints and
mystics toward transcendence. This soul-shrinking conception
of faith is welcomed by some as a simple escape from responsibility and from the questions urged upon them by reality. How-

ever, ever greater numbers are finding it a crippling hindrance to self-realization, to communication, and to action.

"Far truer to the experience of religious consciousness is Tillich's description of faith as 'the state of being ultimately concerned.' This indicates that what is being expressed is an attitude of the whole existing person, an attitude of seeking— and therefore of loving—God with the whole mind, heart and soul. Faith in this sense involves risk and doubt. It is forever driving beyond itself and therefore recognizes the inadequacy of every formulation. This is not to say that it refuses to see the need for creeds and formulae, but it does recognize the need for continual criticism of them."

Faith as the state of being ultimately concerned keynotes the divine vocation to self-transcendence that is basic to man's pilgrim nature. True faith is the commitment to self-transcendence, Abraham's leap into the unknown.

We might profit by recalling Karl Rahner's suggestion that the dogmas of our Christian creed and the definitions of the Roman magisterium, along with the theological explanations of scholars of every century, are "beginning and emergence, not conclusion and end." Rahner continues, in the first volume of his *Theological Investigations*, "In the last resort any individual human perception of truth only has meaning as beginning and promise of the knowledge of God." *Theological explanations should imbue us with an eschatological dynamism and hope, rather than lull us with the idolatrous and false sense of security that hanging on to them as beliefs will infallibly lead to salvation.*

To recall the true meaning of our Christian faith we might reflect again on a man often praised in both Old and New Covenants as the classic example of a man of faith. "Go out from your country and from your kindred and from your father's house and come into a land which I will show you. It is Yahweh who speaks." Abraham has become the model of a man of faith because he accepted the call of the Spirit to embrace his *pilgrim role* as a human being. Man's essential nature and task in this world is that of the man of the exodus, a continual pilgrim. Our Christian faith is then an everyday pilgrimage to the eternal and the transcendent. It is *more vocation than formula*, though the formulae are often useful guidelines. This vocation aspect, then, must always remain primary. When it slips from that primacy, we run the risk of erecting our own human formulae and structures (intellectual as well as institutional) into golden calves that blind us to the land promised Abraham and his faithful sons.

In this context it is interesting that Pope Paul VI dedicated 1967 as a "Year of Faith." At the very moment when every theological explanation and formulation was being challenged, reworked, and rethought, the Holy Father reminded us that as Christians we must be men of faith, not attached to formulae but rather living the vibrant reality of our vocation as pilgrims of that truth which will be revealed to us only at the end of time. Today we see as through a clouded glass. Only at the end of our pilgrimage, when we enter the land promised to Abraham and his offspring, will we see clearly.

It is in this context that we must regain and relearn the very precise and clear distinction that underlies all theological efforts and speculations. The essence of our Christian faith is a person, not a set of dogmas: the Christ, the Word of God. To the Jewish people of his day Christ expressed in his own flesh, in his actions and words, the perfect infleshment of divine love.

Christ's primary revelation was himself. Only after some thirty years did he undertake the ministry of the word, as prophet of the good news that the Kingdom of God has come. And then, only towards the end of his earthly life, did he assume the role of master, instructing and teaching his disciples.

The eternal truths of man's relationship with his Creator were expressed by Christ in the framework of his day. Expressed in the simplest of language and with a profound conciseness, these relational truths have nevertheless been distorted by those Christians who prefer to focus all their attention on the external framework rather than on the essence. Thus Christians continue to parrot the parable of the Good Shepherd without ever trying to extend Christ's incarnation as the Word of God by giving renewed flesh to a profound truth concerning man's relationship with his Father in words and image that will make sense to a child born and raised in the inner city who likely has never seen the countryside, let alone a sheep. The recent humorous, but deadly serious collection of comments and reactions from modern ghetto youth in *God is for Real, Man* should make this lesson obvious.

There should always be for Christians a clear distinction between Christ as the concrete incarnation and revelation of God's invisible reality and our own feeble human attempts to express that mystery. Christ infleshed the ideal relationship between God and man, leaving men to accept humbly their pilgrim attempts to articulate that mysterious vocation which He as the Second Adam so well voiced to us.

This distinction between the underlying message of relationship and its external framework was quite evident in the early days of Christianity when, for instance, the Church Fathers proposed two different interpretations of the Genesis account of Creation. While most theologians accepted the six days of creation as an accurate, literally true account of creation, other theologians in the Alexandrian school proposed a symbolic interpretation of this same account. Arguing from premises of Greek philosophy, the Alexandrian theologians claimed that creation had to be instantaneous. But because an instantaneous creation is so hard to conceive, they suggested that the authors of Genesis were perfectly justified in expressing creation in terms of a six-day narrative.

Much later, when astronomers and geologists gained new evidence of the long history of our universe and earth, theologians began to interpret the six days of creation as very long periods of time, perhaps thousands and thousands of years. More recently, as the scientists learned of man's evolution, these explanations of creation were again modified to fit the new scientific images. In the past half century or more many Christians have come to think of God as intervening in the course of evolution to create directly a soul and infuse this into a body that had evolved from some lower primate stock, thus creating man. In more recent days, new theological explanations have been worked out, more in keeping with the radical change brought about by acceptance of the evolutionary perspective. Yet throughout this long, still incomplete development of our understanding of creation the essential message has remained unchanged. This essence is not at all concerned with origins in time or space; it focuses rather on man's relationship with his Creator, and this alone.

In September of 1955, Pope Pius XII reminded the theologians and philosophers attending the International Thomist Congress that they cannot hope to make a lasting contribution to an understanding of man unless they are well-versed in modern science and its view of the world. This reminder and warning becomes vitally important when we realize that our scientific world image has changed so drastically, so radically, that it is no longer a simple question of re-interpreting or re-explaining this or that individual aspect of our faith. Aquinas constructed a magnificent synthesis, integrating his theological and philosophical insights with a scientific image contemporary with his world. Since then theologians, Catholic as well as Protestant, have been defensively reworking individual pieces of that medieval synthesis only when forced into a corner by new developments in science. It is about time that Christians recognize and accept the fact that modern science has added *a totally new dimension* to our world image. The implications of this new dimension are far deeper and more radical than many theologians are yet willing to admit, and certainly far more extensive and practical than most laymen suspect.

The modern scientific image of an evolving universe incorporates the fourth dimension of time, but most of our theological and religious explanations continue to skirt the temporal, remaining faithful to the cyclic, fixed philosophy of the Greeks and Ptolemy's stable geocentric cosmology. For all practical purposes, Christians today live in a dichotomous world, embracing an evolutionary, up-to-date scientific framework while clinging to anachronistic theological constructs. Our task now, and one we must face with courage and faith, is that of working out a new synthesis of science and religion, of articulating a whole new theological perspective in terms of evolution and process philosophy.

Some very important steps have been taken already in this direction by theologians of various Christian persuasions. And while they still have not explored every aspect of our Christian faith, we now have some key issues explained in terms of the evolutionary perspective. Possibly because scientific evolution had its most vital contact with theological thought in those areas concerned with the origin of man, the new explanations and approaches are most detailed in the areas of creation and man's origins, of Adam and Eve and the human situation we have classically called "original sin." This key area has served as a spring board from which theologians have set out to explore in terms of evolution and process philosophy our understanding of the ultimate nature of man and the universe, the question of natural and supernatural planes of existence, the problem of death and its aftermath, and the role of Christ in cosmogenesis—points we will deal with here./

/ The mystery of creation, of man and his nature, of the origin of sin and mankind's "fall" will never be fully grasped and appreciated by the human mind. They are realities so basic that no human mind can exhaust them. Thus as mankind advances in age, and hopefully in wisdom also, we will always require new, deeper and fuller explanations of these realities. Only by embracing this challenge of human nature will we remain faithful to our vocation as pilgrims in search of the fullness of truth. |

CREATION

When a Christian speaks of creation almost invariably he will call to mind, at least subconsciously, the classic words of Genesis,/ "In the beginning God created the heavens and the earth." For most Christians this simple biblical statement means that God created everything in the beginning and out of nothing. Yet is it all that simple?

We have already seen how early Christian theologians tried various explanations in their attempts to present a fuller picture of God as creator and sustainer of all that exists. Some Fathers of the Church, like Clement and Origen who were leaders of the Alexandrian school of biblical interpretation, claimed that the creation narrative of Genesis with its six days of labor is in fact an allegorical presentation of what was actually an instantaneous creation of all things in the beginning of time. Other Church Fathers, Ephrem, Basil the Great, Gregory of Nyssa and above all, the towering Augustine, held for a more literal acceptance of the Genesis account. Admitting that creation might have been instantaneous, they qualified this by suggesting a quasi-evolutionary explanation of creation. Gregory of Nyssa, for instance, suggested that God created everything "potentially and in their causes" in the beginning. The six days of Genesis then recorded "the development or unfolding of individual things from their causes or principles, according to a fixed and necessary order of succession."

Augustine gave more precision to the seminal views of Basil and Gregory, adding a serious warning that we should not seek in biblical thought any scientific explanation or revelation. He also was more limited in applying the idea of causal creation in the beginning and a subsequent unfolding or evolutionary development, limiting this to the world of life outside man whereas Gregory and Basil had extended it to all of creation.

In these explanations as well as in those proposed by the allegorical Alexandrians, a definite emphasis was placed on a golden age long ago in the beginning. It would undoubtedly be unfair to see this emphasis as caused exclusively by Greek philosophy alone since the nostalgia for a paradise lost appears universally in almost every culture. But it does seem evident that this conception of a timeless golden age in the beginning as expressed by the Greek philosophers was very influential in the early Christians allowing a very important biblical insight to slip into the background and be ignored almost completely. The biblical writers constantly remind us that *creation is not limited to the beginning of time.* As the Son of God said, "My Father works even until now." The biblical image of God emphasizes a creator who never ceases to create in and through the history of man and the world.

Yet as theology developed, and particularly as the theologians began to explain our religious beliefs more and more in terms of the hellenic philosophy of Plato and Aristotle, explanations of creation laid increasing stress on a certain instant in the beginning of time. This was rooted in the Greek philosophical principle that the essence of every being must be perfect and complete from the first moment of its existence. The Christian apologists incorporated this idea in their explanations of creation.

In the hellenic conception of reality and the world, change was not an essential aspect of a thing or substance. It does speak of "substantial change" in the sense that there is an overriding *entelechy* (purpose or substance). If this is altered the thing simply ceases to be itself and becomes something else. Thus when a dog is hit by a car, there is a substantial change. Rover ceases to be Rover and the corpse in the street is no longer a dog, much less Rover. Applied to the totality of things, this means that individuals may come and go, but dogs, cats, trees, and all the natural species will always remain substantially what they have been since the beginning. There cannot be, for hellenic philosophy, anything like an evolution of species. In keeping with this view, Christians have pictured God as creating a perfect and complete world in the beginning and then through his providential care preserving and sustaining all things in their essential, unchanging reality. There was an Eden from which mankind was expelled. For Christians the exile came because of Adam's pride; for the pagan Greek it came because of the gods' perversity. In either case, the temptation, and the logical conclusion, is that this world of time and supposed change is actually an illusion and shadow, basically an unimportant interlude between paradise lost and paradise regained. In such a world image there is no room for time as an essential component of all things. Time in the evolutionary sense of duration means a process of real, substantial changes in which the individual thing is actually in the process of becoming itself—not simply unfolding a preformed pattern, but actually developing anew, being created out of nothing, transcending itself in the process of creation. While the three-dimensional image of the Greek philosophers and medieval theologians and poets speaks of time and change, it never quite comes to grips either with time or with change as we today know and understand these aspects of all reality.

When astronomers introduced the concept of change, duration, and evolution into our image of the heavens and the geologists later disclosed these same features in a new understanding of our earth, theologians hesitatingly began to wonder about the validity and value of an explanation of creation that pictures everything as created perfect and complete in the beginning. With Darwin introducing the concept of change into the world of natural species and even man, the questions became even more pressing. Today, we cannot ignore them, much as some might like to. Is it still possible, given our modern understanding of evolution, to make a clear distinction between God's creative action in the beginning and his sustaining, preserving providence in ages after? Geneticist Theodosius Dobzhansky has said that "evolution is the method whereby Creation is accomplished." But evolution is a true process; it is not a series of discrete steps, nor a staircase of fixed instants or moments in time.

The perspective we have chosen here differs radically from the position common to hellenic thought and Christian philosophy and theology prior to the Darwinian revolution (whose real impact we are only beginning to experience in the past decade). The evolutionary perspective is based on the addition and incorporation of a fourth and utterly new dimension to our image of the universe. This is a true historical dimension of duration, process and evolution, based on the conviction that the temporal processes of on-going change are essential in the very substance of all created reality. Creation is far from finished. It was neither instantaneous, nor perfect and complete long ago in the dark reaches of the forgotten, unknown past. It is rather an on-going process, in which all things strive towards a perfection and completion that lie ahead, in the future. Creation occurs now, in the experienced and known present. It touches the very substance and being of all things because it effects the emergence of entirely new possibilities which were not present before, not even potentially.

Some critics have said that Augustine, Basil, Gregory of

Nyssa and other pre-Darwinian thinkers were true evolution-ists. The truth, however, is that while their thought has an evolutionary aura, it is nevertheless basically rooted in hellenic patterns of thought on reality, being, substance, species and, most of all, time. One might more properly place their explana-tions of creation in the context of the preformation debate of the 18th and 19th centuries when evolution was spoken of as the unfolding of preformed patterns within the individual (the human egg or sperm) or species in general, with this distinc-tion: that the early Christian writers were more aware of the biblical dimensions and hence less afraid of evolution as such. Where Christians in the days of Leibnitz and Kant fought evolution as atheistic and unbiblical, some of the early Fathers of the Church would have embraced it wholeheartedly because of their biblical foundation and their appreciation of the fuller meaning of creation.

We must recognize and admit the strong hellenic strain in our traditional conception of creation. Almost without question theologians from the Middle Ages on have accepted the Aristotelian-Platonic belief in the fixity of the natural species. Added to the Judaeo-Christian conception of divine creation, this idea became for the theologians as well as for the man in the street an imposing dilemma with the unveiling of evolution as a scientifically verifiable phenomenon. God, it was sug-gested, *intervenes* in the course of nature to create a new human being just as he *intervened* in the course of evolution to create life and the first man. Theology became very much, from the days of Darwin on, an apologetic, defensive study of a "God of the gaps." The theologian and the Christian saw certain moments in the process of evolution which seemed to call for the creative intervention of God simply because the science of the day could not come up with a natural explanation.

The trouble with the concept of a "God of the gaps" is not so much that it is based on the rather shaky assumption that science will not come up with a natural explanation of some phenomenon. More serious, it perverts the true biblical mean-ing of creation. As Teilhard pointed out in a letter to Julian Huxley in 1953, divine creativity is immanent in the natural order, and not an intervention from outside. A theology based on a "God of the gaps" makes God more and more remote from both man and the universe. Its logical conclusion is the deist's belief in a God who created this universe and then retired to outer space, leaving man and the universe to its own devices.

In working out an explanation of creation amenable to modern evolutionary science, the biblical view is well worth refurbishing. The Hebrew word, *bara*, which we translate as the verb "to create," portrays God primarily as acting in and through history to rescue his people from their sinfulness. It is rooted in the life of the Chosen People with whom God made a covenant. This is especially true in Deutero-Isaias. For the Hebrews, God's on-going salvific love was the dominant theme of life; his covenant with Moses, Abraham, Isaac and Jacob gave meaning to all reality, so much so that they felt compelled to trace its origins back to the beginning. God's covenant with his Chosen People was prepared for in the relationship Yahweh established with the universe and mankind in the very beginning. It is in this context of relationship that we should view the Genesis statement that "In the beginning, God created the heavens and the earth. . . ."

The phrase "in the beginning" must be viewed in a relational framework rather than as a temporal dimension. Evolution is an on-going process. As such it is not composed of a series of discrete moments or instants in time. We may, for convenience' sake, divide up this temporal dimension into seconds, hours, and light years, but it remains a true dynamic dimension of on-going change. Creation, then, is not some isolated, unique moment lost in the distant past. It is rather God's continuing sovereignty over all nature and all human history. It is the story of a marriage between the divine and the human. Creation is exemplified in the Exodus as well as in the story of Osee. It continues even today in God's wooing of mankind and the universe as He brings into being the fullness of His only begotten Son. Creation is ultimately the full incarnation of divine love in this universe, the extension of Bethlehem's blessed event.

We might learn then from the Statement of Faith recently adopted by the United Church of Christ. The tense of a verb can convey a very important message. Thus this Creed says: "We believe in God. . . . He *calls* the world into being, *creates* man in his own image, and *sets* before him the ways of life and death." Here the on-going nature of creation is emphasized as well as its relation as covenant.

Generally, when Christians talk of creation, they imply or openly add on the idea of creating "out of nothing." Jaroslav Pelikan, at the Darwin Centennial celebration at the University of Chicago, pointed out that the concept of creation entailing "making something out of nothing" is not a biblical notion. It developed after the biblical era as a defense of the goodness of our world and the absolute sovereignty of God against the gnostic belief that matter is evil, or the product of some inferior deity. Pelikan points out how this conception of creation out of nothing gradually crowded out the ancient biblical idea of an on-going creation, immanent in the events of human history and the cosmos. This trend gained real momentum during the late Middle Ages, the Reformation and the Age of Enlightenment, so much so that few Christians today think of creation in any terms except the creation of something out of nothing in the beginning of time. Yet this view is both unbiblical and unscientific.

In his book, *God's World in the Making*, Schoonenberg tries to highlight both the relational and evolutionary aspects of creation. He does this by pointing out that every creature is continually and totally dependent on his Creator at every moment and step in his life. Creation, for Schoonenberg, does not imply "out of nothing," because one creature can evolve into another. One species may evolve into another entirely new species through the creative process of natural selection. This does not mean that the Creator is not active in this process. Likewise parents may create a child in conception, but because this union of human egg and sperm brings into being a totally new person, transcending the reality of both parents, God's creative immanence is required. Again this creative action is not limited to the so-called "moment" of conception.

In the case of man, this creative action *cannot* be limited to the so-called "moment of conception," for the union of egg and sperm is a delicate process lasting about two hours during which the sperm releases its acrosomal filament as it touches the egg surface, the egg builds a fertilization cone around the filament tip and slowly draws the sperm in as the cortical granules start to break down and a fertilization membrane is formed. Once inside the egg, the sperm must then rotate 180 degrees and work its way through the cytoplasm to the female pronucleus. On the way it absorbs liquid and swells to form the male pronucleus. Finally pronuclear fusion occurs and the zygote begins to divide into two cells. But the newly conceived child's transcendence of its parents hardly begins in this process. The creation of a new person, as we will see shortly, is a lifelong task of challenge and response in which the new person gradually affirms his emerging personality against the background of his family, society and the universe.

A misplaced emphasis on a temporal "in the beginning" can distort our whole understanding of creation. If creation is an on-going process of evolution, then the last stroke of the artist's brush is far more important than the first. The end is far more vital and instructive than the beginning, especially if we are fortunate enough to possess a picture of the end of creation in the biblical picture of Christ, the firstborn of all creation.

Langdon Gilkey, in his book *Maker of Heaven and Earth*, points out that the myth of creation presented in Genesis does not intend to tell us anything about the first moment of time any more than the myth of Eden and the Fall tells us about a first human being. What Genesis does tell us, he claims, is that every moment of time, like every contingent and created being, comes to be through the creative power of God. The question of the first moment in chronological time is a question for the astronomer and physicist, and not for the theologian or Christian as such. The creation event of which the theologians speak is not, according to Gilkey, just an initial event within the first moment of time. It is rather the relationship of all events to their eternal source. Thus, as Karl Barth says in his *Church*

Dogmatics, "creation is the establishment of a place for the history of the covenant of grace."

Genesis then records *a relationship, not an event.* The authors of Genesis were concerned with giving a background that would relate all mankind to Yahweh's covenant with the Chosen People. The relationship of man and the cosmos to the divine relegates questions of origin in time to, at most, a very minor side issue. This appreciation has been well documented in the neo-orthodox Protestant tradition by Ian Barbour, Emil Brunner, C. F. von Weizsacker, Langdon Gilkey and Eric Mascall. For these theologians the Christian doctrine of creation is an affirmation of our dependence on God and of the essential goodness, orderliness and meaningfulness of our world rather than an account of our origins in time.

THE NATURE OF MAN

"And God said, let us make man, wearing our own image and likeness." To most Christians the creation of man in the image and likeness of the divine means that we humans have an immortal, spiritual soul, composed of intellect and will.

Man is a mysterious creature. Dust of this earth, perishable and doomed to die, we nevertheless possess a divine spark of immortality. In achieving consciousness of self, man has concomitantly become conscious of death and his own finiteness, a sequence Theodosius Dobzhansky has brilliantly explored in his *Biology of Ultimate Concern.* The question for philosophers and theologians has always been how this mysterious combination of earth and heaven can be adequately and accurately expressed within the limitations of our vocabulary. Many serious attempts have been made over the years and we should look at the two major ones in some detail before we suggest a new approach in terms of our evolutionary world image.

Quite contrary to the common impression, the biblical writings do not give us a clear or full picture of man's nature. More particularly, since the writers were not at all concerned with matters of science or philosophy, they do not impose on us any single philosophical or scientific view of man such as the common body-soul conception. In fact, the most ancient tradition among the Hebrews, a view that appears repeatedly in the Old Testament, views man as "a living person" (Gen. 2:8). In the earlier books of the Old Testament no distinction is made between body and soul, or between matter and spirit. These distinctions first arose in the philosophical thought of the Babylonians and Greeks, so that our first encounter with them in biblical writings comes in the sapiential books of the Old Covenant. These works, written after the Hebrews had been exposed to the currents of pagan philosophy in the Babylonian exile, offer the original holistic Hebraic view of man as person side by side with the pagan conception of man as a (philosophical) dualism, the dynamic union, or in some cases, the unity, of two principles of being, one material and the other spiritual.

In the New Testament writings, a Greek philosophical conception of man as matter-spirit, or body-soul, becomes more common, though the original Semitic view of man as person is never replaced fully.

Three hundred years before Christ, Plato spoke of man's god-like spirit being imprisoned in the body. Aristotle realized the weaknesses of this approach and suggested a philosophical explanation now known as the hylomorphic theory. Briefly, this approach suggests that we view man *philosophically* as an *indivisible* unity rather than as a Platonic type of union. For Aristotle, man is an essential unity of a material principle of being, prime matter, and a spiritual principle of being, the substantial form. But Aristotle's philosophical explanation of man cannot be applied to the concrete realities we call our body, though many are misled to this conclusion. Actually, a living human body is not simply matter in the philosophical sense. Even inanimate rocks and stones are, in the Aristotelian view, unities comprised of prime matter and substantial forms. As philosophical principles of being, neither prime matter nor substantial form can exist alone as such. They are always found together in the concrete reality we see.

Much later Thomas Aquinas adopted the Aristotelian philosophical conception of man and all reality, expressing it in terms of matter and spirit, or body and soul. Then, because the Thomistic synthesis became almost the sole source of Roman Catholic theology and philosophy in post-Reformation times, this conception was quite naturally incorporated in dogmatic definitions and explanations of man. Even so, the Roman Church has never made this philosophical explanation an essential part of its faith. Those dogmatic definitions which speak of man in terms of Aristotelian-thomistic philosophy always use this approach as a *working basis* for the definition of a specific religious belief.

An immediate problem with this approach arises today in the area of catechetics and apologetics. Though this is not our prime objection to the continued use of the hylomorphic explanation of man, it is worth examining in some detail.

While the philosopher and theologian may speak of man in the abstract terms of hylomorphism, the ordinary Christian, untrained in philosophy, is much more at home in the concrete realities of daily life. He constantly tries to bring the abstract conceptions of the philosopher down to realities he knows by experience. Hence, for most Christians the living human body is viewed as matter, purely and simply, and man's soul as some sort of ethereal, nebulous spirit dwelling within this body. How often, for instance, do we hear people speak of a man's body ending up in the grave after death? A human corpse is not the same as a human body which results from the dynamic, vital unity of prime matter and substantial form in the Aristotelian-thomist view.

The problem of popularizing, or making concrete the philosophical approach to man suggested by Plato and Aristotle leads quite naturally to an even more dangerous result in the perennial tendency of people working in a pre-Darwinian perspective to resolve the mystery of man in terms of dualism. This facile, but extremely dangerous solution views man in terms of two basic realities, a spiritual soul created in the image and likeness of God, the source of all good in man, and a material, physical body, the cause of all those conflicting emotions and passions which seem to divert man towards evil and away from his creator. In many, if not all, Christian heresies everything associated with man's body becomes evil, or at least strongly suspect. This subterranean temptation can be easily traced from Neo-platonism and gnosticism through many centuries in the beliefs of Manicheanism, Albigensianism, Jansenism, Puritanism, Victorianism, and on to our modern playboy mentality of sexuality as a commodity rather than personal involvement. Man, so some later followers of Plato suggested, is a divine soul imprisoned in an evil body. In the Manichean belief, which strongly influenced Augustine's view of marriage and human sexuality, for instance, our body was created by the devil or an evil god. This common but heretical view frequently comes to the surface, almost unconsciously, when we speak of sending missionaries to foreign lands to save souls. Why is it that we think only of saving man's soul? And how often do we talk of the spiritual or religious life in terms of conquering the body—as if it *alone* were the obstacle blocking man's love of his creator? How often do we view the body and material things as not exactly nice?

Some of this confusion undoubtedly stems from the terminology used by the apostles in the New Testament, and more directly to its inadequate and partial translation into modern languages. As Hebrews concerned with communicating a religious message, the apostles were not interested in any philosophical conception of man. They were concerned only with man's *relationship* with his Creator. Thus when the biblical writers spoke of man being created in God's image and likeness or of man becoming a living soul, of man receiving the "breath of the spirit," they did not have in mind anything even remotely connected with the Aristotelian-thomistic hylomorphic theory of man. Expressions like these refer to an openness of heart to others which every man must have to live fully the divine life of love in his image. Both in its source and its ultimate goal this openness to others is rooted in God; it is the motive behind creation as well as the climax of all creation. But granted this, the realities of daily life and experience force us, as they did the biblical writers, to recognize a terrible tension in man's personality. The biblical writers pictured this as the conflict in man between the flesh and the spirit, between the fear and re-fusal to love others and the true openness that characterizes the man who is being created in the image and likeness of God.

The biblical writers saw man as constantly torn by a real warfare between the "perishable flesh" which ends as "dust" and the eternal spirit. To epitomize the opposition of the flesh to God the biblical writers often spoke of the "world." They were not referring to the world as we know it, but rather to a *religious attitude* characteristic of men who place all their treasures in perishable finite goods and refuse to recognize the immortal value of persons and selfless love. The hearts of these men have been hardened. They have rejected love and set themselves up as gods.

Flesh, world, spirit, heart, and other similar terms so com-mon in the biblical tradition belong strictly to a religious mes-sage, the story of the covenant and of creation in which God gradually forms the human race in his own image, in the image of his Son. Hence we miss completely the message when we try to apply these terms to any philosophical attempt to under-stand man's nature. The very practical problem remains that many Christians not only miss the true meaning of biblical thought on this point, but actually distort it in a very pagan, dualistic way because of undercurrents from Plotinus, Descartes, and the whole Manichean heritage which unconsciously per-meate our whole pattern of thought in western Christendom. The biblical concepts of flesh and the world are repeatedly con-fused with man's body and the material world, while the bibli-cal concept of spirit is distorted by equating this with the phil-osophical concept of soul. It is well to recall that the dualism of matter and spirit, of body and soul, came from the Greek phi-losophers and not from the original biblical tradition.

This practical problem could be eliminated by an intensive effort to reeducate Christians everywhere. My own conjecture is that this effort would take generations before it ever came close to restoring the proper perspective to our understanding of man, both philosophically and theologically. But even granted this could be done, there is a more essential objection to our continued use of the Aristotelian-thomistic approach to man's nature. This objection touches the very heart of the thomistic synthesis. It is a very sensitive point since, if accepted, it completely pulls the floor out from under the feet of the thomistic or scholastic approach. This fact is undoubtedly what prompted Jacques Maritain, the great pioneer of neo-thomism, to react so vehemently against the process or evolutionary theology of Teilhard de Chardin, Piet Schoonenberg and others in his *Peasant of the Garonne*.

In the past hundred years theologians and philosophers have slowly come to grips with the evolutionary perspective. Their first and often only response has been to rework their three-dimensional, fixed conception of man with some fancy footwork and anachronistic reinterpretations that would allow them to transfer these ideas directly to the four-dimensional evolutionary world image.

In this context, Teilhard suggested in 1926 that we "might perhaps say . . . that Aristotelian hylomorphism represents the projection, upon a world without duration, of modern evolutionism. Transferred into a Universe to which duration adds an extra dimension, the (hylomorphic) theory of matter and form becomes almost indistinguishable from our modern speculations on the development of matter." Thus some quite eminent and professional philosophers are convinced that the hylomorphic theory of reality can be transferred without radical change into our four-dimensional modern world image. Bernard Lonergan, for instance, has suggested that we view the classic prime matter as "empirical residue" while Joseph Donceel proposes "undetermined cosmic energy." Seminal as these suggestions are, my own conviction is that such a transfer is impossible here because of the *totally different dimensions* that are involved in the two world images. The coordinates and terminology of three-dimensional Euclidean geometry cannot be transferred to poly-dimensional non-Euclidean geometries without complete distortion, irrelevance and confusion resulting.

Furthermore, I am puzzled by the insistence on maintaining three-dimensional conceptions which do not solve the basic problems posed by these conceptions for a person living in a four-dimensional evolutionary perspective. To integrate the body-soul conception of man with process thought, it has been suggested that we accept "natural" evolution along with a direct divine intervention through which a human soul is created and immediately infused into a body that has evolved from a subhuman primate stock. In the evolution of both the species and the individual human a question immediately arises: just when does God infuse the human soul into this developing body? Is it, in the case of the individual, at the "moment" of conception when the fusion of egg and sperm occurs? Or is it perhaps, as Thomas Aquinas suggested on good Aristotelian evidence from embryology, weeks after this fertilization? Considering Aristotle's studies of miscarried human fetuses, Aquinas suggested that there is a sequence of animating principles or souls, a vegetative "soul" being succeeded by an animal and finally human soul, forty days after conception for male embryos and eighty days after conception for females.

If the human soul is infused at the "moment" of conception or shortly afterwards, then what happens a few days later when the inner cell mass of the developing zygote splits to form identical twins, triplets, or quadruplets? Does the soul also split? And what becomes of nearly one-third of all the male fetuses conceived, since on an average 54 out of every 160 male fetuses miscarry during pregnancy as compared with only 6 out of every 106 females? Just when does a fetus become human? Is the fertilized egg, as Schoonenberg suggests, pre- or pro-human rather than fully human? And when does the embryo become human? The medieval theologians and scholastic philosophers had at very most only a faint hint of these perplexing questions. With our modern science these questions have become more and more pressing. The possibilities of obtaining a satisfying answer from the classic conception of man have likewise become more remote.

Perennial questions about death also become more pressing and perplexing as we enter more into an evolutionary scientific view of man and the universe. In the Aristotelian-thomistic perspective, prime matter and substantial form cannot exist as separate entities. They are always and everywhere conjoined. Thus our common description of man's death as the

separation of body and soul is not only misleading, it is philosophically impossible. Aquinas and other theologians have
never been able to solve this problem of death satisfactorily
within the classic context. Recent developments make the question even more troublesome for the three-dimensional philosopher. St. Vincent Hospital in New York City, and many other
hospitals around the world frequently face a Code 99 case, a
person pronounced clinically dead and then, through heart mas-
sage or other new techniques, restored to life.

Still other questions have been raised by modern medicine.
What life principle, for instance, animates the human heart,
kidney, or brain preserved alive *in vitro*? What life principle
animates an organ transplanted from one person to another?
Transplanting a kidney or heart is one thing, but what happens when brain transplants, already fairly successful in dogs
and monkeys, are applied to man? What life principle animates
the living DNA chromosomal core of a bacterium if this is
incorporated into the hereditary content of a human body as
has already been done with rabbit virus and man? Modern
psycho-pharmacology raises still other questions. Explaining
the action of the psychogenic drugs, LSD 25, STP, the tranquillizers, the sex hormones by suggesting that these "inert"
chemicals only act on our material or chemical nature to
modify the expression of our personality involves some fancy
but basically unsatisfying footwork within the Aristotelian-
thomistic framework. Such footwork, however, evades the basic
questions raised by psycho-pharmacology.

The classic body-soul conception of man will undoubtedly
be with us for many years to come. Nevertheless, we should be
aware of the problems this view raises when we transfer it from
its congenial milieu in the Ptolemaic-thomistic world. Even as
we continue to speak of man's body and soul we should be increasingly aware and appreciative of the new conceptions that
are already being worked out by theologians and philosophers
who take the evolutionary framework as their inspiration and
ground of thought.

Some indications and outlines of this new conception of man

are already clear, though still quite tentative. Rooted in the dimension of process, modern psychology and philosophy suggest that we look at man as a dynamic, evolutionary unity. If one were to give this view a philosophical label the best approximation might be to call it an "evolutionary monism." In many respects this new view recalls the wholeness of the early biblical conception of man.

Instead of picturing man as the fixed, though active unity of prime matter and substantial form, of body and soul, would it not be more appropriate to our modern understanding to look at man as a whole, an inner consciousness or spiritual (personal) aspect emerging out of our materiality, our outer aspect seen in the relationships and dependence on persons and things outside which form the background of being for our emerging selfhood? In simpler terms—and without confusing these with the three-dimensional view—could we not speak of man's *personality*, that which makes each of us unique individuals, emerging out of our necessary dependence on others, our *materiality,* or as Schoonenberg suggests, our *corporeity*? Man is a bipolar unity in process. As Teilhard noted so emphatically, the two aspects of man, personality and materiality, are dynamically and *genetically* related in a life-long process. Thus, man's personality gradually emerges from the universe in which he is conceived, from our necessary dependence on others, on the structured complexity of human society and the world in general. In no way is this view a polished-up version of the classic body-soul, matter-spirit conception of man. And this is especially to be noted since theologians and philosophers, both Teilhardian and post-Teilhardian, often revert to the old terminology simply because we have not yet found the precise terms we need to express the new conception of man.

Ansfried Hulsbosch, in his book *God in Creation and Evolution*, has emphasized the compatibility of this modern evolutionary conception of man and the ancient biblical view. The latter, as Hulsbosch outlines it, pictures man on this earth as a two-sided being, on the biological side related to the animals and on the personal side related to God in whose image we are being created. This, as Hulsbosch stresses, is not a dualism, but rather *the content of a mission to self-actualization.*

Genesis tells us that *man* is made from the slime of the earth, man, body-soul, and not just the body! Thus the "image and likeness of God" spoken of in Genesis refers to the whole man and not just to the soul. St. Paul adds new depth to this insight by explaining the full religious meaning of "image." Thus, image is feminine in relation to reality which is masculine. In *Teilhard and the Supernatural,* Eulalio Baltazar points out that Paul compares man, the image of God, the pride and glory of his creation, with the wife who is the image of the husband, his pride and glory (1 Cor 11:7). Woman is a perpetual symbol, given by God to remind and teach us of man's true relation to him. Outside the conjugal union, woman is barren. Outside a personal union with God, man is barren.

Man is a bipolar process. Ontologically, epistemologically and methodologically, as Baltazar claims, man is intrinsically ordained to the other by his very finiteness, more particularly to *the* Other, the ultimate in personality who is God. The human bipolarity involves a mission to self-actualization, the emergence of spirit out of materiality, of being-in-oneself out of self-estrangement or the necessary dependence on the outside world where we are involved in and at the mercy of processes taking place in the world.

The creation of man, like the creation of the universe, is an on-going process completed only in "the fullness of time." Man's ultimate goal is to become more like God, in the sense of more personal and more a being-in-oneself, more "spiritual." This mission to self-actualization is achieved through our groping towards maturity as human persons.

This interpretation is closely related to our conception of God. In the fixed, hellenic philosophy of nature common before Darwin, God was seen as a pure spirit, infinite and uncreated. In the evolutionary perspective, we can describe God as the ultimate in personality, infinite in the sense that there is no materiality in his nature, no necessary dependence on others, no limits placed on his being-in-himself.

When joined with an evolutionary conception of man, this view of God reveals some new insights. The ultimate goal of man's creation-evolution is a truly personal (God-like) man. This goal is achieved as man participates and cooperates with God in his own creation, in the groping process of maturing. Each of us has been conceived in an evolving universe. Each of us is being created and each of us is creating ourselves as we development of myself as a person is a gradual, life-long proc-express our personality more fully with each passing day. This ess marked by some very critical steps: conception, embryonic development, birth, infancy, childhood, adolescence, and, hopefully, psychological and spiritual maturity.

Two aspects of this view deserve some discussion, the problem of conception and the life-long emergence of self out of the universe and human society. In both these aspects, the key concept is that of transcendence, which we must examine at least briefly. But first the two problematic areas.

The human egg and sperm are living organisms, distinct from the parent body that gave birth to them and endowed with a life of their own. But the life of the sperm and egg can hardly be said to be human. Merkelback, a leading theologian of the early 1900s, suggested that the fertilized egg (zygote) is not very different in its life processes from the unfertilized egg. It is perhaps closer to being human, but still far from being fully human.

In talking about "being human" I suspect most readers might think of this phrase quite naturally in terms of a fixed category. To be human is still understood as meaning some sort of agreement with or participation in an archetypal, fixed nature we call humanity, or human nature. Man does not possess humanity, personality, or consciousness. These are not something superadded to man in an accidental way. Humanity, personality and consciousness are a manner of being. Man in an evolutionary universe is in process to being-in-himself, transparent to himself, self-conscious, a growing emerging person in the process of becoming more fully human. In an evolutionary framework "natures" are not fixed realities, archetypes, or ideals, but rather *goals*. There is no point in our life when we can be said to be fully human, at least until we reach our ultimate goal of personal union with God, the cosmos and all mankind.

And yet conception, the union of egg and sperm, marks a crucial turning point in the emergence of a new person, even though the "moment of conception" may last upwards of an hour or two. Conception initiates a single unified being in which a new operation is organized and focused on the goal of complete "personhood."

To explore further the idea of conception, we might deal for a moment with the "nature" of the gametes, the egg and sperm. From one point of view, certainly the more common assumption, the "nature," goal or function of every gamete is to develop into a human being. But, as North has pointed out in *Teilhard and the Creation of the Soul*, there is another viewpoint, much more realistic and existential and certainly more in accord with our modern scientific knowledge. The real "nature" and the normal fate of a gamete is *not* to develop into a human being. The vast majority of gametes are destined to disappear without producing anything. This is nature's plan, not a frustration of it! Only one out of some two to three million sperm in a single act of intercourse can fertilize the egg. Most acts of sexual intercourse occur when the woman is not fertile. And how many eggs are released in the cycles of unmarried women with no chance of being fertilized? These questions have bearing not only on our understanding of conception, but also on questions of sexual ethics, primarily, the morality of contraception and the growing awareness that human sexuality and intercourse is fundamentally a mode of personal communion rather than reproductive in function. Human sexual intercourse transcends the biological to enter the realm of the personal. It remains creative in function, but this creativity can be and often is much more than biological reproduction.

The fertilization process is indeed a crucial turning point that initiates the emergence of a unique individual person, but it is only the first of many steps in a life-long process.

The mission to self-actualization demands on the part of the emerging person a growing transcendence or transformation of the limitations and necessary dependence basic to his ground of being. Thus, the newly conceived child is distinct and independent of both father and mother in one sense, though his biological dependence on his mother and the confines of the womb limit very much the expression of his personality or self-identity. At birth this biological dependence is lessened when the umbilical cord is cut. As weaning, schooling and adolescence, with their biological and psychological-emotional maturation, follow, the growing human person slowly and painfully learns to transcend the dependence on others heretofore imposed on it by biological or social necessity. This, however, is not a denial of that dependence which is characteristic of the finiteness of our human nature. It is rather a transcending or going beyond its *necessary* and *imposed character*, a transformation in love and free acceptance. Man is not God, he is not a pure infinite (unlimited) person. Hence we will never be able to free ourselves entirely from our "material nature" of dependence on others, on our fellow man and on God. By his very nature as a finite, social creature, man must always depend on others. He cannot exist apart from them. However, we can transcend and transform that necessary dependence by embracing it freely through loving unions with others. As the child grows to maturity, he must learn to embrace lovingly his need for others. In affirming his self-identity, the teenager cannot cut himself off from his family. He must transcend the dependence on his family imposed by circumstances but immediately affirm his loving dependence on them.

By lovingly embracing our need for others, we recognize our own finite nature as creatures, affirming our human personality as it truly is. At the same time we also transform our materiality, "spiritualizing" it, as we learn to become more fully human, personal, and hence more God-like. Biological freedom, self-consciousness and being-in-oneself expand as we mature in the psychological, social and religious spheres of our personality.

The second area, the role of human society in this process, emphasizes the fact that the dynamics of the human person are inseparable from our existential situation within a certain human society. In other words, we are not only exploring a new expression of man's nature in terms of an evolutionary monism relating genetically the person and our necessary dependence on others, we are also suggesting that *it is impossible to understand the human person and his emergence without at the same time recognizing the prime role of human society as the ground of being for this germination.* In an evolutionary, existential, relational and personalistic world, it is impossible to speak of man's nature in abstract, idealistic, or fixed archetypal terms.

The place of conception and human society in the emergence of human personality raises the question of transcendence.

The newly conceived fetus, because it is a new and distinct person, transcends both parents. This, according to Schoonenberg, is what we really mean by the "direct or immediate creation of the human soul." God works *through nature* in giving the power of transcendence to this new being. In the philosophy of Teilhard, psychic or radial energy is the power to transcend materiality or the necessary dependence on others. It is the capacity of being-in-oneself, centered. But the human person is a dynamic emerging process. Hence, if we talk only of God creating in the beginning and then acting or intervening at key points in the birth of the universe or man, we actually reduce his transcendence, making him just one of many causes at work in the emergence of man. To say that man's inner aspect, his soul, is created directly by God means that the soul is the principle and pole of personal being-in-oneself by virtue of which man in his coming-to-be is and becomes more independent of his parents, society and the universe. But this transcendence exceeds the capacities of the parents, society and the universe as well as the powers of the emerging person. Hence, as Schoonenberg suggests, "the creation of the human soul is neither more nor less than the beginning of a new person in a whole world, which is constantly created by God as a world in which there is an increase in human persons."

For Teilhard cosmogenesis culminates in hominization and personalization. Nowhere is this more apparent than in the role the universe, human society and our families play in our own emergence as persons. It is an intriguing process, as Delfgaauw points out, in which a seeming paradox exists: the higher proceeds from the lower and yet cannot be reduced to it. Perhaps this is because God's creative spirit (person-love) is at work continually in nature, bringing *new* beings into existence by carrying them along the current of evolution to that critical threshold where the continuous injection of energy produces an alteration of entirely discontinuous character, a new creature or personal being. Commenting on Teilhard's view, North has pointed out that the continuous injection of energy on the without (complexity) produces a discontinuous effect on the within (consciousness) when a critical threshold is reached, a boiling point that results in the "creation" of the human soul or personality. From matter, then, emerges the spirit; from the universal ground of being, the unique person on his way towards the fullness of Christ.

This evolutionary perspective must logically be carried over into the realm of human sexuality. In the pre-Darwinian conception of man, explanations of human sexuality focused on mystiques of the eternal masculine and feminine. The assumption was that there actually existed some sort of eternal archetype of the masculine and the feminine. Added to this was the premise of Aristotelian-thomism that sexuality, like personality, is accidental to man. In this context certain roles and characteristics were predicated of men and women as if there were an invariable and eternal position for men and women in society. Human sexuality was reduced to procreation, and its existence in man justified solely, if reluctantly, in terms of the continuation of the human race. What the new perspective reveals is the essential equation of sexuality-personality as essential and basic in man. But the dynamism of human sexuality is flexible and ever changing. Rooted in genetics, hormones and biological structures, human sexuality nevertheless cannot be reduced to any or even all of these. Human sexuality emerges out of human dialogue. It does not exist except in the relational, existential context of human society in which I become more and more a man as a result of my on-going dialogue with other human persons, male and female, who likewise are in the process of emerging as persons, male and female.

While the process image of man outlined above is far from complete, it is, I am convinced, a step in the right direction. It offers many advantages over the classic image of Aristotle and Aquinas: a way to avoid the subtle Manichean-puritan dualism; a way to restore the radical humanism and materialism of a Christian way of life that must take root and grow in this world; an answer to some of the problems raised by modern pharmacology, psychology, embryology, evolution; a theology of death; and finally a way to explain man's nature in a meaningful Christian way to modern man.

THE NATURE OF THE UNIVERSE

Having at this point opted for an evolutionary explanation of man's nature, we can return to the question we raised in our survey of the modern scientific image of evolution (Chapter Two). If our universe is as consistent and logical as the scientist assumes, then there must be a consistency and logic throughout our image of the world. If we opt for a new evolutionary explanation of man, then to be consistent we should also opt for an evolutionary image of the universe itself. If we reject as meaningless today the fixed image of man as a body/soul unity, then we must also reject as unacceptable today the fixed image of the universe as a composite of matter and spirit. Both concepts, of body/soul and of matter/spirit, are rooted in the fixed cosmology of Plato and Aristotle, Ptolemy, Dante and Aquinas. They are without relevance and meaning for modern man who thinks and breathes the air of constant change and evolution.

This conclusion may sound very daring and probably heretical to some readers. But it is a conclusion that is inevitable simply because it has emerged from an organic development of human thought, debate and controversy stretching over the last two hundred years. Even more to the point is the fact that this conclusion finally resolves the problem of integrating the fixed cosmology of the pagan Greeks with the evolutionary theology of process found in biblical thought, a dilemma only faintly understood by the great theologians of the past.

The problem of describing and understanding the ultimate nature of the universe has a fascinating history. Working from their own immediate experience and intuition of self and the world, philosophers and theologians have from the beginning of recorded history viewed man and the universe in endless variations on a single theme, seen best in the dualistic analysis of Plato. On one side of the fence is the inert, inanimate, inorganic world of matter; on the other side is the world of life, spirit and soul.

As a biologist-philosopher, Aristotle opted for one end of the dilemma's horns. Faced with the problem of life and non-life, he suggested that some unobservable *vital principle* is responsible for the phenomenon we call life. Basically, he felt there are three forms of entelechy or life principle: the vegetative, animal and rational psyches. Along with this philosophical approach, Aristotle tried to view the problem as a biologist, in terms of embryonic development. His careful studies of the embryonic development of the chicken egg led him to believe that a whole new organism develops out of amorphous and unstructured raw material. He explained this by suggesting that some unobservable vital force or principle guides the development of this entirely new organism. He thus established the epigenetic school of thought in biology as well as the vitalistic school of philosophic thought.

The other end of the dilemma was well defended in the same era by two other Greek thinkers, Democritus and Hippocrates. These two scientist-philosophers have often been honored as the co-founders of mechanistic philosophy and preformation thought in biology. The mechanistic approach to life suggests that living organisms are not basically different from the complex operations of a machine or clock. The only difference between man and a rock is the greater complexity of the human machine.

In biological thought, Hippocrates anticipated by some two thousand years Charles Darwin's concept of pangenesis, the blood theory of heredity which claims that minute particles or models are produced in each organ of a living body, transported through the blood and finally incorporated into the seminal fluid in the testes. For people who knew nothing of genes and chromosomes, or of the human egg and sperm, it seemed logical to explain reproduction in terms of these minute models gathering in the seminal fluid. In the mating process this fluid would bake the menstrual blood and form it into a baby. This belief that the embryo is preformed in the seminal fluid gained even greater popularity during the eighteenth century when philosophical evolution seemed to threaten all Christendom.

The evolutionary philosophers of eighteenth-century Germany and France claimed that if we admit a true development of the individual, an ontogeny, then logically we should also accept an evolution or development of species of life, a phylogeny. The strongest refutation of this dangerous evolutionary view was to show scientifically that there is no true ontogeny. Among the embryologists of this era, Malpighi (1628–1694), Spallanzani (1729–1799) and Bonnet (1720–1793) claimed they could see a well developed, though minute, human being all curled up within the Graffian follicle of the human ovary. Working with equally primitive microscopes and an equally fertile imagination, Leuvenhoek, Hamm and Hartsoeker suggested that the female had nothing to do with reproduction except to provide a place for the seminal fluid, or the newly discovered sperm, to develop. This was obvious since one could see a tiny human, a homunculus, all curled up within the head of the sperm. Evolution could not possibly be if the living organism was already preformed within the egg or sperm.

The preformation theory dominated biological thought long after Caspar Wolff disproved it in 1759 with his studies on the development of the intestine in the chicken embryo, possibly because it complemented so well the mechanistic philosophy resurrected by Descartes in 1637. "I do not accept or desire any other principle in physics than in geometry or abstract mathematics, because *all phenomena of nature* may be explained by their means and sure demonstration can be given of them," was the way Descartes summed up his mechanistic approach to nature and life. A century later, La Metrie's *Man the Machine* (1748) suggested that man is just like every other living organism, a machine devoid of spirit or soul, a little more complicated than brute animals and far more complicated than non-living things, but nevertheless a machine in essence.

At the turn of this century, the battle between mechanists and vitalists again erupted with overtones of the preformation-epigenesis debate.

In 1914 Hans Driesch published his *History and Theory of Vitalism,* presenting philosophic conclusions from his many experiments with sea urchin embryos. Driesch separated the two, four and eight cells of the very young embryo and found that each cell or blastomere would develop into full, complete larvae. When he combined two fertilized eggs by pressing them together between glass plates, he got a larger but quite normal embryo. The conclusion was obvious: there cannot be any preformed structure or machine in the fertilized egg. If such a structure were present in the embryo, then separating the cells would leave each cell with only part of the structure. The result then could only be abnormal embryos.

Jacques Loeb, the author of *The Mechanistic Conception of Life,* defended the opposite view and the battles waged hot and furious both in the lab and in the public forum. In general, embryology followed a vitalistic-epigenetic theory while the new science of genetics favored the mechanistic-preformation explanation suggested by the discovery of genetic and chromosomal heredity. In the present century Henri Bergson, Pierre Lecomte du Nouy, Edmund Sinnott and others have staunchly defended new forms of vitalism which, despite their new terminology, are still heir to the weaknesses of earlier vitalistic thought.

Ludwig von Bertalanffy has compared this dispute to a "game of chess played over nearly two thousand years. It is essentially the same arguments," he suggests, "that always come back, though in manifold disguises, modifications and forms. In the last resort, they are an expression of two opposing tendencies in the human mind. On the one hand, there is a tendency to subordinate life to scientific explanation and law; on the other hand, there is the experience of our own mind, taken as a standard for living nature, and inserted into the supposed or actual gaps in our scientific knowledge."

The solution to this ancient debate, I would propose, cannot be found within the context of a fixed world image. Life and man cannot be adequately explained in that framework because it is defective and untrue to reality. A fixed world image allows only a dualistic and static approach to life and non-life, matter and spirit, body and soul. The solution, I believe, can only be found by approaching phenomena in the context of an evolutionary framework.

Two men of solid scientific background have ventured seminal approaches to the age-old problem of the nature of things. Both have adopted the evolutionary dimension as a basis for their suggestions. The first began his explorations during the First World War and continued wrestling with a new insight until his death in 1955. He is the well known author of *The Phenomenon of Man* and other works, the Jesuit paleontologist-geologist Pierre Teilhard de Chardin. The second scholar worked in much the same era. His theory of "organismic biology" was first proposed in 1933 in a book entitled *Modern Theories of Development: An Introduction to Theoretical Biology*. In 1952, Ludwig von Bertalanffy expanded his ideas in *Problems of Life: An Evaluation of Modern Biological and Scientific Thought*. Of his own explanation, Bertalanffy noted that it "does not consent to either of the classic views (of vitalism and mechanism), but transcends both in a new and third one." The same evaluation applies to Teilhard's approach.

Because the theories of these two men so closely parallel each other I will attempt a synthetic summary that highlights their basic contributions and insights. In this way I would hope we can move ahead towards a more substantial understanding and explanation of reality in terms of an evolving world image.

To begin we might compare Bertalanffy and Teilhard in their terminology. Bertalanffy speaks of the two aspects of all reality as involving structure on one side, and forces, energy or fields of energy on the other side. These are inseparable and dynamic aspects of all reality. Teilhard's approach likewise speaks of viewing all phenomena from two angles: the "without" of complexity and the "within" of consciousness, freedom, spontaneity, and in the case of man, person. This approach appears similar to that used by Aristotle, Plato and Aquinas whose explanations we have rejected as inadequate today, but the similarity is only superficial. It is the dimension and perspective in which these concepts are framed that is crucial, and on this point Bertalanffy and Teilhard are at opposite poles to the fixed cosmology of earlier thinkers.

"We find in nature," Bertalanffy tells us, "a tremendous architecture, in which subordinate systems are united at successive levels into ever higher and larger systems. Chemical and colloidal structures are integrated into cell structures and systems of organs, these to multicellular organisms and the last finally to supra-individual units of life."

At the base of the evolutionary pyramid stand the elementary units of subatomic particles. Further up the scale are the atoms, and molecules, each structured in a very definite pattern and bound into systems by positive and negative electrical charges. Molecules of small molecular weight, both inorganic and organic, have very precise and definite formulae. Water, for instance is H_2O, ammonia NH_3, and methane CH_4. But the more complicated a molecule becomes and the more atoms it integrates, the less defined and precise is its structure. This becomes very evident in the organic molecules with their chain backbone of carbon atoms. In the common organic molecule cellulose, for instance, three hundred or more double sugar molecules are linked together in multivalency chains by ordinary chemical bonds. Forty to sixty of these chains are then bound together by secondary valencies, or van der Waals forces, into the pliant fibrous micella we know as cellulose. Proteins, on the other hand, are generally smaller than this and more structured along definite periodic patterns and sequences of the basic amino acids.

From this general pattern to which we referred in our survey of cosmic evolution (Chapter II), Bertalanffy distills three important elements. First, he suggests that the valency forces of classic chemistry which explain the structure of basic atoms and small molecules must be complemented by a scientific analysis and study of broader fields of force which come into play in the cohesion of all phenomena in our universe. Thus more study should be given the van der Waals forces which explain the action of the so-called imperfect gases and produce lattice crystalline structures, as well as other broad fields of force. Second, he suggests that essentially new structures and orders of reality appear as we ascend the evolutionary pyramid. Thus the concepts of "molecule" and "chemical compound" cannot be applied to the cellulose structure since its formula is so unlimited, i.e., $(C_6H_{10}O_5)_N$ where n indicates an undefined number of subunits. (Over forty individual chains, each containing over three hundred sugar residues, are bound into a single micella of cellulose.) And third, working from cellulose and other similar undefined and large structures, Bertalanffy suggests that these may be arranged into ever larger (higher) structures, less well defined but nevertheless formed by forces susceptible to scientific investigation.

Approaching the realm of reality which in our common sense observations we classify as living beings, distinct from the inorganic realm of dead matter, we find a gray indistinct zone where our common sense distinction simply does not apply. With a molecular weight of forty million and upwards, the virus is nothing but a single strand of chromosomal material, DNA, wrapped in a protein coat. Yet this form of reality reacts as a "dead" crystal in some circumstances and as a "living" reproducing organism in other situations. Bertalanffy has suggested that the DNA molecule, the double helix of the chromosome, and viruses might best be described as "metabolizing crystals" while Schrodinger prefers labeling them as "aperiodic crystals" in the sense that they differ from the inorganic crystals by combining a variety of amino acids, sugars and bases in a crystalline pattern. The problem is not just one of semantics either. When Kornberg was asked whether he had created life in a test tube when he synthesized a DNA chain *in vitro*, he asked the person to define life first and then he would answer the question. The gray zone between our common sense distinction between the living and the non-living emphasizes the dynamic process of evolution as a continuous stream of minute steps. The chromosomal structure is the result of definite forces, whether we view them as the electrostatic charges within the nucleic acid chains as Friedrich-Freska suggests or as quantum-mechanical resonances as Jordan proposes. This interdependence of structure and forces or energy fields is the key to the evolutionary process according to Bertalanffy. Structure (matter) is constantly and dynamically paralleled in all phenomena by energy forces binding and uniting and forming. Nothing in this universe is simple inert matter, nor does pure energy exist anywhere. Matter (structure) and energy exist as dynamic, convertible aspects of one and the same reality. In an evolutionary world image, the traditional fixed conceptions of matter and spirit are a meaningless anachronism.

Since 1955 when publication of Pierre Teilhard de Chardin's many writings on science and theology began, many Christians unfamiliar with modern science have begun to face the new perspective of an evolutionary world. Despite the many books and countless articles written about Teilhard's synthesis, no one has yet plunged to the heart of his truly revolutionary approach to the ultimate nature of our world. Teilhard himself obviously did not see the full implications of his seminal insights on this point. He is patently ambiguous in practically all his discussions of the ultimate nature of things, wavering and fluctuating between the classic fixed conceptions of matter and spirit, body and soul, and his embryonic insight into an evolutionary ontogenesis. Teilhard simply could not make the complete transition from a Platonic/Aristotelian/Thomistic ontology to a fully evolutionary ontogenesis, though he undoubtedly set the essential piers bridging these two views. At times Teilhard speaks in terms perfectly in accord with the fixed philosophy of his school days. At other times he seems to burst into the full light of an evolutionary perspective. But more often he hovers somewhere in the middle of the incompleted bridge, suspended between two worlds of thought, leaving the reader quite confused as to his actual meaning.

Basic in Teilhard's understanding of the ultimate nature of things is his belief that the *étoffe de l'Univers* has two integral aspects which are genetically and dynamically related one to the other in an evolutionary process in which one aspect is root and the other terminus. In this explanation Teilhard borrows the German term *Weltstoff* to indicate the most generic and universal traits of all phenomena as well as the energies and potentials and structures that become actual in the realms of life and mind. Teilhard's notion of *Weltstoff* is much richer, as Smulders has pointed out, than the old sense of the word *matter*. Teilhard, in fact, adopted the German term to avoid any implication of dualism and the oversimplified, fixed dichotomy of matter and spirit.

It is interesting that theologians and philosophers alike have simply transliterated *Weltstoff* and *étoffe de l'Univers* into English without any hint of going beyond the surface and analyzing the fuller meaning of these terms. Perhaps it takes an awareness of and attention to details characteristic of a good translator to notice, as Arthur Gibson did in translating Smulders' book *The Design of Teilhard de Chardin*, that *world stuff* and *stuff of the universe* are not valid translations of *Weltstoff* and *étoffe de l'Univers*. As Gibson explains in a note, "We have . . . deliberately chosen in this translation the English term *fabric*. We wished to avoid the extensively material and somewhat foreign sound of *stuff*. But there is a deeper reason for our choice. Unless *Weltstoff* is to revert to nothing more helpful than precisely 'material to be worked up in the manufacture or out of which anything is to be or may be formed,' it must be made to mean something more generic. Now Webster, from whom the above definition of *stuff* has been taken, defines *fabric* as 'a structure; cloth woven or knit from fibers,' thus clearly highlighting the notion of structuring and of an advance over the primordial 'stuff'. Note precisely that in Teilhard's enucleation, the *Weltstoff itself* proceeds in a way that constitutes 'a "convolution" of the fabric about itself'; now, either this is an improper simile or else the *Weltstoff* is *ab initio* more than *mere* primordial stuff, and contains *within itself* in potency the very convolutions it later assumes. *Fabric* incidentally is given as Webster's fifth definition of *Stuff*; hence it cannot be maintained that our choice tips the scales too heavily on the side of manufacture!"

Gibson's suggestion is well taken and a helpful insight, but when he raises shades of preformation and fixed Aristotelian overtones of act and potency towards the end of his note, we might well wonder whether, having taken an important step towards an evolutionary or process philosophy of nature, he has not slipped back into the very cosmology Teilhard tried so hard to lead us out of.

There is, for instance, an important second advantage in the suggestion that we speak of the fabric rather than stuff of the universe, an advantage which Gibson himself ignores. For Teilhard *Weltstoff* is always and everywhere composed of an interiority coextensive with and equal to its exterior complexity. "Since the fabric of the universe has an inner aspect at one point of itself, there is necessarily a *double aspect to its structure*, that is to say in every region of space and time . . . *coextensive with their Without, there is a Within to things*." Or to take advantage of Gibson's insight, every fabric, every phenomenon in this universe, is woven of two integral aspects, warp and woof.

In our earlier book, *Perspectives in Evolution*, we examined the terms Teilhard used at various times to indicate the two aspects of *Weltstoff* within an evolutionary framework. Continually groping for a really good pair of terms to express the two aspects of things, Teilhard spoken variously of the Within, spirit or spirituality, person, being-in-oneself, centered unity, centreity, consciousness, love, spontaneity, liberty, freedom and psychic or radial energy. Likewise for the exterior aspect of things Teilhard devised a number of terms, none of which really satisfied him: the Without, matter, materiality, dependence on others, plurality and multiplicity, complexity, and physical or tangential energy. Teilhard himself repeatedly saw the danger of selecting any one of these pairs. Almost unconsciously we tend to read into them our own subterranean overtones of dichotomous cartesian and platonic dualisms. Today it seems to me we are still stymied by this problem. Neither Cuenot's *Nouveau Lexique Teilhard de Chardin* nor Cuypers' *Vocabulaire Teilhard* give us a sufficiently detailed and critical analysis of Teilhard's terminology on this point. The same defect is apparent in critical studies of Teilhard's thought. Even the masterful tome *Bergson et Teilhard de Chardin* by Madeleine Barthelemy-Madaule and the Appendix of Emile Rideau's voluminous *Introduction to the Thought of Teilhard de Chardin* either skirt the issue or deal with it on the surface. The only really creative tackling of the topic is in the little-known two-part *La Montée de Conscience* by Georges La Fay. Somewhere along the line some scholar will have to devote a lengthy tome to analyzing and detailing every statement of Teilhard's on the basic nature of the universe. Until this is done and done with critical scholarship, we can only admit our present limitations. We do not yet have an ideal terminology for the two aspects of *Weltstoff*. Somewhere in Teilhard's many writings it may lay hidden, but until we find it we can only go on what is at hand.

From a correlation of Teilhard's and Bertalanffy's pioneering insights some interesting clues have already emerged. The threads of ever-increasing complexity (structure) and consciousness (spontaneity or freedom) can be traced throughout the history of cosmic evolution in the continuity of a single process, groping, halting, sidetracking and even dead-ending at times, yet always in the main stream moving upwards. Creation then is a continuous, on-going process. And certainly not the given datum of a fixed material nature, complete in the first moment of a thing's existence and subject only to superficial, accidental changes.

Continuity in the process of ever increasing complexity and structure has already been outlined from both Bertalanffy's and Teilhard's vantage points. As for the correlation between structure and interiority, Bertalanffy had expressed this quite well when he noted that "at every new structural level the degree of freedom increases."

We have already noted our problem with terminology, particularly our present lack of a single term that will satisfactorily express the interiority of the atom, molecule and cell, as well as of the living organism and man. At the moment, spontaneity, centeredness, freedom and, possibly, energy are the least objectionable, and provide a base for operations and further discussion.

In discussing the inner aspect of reality, Pitirim Sorokin recalls in *The Ways and Powers of Love*, that from the earliest Greek thinkers, philosophers and theologians have "viewed even the unifying physical forces of gravitation, of the unification of electrons and protons in the atom, of chemical affinity, of magnetism, and so on, as the manifestations of love energy (the affinity of beings for each other) in the physical world; the 'instincts' of solidarity or gregariousness, biological mutual aid and cooperation, as the manifestations of love energy in the organic world; conscious love, sympathy, friendship, solidarity, as its manifestation in the psychosocial world."

This is obvious to anyone who has delved into the history of philosophical and theological thought. But we should not be misled by appearances into equating this tradition with the modern process thought of Teilhard, Bertalanffy, Whitehead and others. True, Teilhard himself stated that "transported into a universe in which duration adds a further dimension, the (Thomistic) theory of matter and form becomes almost indiscernible from our speculations today on the development of nature." Physicists today commonly refer to matter as "canned light" or "canned energy." From the theological and philosophical side, Karl Rahner has suggested that we speak of matter as *gefrorener Geist* or "frozen spirit," while Bernard Lonergan proposes "empirical residue" and Joseph Donceel "undetermined cosmic energy" instead of prime matter. To equate the approach of modern science with the up-dating attempts of the theologian and philosopher, no matter how brilliant these might prove, is to me falling into the trap of anachronistic thinking, projecting our present evolutionary insights into a world dominated by an entirely opposite cosmology and claiming that because of certain similarities of terminology the theological explanations of the past merely need some surface polishing to bring them up to date and relevance. There is throughout the Judaeo-Christian tradition a certain process, an evolutionary orientation. The Judaeo-Christian tradition is based on a linear conception of time, as we pointed out in *Perspectives in Evolution*. However, the philosophical categories which dominate practically all our theological explanations, from the early Fathers, through Augustine and Aquinas, down to the present, have been drawn from the Greek world where cyclic time and a fixed cosmology reigned almost supreme.

To agree with the up-dating of Rahner, Lonergan and Donceel seems to me to avoid the basic and fundamental objection raised by Teilhard in his essay "From Cosmos to Cosmogenesis:" "In the realm of the Cosmos, a ruinous dualism has unavoidably been introduced into the structure of the Universe. On one side, the Spirit—on the other side, Matter; and between the two nothing but the affirmation of a verbal interdependence between Matter and Spirit, all too often comparable to a slavery of the body to the soul. All this because *the two terms, arrested and fixed, have lost all genetic connection.*"

Fundamental in the evolutionary view is the rejection of matter and spirit as fixed categories. In the Aristotelian-thomistic view, matter and spirit represent fixed realities, created as individual, unchanging realities, perfect and complete in their essences as inseparable unities in concrete things. In the evolutionary view, matter and spirit are still parallel to each other but there is a dynamic transformation in process, a transformation which integrates and centers matter on itself, thus giving continual birth to the evolution of spirit. The vocabulary limps and there is little we can do about it. Teilhard continually ran into the problem, as, for instance, when he wrote: "Concretely, there is not Matter and Spirit. There exists only Matter becoming Spirit, for there is in the World neither (pure) Spirit nor Matter. The 'Fabric of the universe' is Spirit-Matter." Just as a person emerges out of the structure of the universe and human society in a life-long process of participation with God in his own creation, so too does the universe operate in its own creation through the laws of increasing complexity-consciousness and of natural selection to produce here and there new and more centered unities, atoms, molecules, cells, animals and plants, and finally man and mankind.

There is in both man and the universe a single organic process at work, the transfiguration of reality in love. Or if you prefer more traditional language—with its implicit Cartesian /manichean overtones—the spiritualization of matter. In his *Essay on Love*, Solovyev suggested that in the inorganic world the physical counterpart of human love is shown in all the forces that unite, integrate and maintain the whole inorganic cosmos in endless unities, beginning with the smallest unity of the atom and ending with the whole physical universe as one, unified, orderly cosmos. In a cosmos, as we pointed out in the opening pages of Chapter Two, the universe is organized, a system, the opposite of chaos, and man's task and vocation is to discover that order. In a cosmogenesis man's task takes on an additional challenge since he continues and extends the universal process of creation and unification. In his mind and heart, man lifts the evolutionary forces and energies of love and centreity to a new and higher plane. In man evolution becomes conscious of itself; man takes into his own hands the cosmic creation still in process.

Two crucial questions arise in this context, the problem of discontinuity within a continuous evolutionary process and a question of emphasis in man's emergence, the relationship of structure and person in man.

First, the evident continuity within the evolutionary process prompts us to ask whether man is not simply a little more complex than the animals, and not essentially, or better, qualitatively, different from them. Is there only a quantitative difference in the degree of complexity between brute animals and the human animals?

On this point Teilhard has suggested an interesting solution, pointing out that if you heat water degree by degree you finally reach a critical threshold, the boiling point where the addition of one more calorie of heat energy brings about a revolution, the emergence of a totally new state of being. A liquid becomes a gas! Thus in the evolution of life, structure and interiority grow simultaneously in the interwoven process of increasing complexity and consciousness or spontaneity until a critical threshold is reached where one more step in the quantitative advance of complexity causes, by feedback, a self-conscious, reflective, moral creature—man. As Bertalanffy suggests, the whole is greater that the sum of all its parts. In this approach we move beyond the anachronistic problems of matter, spirit, body and soul, the special creation of the human soul and the question of when this is infused. We also move beyond other problems: the question of death, for instance, which we will take up in our next chapter.

The second question arising in the evolutionary context concerns the relationship between our evolutionary view of man and of the universe. In speaking earlier of an evolutionary monism in which man's personality emerges out of his necessary dependence on others we must find some common ground with our dynamic view of the universe as an evolutionary process of increasing complexity/consciousness. How can we express the genetic and dynamic continuity between man and the universe?

In dealing with the general fabric of the universe and its evolution we have suggested with Bertalanffy and Teilhard that the inner and outer aspects of things exhibit a coordinated increase. Looking at man, it would seem that his evolution in complexity has almost ceased. Physically, man has not changed much in at least fifty thousand years; his brain is about as centrated as it can be. Has man's consciousness then also halted its evolution? An answer lies in the fact that with the appearance of man evolution shifts its emphasis from the without of things (complexity and structure) to the interior of the psychosocial. Man's bodily structure has reached a high point in terms of cerebralization with a minimum of organic specialization. Now the emphasis appears to rest on *the continued evolu-*

tion of structures on the psychosocial plane of supra-individual unions in love: the family, the tribe, the nation, a united mankind. Structure continues to increase in man as does spontaneity, freedom and personalism.

In this context we describe man as personality emerging out of the necessary dependence on others. The key here is twofold. First, man as a person is not synonymous with individuality. Second, man as a person exists only within the structure of human society rooted in the physical and biological realms. Man cannot affirm his true identity as a person except within the context and fabric of a human society based on love. Man cannot exist isolated from society in his individuality. His personality emerges from, but remains in dialogue with, society. Man's personality then emerges in and through a transformation or transcendence of the necessary dependence on others imposed on him from the first moment of his existence and imposed by his very existence in this world as a finite, incomplete creature. As a man becomes more human and more a person ("spiritual") he does not escape his "materiality." But rather he transforms that structure by a loving embrace. He transfigures it. He "spiritualizes" it. Man's continued, lifelong creation-emergence as a person involves two inseparable and complementary aspects: the growing affirmation of his being-in-self as distinct from others and his loving embrace of his dependence on others within the structure of a loving human society. Thus the law of increasing complexity or structure continues with the creation-evolution of man as a social being.

Now we must turn to questions of man's origins in an evolutionary context and his future.

5

mankind—fallen or rising?

The perennial nostalgia for paradise. It is somewhat paradoxical that our technological scientific culture still betrays man's deep yearning for an idyllic state away from time, change and the painful ebb and flow of daily life, a sacred place where the heart can find immortal bliss. But the paradox is not as strange as it may seem at first sight. Man's past nostalgia for a paradise lost has been well documented in a variety of cultures by Mircea Eliade and Sister Sylvia Mary, an Anglican historian. This background becomes quite instructive when we add to it the studies of the Lutheran theologian-historian Ernst Benz, who has traced the gradual transition from the other-worldly eschatological hopes of the Hebrews and early Christians through the social and technological utopian writings of the Renaissance, Enlightenment and nineteenth century, to our modern scientific and technological this-world eschatology. Just as creation occurs in the beginning for a fixed world image and at the end of time for an evolutionary image, so Eden and Adam shift from the beginning to the end in modern process theology. This shift requires some detailed explanation, particularly since it entails a whole new theological understanding of the origins of mankind and "original sin."

Past generations have witnessed many attempts to explain man's situation and his nostalgia for a paradise lost. In terms of Greek philosophy and a fixed cosmology, everything is created perfect and complete in the beginning. With man came the "fall" and our present situation. Within this context the classical explanation of man's origins has undergone many developments since the Hebrews compiled the story of Adam and Eve in the Garden. In the late fourth century, for instance, theologians coined the term *original sin.* Augustine found this conception very useful in refuting the Pelagian heretics who among other things rejected the concept of a fallen mankind. In this classic explanation the first man, from whom we have all physically descended, was created perfect by God and raised to supernatural life, only to fall into sin and rebellion. Thus, every member of the human race has inherited from his parents and ultimately from Adam, a sinful guilt, the lack of supernatural grace which is the prime effect of that original sin. Augustine and many other theologians since believed this guilt was handed on from generation to generation in the passions and uncontrollable "concupiscence" involved in sexual intercourse. This aspect of the classic explanation was generally rejected by theologians within the last century, and other modifications have been worked out in attempts to bring the classic explanation more into line with our growing awareness of man's evolutionary origins.

More recently theologians have tackled the problem head-on. In July of 1966, Pope Paul VI called a conference of twelve theological and scientific experts in Rome to discuss the reinterpretation of "original sin" in terms of evolution. A careful analysis of the opening papal address and of the papers presented at the conference indicates the appropriateness, necessity and validity of the summary of new views we present here.*

In reinterpreting the mystery of man's situation and his position in an evolving universe, modern scholars have suggested three basic approaches or insights. These approaches we must emphasize are simply that—approaches and partial insights rather than complete, full explanations of a reality that can never be fully understood or explained. While the classic explanation of man's situation as fallen and the result of an

___

* An analysis of the papal address can be found in "Antediluvians and the Search for Adam," by Robert T. Francoeur. *The Critic.* 25:4 (February-March, 1967).

original sin on the part of Adam captures the essential religious truths contained in Genesis and the whole of biblical literature, it nevertheless has two distinct disadvantages for modern man. First, it is very difficult to integrate in an evolutionary perspective, and second, it is almost meaningless and totally irrelevant to modern man. Was Adam an Australopithecine, *Homo erectus*, or Neanderthaloid? And why should I be punished for something Adam did perhaps a million or two million years ago? While the new approaches outlined here are far from complete or satisfactory, they do have the advantage of expressing the essence of the biblical conception of man and his situation in terms both intelligible and acceptable to modern man.

1. THE APPROACH OF PROCESS PHILOSOPHY

Philosophy attempts to deal with the ultimate realities of our world as seen by man's intellect and reason. The philosopher tries to go beyond everyday observations and arrive at general principles and conclusions. Thus philosophers of every age have accepted the basic principle that everything we know from experience is finite. According to Anselm, anything finite is by its very nature then incomplete. For Anselm, Thomas Aquinas and others, this lack of something necessary for complete existence amounts to an *ontological defect*, a limitation inherent in every creature by the very fact that it is a creature.

This philosophical view of the universe and man was generally ignored as unimportant by most thinkers, though it was revived and extended by Martin Luther and Leibnitz among others.

It is not really understood in its full impact until one steps into the evolutionary perspective. In this dimension, the philosophical conception of an ontological defect takes on a new dynamism since it now becomes the basis for a continual ongoing creation process. It becomes a challenge rather than a mere defect or lack. And though it applies to all creatures as we will see shortly, it finds its main focus and emphasis in man, for he alone of all creatures is conscious of the defect and can ratify and accept it in the expression of his personal growth. By his very nature, man is finite: he must find his completion and fulfillment, consciously and willingly, through transcendence of self. Man's finite nature and his basic need for transcendence find expression in his social needs. Without companionship, without a loving union with others, man cannot exist. Genesis has put it very well, "It is not good for man to be without companionship." Every human being, as he grows up, soon comes to realize that his growth as a person involves a dependence on and recognition of others. And still, each of us is somehow afraid to open up to others and admit we need them. Whether through pride or fear, or both, man hesitates to love, even though he knows he must love in order to achieve his fullest being. How often does the teenager express this fear that in opening himself to another in love he runs the risk of seeing his own personality absorbed, weakened or destroyed by the very person he loves. Our finite nature bears with its finitude the divine vocation to unite with others in love. Yet along with this challenge to transcend the finite world of self, there is in each of us a natural and radical incapacity and unwillingness to go out of our own little protective shells. Almost unconsciously we resist our divine vocation, thereby ratifying the "ontological defect" of which early philosophers have spoken so well in a fixed image.

Here we are applying that concept to the evolutionary image, and specifically to man's on-going process of creation in which each of us shares. Only when a man opens himself up to another person in love does he effectively admit and embrace his own finite nature as creature. Only when a man loves selflessly does he recognize his true role in this universe. Yet through fear and pride man can refuse to admit and accept his finite nature, not in some philosophical, abstract way but rather in the concrete realities of daily life. Self-idolatry, setting self up as God and claiming to be self-sufficient or infinite, is after all the very essence of sin whether we call it original and blame Adam or simply speak of each man's rejection of love in daily affairs. Like "Adam," each of us is on occasion so enraptured with ourselves that we refuse to recognize our need of others. But what man experiences as a dynamic tension on the personal, conscious plane, all created nature shares in on various levels. There is, as we noted in Chapter Two, a constant dynamic tension and interplay between the forces of attraction and repulsion on every level of our created world. At work throughout nature are forces of attraction leading on to ever higher levels of union, complexity and consciousness. Unless the atom transcends its own finite realm and "reaches out" to other atoms, the molecule cannot come into being. The same can be said of subatomic particles, molecules and cells. Yet, throughout nature, this attraction towards union is resisted by the forces of entropy. Synthesis is opposed by disintegration. All created nature seems to resist the call to higher unions despite the fact that it is only in differentiated unions of elements incomplete in themselves, unions which differentiate and preserve the essential integrity and uniqueness of the components, that these same elements can find fuller development and contribute to the evolutionary process of creation.

On this point, Teilhard de Chardin frequently spoke of cosmic evolution as a process in which all things gradually center on Christ in unions based on love. Certainly on the human level true selfless love is the only force that can unite men without destroying the individual persons so bound together. In applying this conception to the whole universe we might do well to recall an insight common to pagan philosophers like Empedocles in the fifth century before Christ as well as Christian theologians like Thomas Aquinas. These two thinkers, and many others, suggested that the basic *energy* or *force* at work in the universe is that of love, the affinity of one being for another. Thus, love which is conscious, personal and free energy at work within human society can also be seen at work in various forms on the subhuman and even inorganic levels. Viewed in the context of modern evolutionary science, this classic philosophic insight sheds some interesting light on the problem of "original sin" or the human situation. If love, the affinity of one creature for another, is the ultimate force behind evolution, then any resistance to this movement constitutes *a refusal and rejection not only of the creature's finite nature but also of its role in cosmic evolution.*

There are many forces at work in our universe that lead to fragmentation. Among the atoms, molecules and even living organisms, entropy leads to decay, disintegration, dispersion and a state of complete uniformity and inactivity, the motionlessness and homogeneity of absolute zero. Among men, forces of hatred, animosity and discrimination repeat the fragmentation so vividly portrayed in the story of the Tower of Babel.

Yet throughout the history of cosmic evolution, and especially in the history of man, forces of affinity have led to unions of ever increasing complexity and consciousness. Chemical bonds, Van der Waal and other forces, gravity at work in the atomic and molecular worlds, neg-entropy (negative entropy) forces in the world of living organisms, and conscious personal love among men. In the Christian perspective, the "Church," the "Mystical Body of Christ," the community of mankind united in love, embraces the whole universe since "in Him all things hold together."

The value and importance of this process conception of man is more than apparent in the writings of the French Marxist Roger Garaudy. One of the leaders in the Christian/Marxist dialogue, Garaudy quotes at length Teilhard de Chardin's evolutionary explanation of original sin, pointing out its dynamic process dimension as the key reason why he as a communist philosopher finds this view of mankind's "original sin" not only acceptable but even more, completely compatible with his own Marxist interpretation of the nature and future of man.

2. A PSYCHOLOGICAL OR RELATIONAL APPROACH

Among the many psychologists who have probed the depths of the human mind and heart, two have specifically directed their attention to a new view of the story of "original sin" presented in the myth of Adam and Eve in the Garden.

Erich Fromm, the renowned author of *The Art of Loving*

and other books, has suggested that any theory or explanation of human love must begin with a clear understanding of man and his human existence. While various bonds and attractions towards union are found in the inorganic and animal worlds, man's love transcends these chemical, physical and instinctive bonds. He has his roots in them and yet he leaves them behind. (This point of transcendence is not evident and hardly noticed in a number of recent works, notably *The Naked Ape* by Morris, Ardrey's *The Territorial Imperative* and Lorenz' book *On Aggression.*) Where man's ancestors once enjoyed a oneness with nature, self-consciousness and awareness of the world have led man out of Eden. In reflective man, the evolving universe becomes conscious of itself. But having left a paradisal oneness with nature, man cannot turn back. With flaming sword, the mythic cherubim blocks all man's attempts to return to the animal world. The only road open to us lies ahead, in the further development of our intellectual life and our capacity for love. Only by moving forward can we achieve a new harmony with the universe, a harmony no longer based on blind instinctive behavior but on free, conscious love that far surpasses any peace existing in the world of nature below man.

Fromm's approach concentrates on a common western characteristic, the awareness of individuality. This view may not apply to certain cultures, as for instance, the Pueblo Indian and certain eastern cultures. Nevertheless, it is quite instructive for those in the European-American tradition. Fromm suggests that when man became conscious of his fellow man, his past and possibilities for the future, he also became aware of himself as a separate person. This separation and individuation has many faces. It comes with an awareness of the shortness of human life and of the fact that we come into this world at the bidding of others and will leave it against our will before or after those we love. Alone and separated from the world, man often finds himself helpless before the anonymous forces of nature and society.

In this situation anxiety and isolation would soon drive man insane if he had no hope of breaking out of this prison, no hope of breaking down the walls that separate him from others. To be separated completely means to be cut off from others, helpless and unable to respond actively to others. It means that others, people and things, can invade my world without my being able to resist them. Such separation is for man the source of the most intense anxiety and fear.

This context leads Fromm to look again at the myth of Adam and Eve. In eating the fruit of the forbidden tree Adam and Eve exercised their freedom to choose between good and evil. They expressed their freedom from an imposed, instinctual harmony with nature, and saw that they were naked. We could, of course, interpret this nakedness and their resultant shame in terms of our Victorian and puritan embarrassment over human sexuality, but Fromm indicates that this perhaps is not the real meaning of the biblical authors. It may be more in keeping with the authors' intent to see here a message of our relationship with our creator and our fellow man. When Adam and Eve first became conscious of each other and of themselves as unique individual human persons, they also became aware of each other as distinct and separate persons. But in recognizing their separateness as man and woman, they still remained *strangers.* Though united as husband and wife, they had not yet learned to overcome their separateness through love. This is made quite clear in the reaction of Adam after eating the fruit, for instead of defending Eve as a man in love would have, he tries to throw all the blame on her. And Eve, in her turn, blames the serpent. This unwillingness of Adam and Eve to accept each other in love can only result in shame, anxiety, and a true sense of guilt over their acceptance of their separateness and their refusal and rejection of the true union of love.

This explanation of Genesis by Erich Fromm highlights the very close connection that exists between the "original sin" and every man, between the human situation and the necessity for a loving openness to our fellow creatures and our God. As a complement to this approach we might look briefly at the emergence of the human personality as experienced by a child in the first months after birth. Again, this interpretation, like that of Fromm, emerges from a Western conception of man and is very much within the European-American tradition of thought. The psychological basis is that of Freud and Horney, but the substance and details have been worked out by Henry Elkin.

In Elkin's view, the new-born child enters a non-physical world of self and non-self, a world of sensations and experiences which he must organize in order to find for himself a place of integrity as an individual person. This first step in the affirmation of personal identity, our primordial consciousness, seems to be closely associated with our first and perhaps only instinctive bodily movement. Instinctively, yet with purpose, the infant will turn his head to focus his perceptions and attention on his mother's breast. This simple movement, sooner or later, brings the child to a dim but marvelous apprehension of his own psychic identity. In gradually centering his attention and transforming the all-encompassing, dimensionless and ever shifting field of visual perceptions, this elementary movement brings the infant to a dawning awareness of his primal *Self* as distinct from the impersonal non-self or *other*.

As this primordial consciousness of *Self* deepens, it is marked by a growing sense of numinous omnipotence in the infant's mind. The *other* appears both impersonal and controllable at this point, for the child can "control" everything he sees simply by moving his head. Thus his primal image of self contains the seeds of an initial, grandiose illusion of personal independence and divine omnipotence coupled with an absolute, self-centered pride which Freud would call "primary narcissism." Theologians in the Christian tradition might give it the more familiar name of "original sin."

The term *numinous* or *numinosity*, as used here, indicates something supernatural, something dedicated to or hallowed by an association with a deity, sacred or possessing talismanic properties, magical, filled with a sense of the presence of divinity and hence holy. The term also refers to an unseen but majestic presence inspiring both dread and fascination, according to Webster. Elkin notes that the non-rational element characteristic of many living religions has been referred to as numinous and it is this non-rational or pre-rational, hence pre-ethical or pre-moral, aspect that concerns us here.

At first the primordial *other* is impersonal. It begins to assume personal qualities only when the child starts to respond and dialogue with others. He smiles in response to a human face and tries to form sounds imitating those he hears coming from the *other*. These signs of personal recognition probably begin about the third month and slowly develop in depth and consciousness.

The subjective illusion of the numinous omnipotence of *Self* is characteristic only of the earliest phase of personality emergence. Nevertheless, it underlies every falsehood and evil in human life since it distorts reality and frustrates the true affirmation of our personality as it must come to be in a social world of finite and incomplete persons. As the range of primordial consciousness expands to encompass new elements and experiences, the infant soon learns that the *other* is not always as manageable as he first thought. The infant soon learns that the *other* oftens fails to respond adequately to the demands and needs of his "omnipotent" *Self*, even if only for an occasional moment. Instinctively the infant cries for food and his mother is not there immediately to fill his need, or she may misinterpret the message.

At this point a momentous primordial drama occurs in the infant's emerging consciousness, a drama involving his image of *Self* and *other*. As the moments of conflict are repeated, as the *other* fails to meet the demands of *Self* even for a moment but again and again, a primordial frustration shakes the infant. He experiences a very personal eternity of agonizing, primordial doubt in which he finds himself doubting the reality of *Self*. His once omnipotent *Self* becomes increasingly ineffective in coping with the *other*. Hence this doubt focuses on the reality of both *Self* and *other* as he has known them up to this point. Shocked by an awareness of his own frustration and beset by instinctive fears of the unpredictable *other*, the infant falls into a state of primordial anxiety, a mystically ineffable and aweful, holy terror, as Elkin puts it. Excruciatingly aware only of its unanswered needs in a world where it has not yet learned to accept the existence of an *other* he cannot control, the infant may slip into a paralyzing state of primordial despair, of numb insensibility and spiritual darkness.

(We might, at this point, note that we have capitalized *Self* and *Other* in certain instances to indicate a numinous or omnipotent quality attached to the term in a particular context.)

Fortunately the merciful intervention of a personal and loving *other* can rescue the infant from this tormenting doubt and anxiety. In a very real sense, this deliverance brings about a spiritual resurrection in which the child is introduced into a new and regenerated world marked by a shift of numinosity and omnipotence from *self* to *other*. Primarily through the mediation of the mother, a child can come to realize that the very existence of his *self* depends on the omnipotent and merciful love of the *Other*, his mother, father, family and relatives. It is only when the child learns to rely trustingly on this divine love of the *Other* that his spirit can remain secure in the light of a primordial consciousness reflecting the communion and co-union between *self* and *Other*.

An important development seems to occur in this process of personality emergence around the age of six months. Before this, the infant is unaware of his mother as a separate and *personal* being, or in fact, of anything else in his world as a separate entity. Until about six months, the child lives immersed in and surrounded by the primordial *Other* in all its varied manifestations, of which the mother's is only one aspect. Then, about six months after birth, the infant enters the physical world. He becomes aware of the existence of the physical world as such, composed of distinct objects. The spring-board for this discovery is the infant's growing experience of self as a body-self, his development of a body-image. An important part of this discovery are the attempts the infant makes to grasp and manipulate objects in his hands. The manipulation is far more important than the mere instinctive grasping of things which begins shortly after birth.

In this second phase of personality emergence, the infant begins to appreciate his mother as a separate, distinct and personal being, possessing certain distinguishing characteristics. In some ways each infant experiences his mother as a "good mother," a merciful, loving mediator between his now uncertain world and the earlier primordial world wherein he made his first step in solving the relationship between self and other. But the infant can and often does experience his mother as a "bad mother." Fear, hatred and guilt, the foundations of psychological pathology in adult life, naturally arise in this context, for hatred and rejection by the "bad mother" bring back into play the infant's temptation to claim numinosity for himself as a defense. Rejected by the other, the infant naturally falls back onto the only secure world he has known, the primordial world in which he was God.

No human being and no mother is perfect or all bad. Thus, at this point, the mother can play the role of a merciful mediator, resolving her child's dilemma by showing him how his finite personality, *self*, can be affirmed and thrive in the loving society of *others*.

In the primordial state of personality development, the temptation was to confuse self with God. Unless properly resolved, this confusion leads in adult life to psychoses, criminality and perhaps, as Elkin suggests, to some unclassifiable creative geniuses. In the second stage, there is the temptation to confuse some other finite creature, particularly the mother, with God. This confusion can easily lead to a stunted and mediocre life of crippling dependence.

The images and feelings connected with the primordial *Other*, focused on the mother, are the very foundation of one's personality. Gradually these are carried over to the growing phenomenal world beyond the mother as the child again adapts to an expanding world. Once again his security in the spiritual realm of merciful, abiding and trustful love created by the mother is threatened, this time by the emergence of a whole new order of values. In entering the physical world the child gradually becomes conscious not only of handling, manipulating and mouthing objects, but also of being handled by personal others. The new, quite natural values that emerge in this encounter are related to physical power and weakness. They belong to the objective, physical world. Hence the numinosity that slowly shifted from *Self* to the protective, loving and merciful mother, can now be attached to mere physical powers. Elkin suggests that we might see in this regression of the numinous from the personal to a physical basis an indication of man's spiritual "fall from grace."

At first the child views himself simply as a subject of these physical forces outside. This gradually changes as the infant learns to identify himself with his body-image. He then *sees* himself concretely as a physical object, a thing which can be manipulated or destroyed by others much as he himself tears up things, bites and swallows things. Tormented by fears of annihilation stirred up by these possibilities and depressed by his own helpless inferiority, the child again falls into the basic pattern of all anxiety. He begins to doubt, once again, the reality of self and other. His personal identity as it emerged from his primordial experience is shaken since both the reality of that experience and his own resurrection through the merciful love of his mother, the omnipotent *Other*, form the very basis of his identity as a person.

Here again the mother must mediate mercifully and lovingly the emergence of her child's personality to preserve its integrity as self within the threatening physical world. The child's ego (self) has already formed itself in relation to the mother. Now it must gradually take over her role of mediation between self and the surrounding world.

The result of all this is a healthy, mature human person who recognizes and affirms his finite personality within the context of a human society and community of love. True personality requires the recognition of our dependence on others and our relation as creatures to our Creator.

It is easy to see in this picture a revolutionary and quite new approach to the realities theologians have traditionally termed "the original sin" and "man's fall from divine grace." Since the child's awareness and affirmation of self emerge through a resolution of the conflict between self and other in which he rejects the universal temptation to claim numinous omnipotence for himself or some other finite creature, the emergence of personality as portrayed by Elkin actually involves the essential temptation symbolized by the Genesis story of Eden. Unless the infant learns to accept the fact that he is not omnipotent and divine, he will not be able to accept his need for others. Unless he learns to attribute divine omnipotence to a merciful and loving God in a series of steps involving the mother and through her mediation the organization and integration of the physical world, the child will constantly try to affirm the *lie* of his own, his mother's, or the physical world's numinous omnipotence—"Eat the fruit of this tree and you shall be like unto God."

An interesting parallel to this psychological/relational approach appears in William Golding's *Lord of the Flies* where a group of polite, cultured and proper English lads are marooned on an island during the war. Cut off from all adult influences they nevertheless gradually express all the fears of mankind, the egotism of uncertain selfhood, the inhumanity of man towards those who are not part of the crowd or who behave differently, the fear of loving and yet the need to love. *The Lord of the Flies* is a fine modern parable of the human situation we know as "original sin."

In certain aspects the human situation presented in *The Lord of the Flies* reflects the contemporary image of man's situation. Yet there are certain existentialist tensions in this view which reflect a quite traditional view of man supposedly rejected by their advocates. This conflict can perhaps be traced to the Christian perspective of Søren Kierkegaard, the originator of existential thought, who maintained a solid vested interest in the traditional Augustinian conception of original sin and man's fallen state almost as the keystone to his philosophy of man. Though his disciples, Sartre, Camus, Jaspers and Heidegger, often moved far away from Kierkegaard's Christian vantage point, in most cases flatly rejecting it as irrelevant and false, these same thinkers found somewhat devious ways to integrate within their own existentialist emphasis on individual freedom a quite traditional "guilt" which pervades all mankind and unavoidably touches every individual man. Camus, for instance, goes so far as to maintain that man's longing for a lost or rejected paradise drives him to excesses and to inhumanity towards his fellowman despite his best efforts to the contrary. With some hesitation we might recall in this context Jung's psychology of the collective unconscious for, despite the overwhelming behavioral orientation of European and American psychology, there are some illuminating parallels between Jung's collective unconscious and both the traditional and modern explanations of the original sin.

3. THE BIBLICAL OR SITUATIONAL APPROACH

Perhaps the most important contribution to a more balanced appreciation of the human situation has come from the distinction now being drawn by biblical scholars and theologians between the classic concept of an "original sin" as formulated by Augustine and others after him and the biblical conception of "the sin of the world."

It is instructive that the Old Testament makes only one clear reference linking the human situation and the sinfulness of mankind with the historically first man, Adam. Yet very few passages of any length can be found that do not make some kind of reference, either direct or oblique, to this situation. Thus, in a workshop paper presented in 1968 at Woodstock College, a Jesuit scripture scholar, Joseph Fitzmyer, summarized the teaching of the Old Testament on what we have classically called the "original sin" under four headings: 1) sinfulness is with man from his birth, 2) this sin is in some way contagious, 3) man's sinfulness creates a solidarity in sin, even with successive generations, and 4) man is a sinner not only as an individual but also collectively.

In the New Testament we find the same broad, universal treatment of the human situation, again with but a single, passing reference to Adam as the cause of our situation in Paul's letter to the Christians of Rome (5:12).

It is strange but understandable how, in the development of Christian theology, an increasing emphasis has been placed by both the theologian and the man in the street on the two references that link the first historical man with the human situation. As we noted before, the very concrete term "original sin" was not coined until early in the fourth century during Augustine's controversy with the Pelagians. It seems obvious that the coining of this very precise term as a label for the sinful situation of mankind, coupled with the theologians need for a concrete source of that situation, played perhaps a dominant role in developing a one-sided and very unbalanced explanation of the biblical message. Added to this is the psychological convenience of an explanation of the human situation which, consciously or not, provides a handy scape-goat in Eve.

Christians of every age have been fascinated by the biblical account of Eden. It seems to offer answers to so many questions, not just of religion, but even of science and history. For centuries, when science and history were only embryonic disciplines, this appreciation of Genesis was tolerable and perhaps even useful despite its latent dangers. Today, however, this simplistic approach is causing more and more problems, particularly as science and history often give answers quite the opposite of those supposedly found in Genesis regarding the origin and history of mankind and the universe. By now it should be quite evident that the biblical writers lived with an entirely different world image from that of modern science. The authors of Genesis knew nothing of how our universe actually came into existence or how man originated. They knew nothing of the prehistoric fossil men of South Africa, Java and Peking, nothing of the dinosaurs and their demise long before man appeared, nothing of exploding galaxies, whirling nebulae, a heliocentric solar system, or a round earth. Needless to say, the divine inspiration and revelation Christians have traditionally attributed to the writers and editors of the various books of the Bible have often been extended, and wrongly so, to include answers to questions of science and history within the message of the Judaeo-Christian tradition. Divine inspiration and revelation have nothing to do with questions of *how* and *when* man and the universe came into being. It encompasses only answers to the questions of *why* and *by whom*, and this always in the context of man's relationship to his creator, his vocation and goal.

Yet the biblical description of Eden is filled with cosmological, mythic and folklore details such as the four great rivers, the six days of creation, the tree of life, the serpent, and others. Contradictions abound in these details, especially since the biblical editors incorporated two or even three versions of a particular story in their collection. Thus the story of creation is told in two different versions; one transpiring in six days, the other in one day, the first picturing man as created last and the second picturing him as created first.

These contradictions in details are superficial and do not at all affect the veracity and inerrancy of the biblical message provided we understand properly the authors' intent. Practically all these details were borrowed from pagan sources and arranged by the biblical authors as a suitable framework for their message of man's relationship with his creator. These details touch on the *how* and *when* of origins rather than on the relational *why* and *by whom*. In some cases the authors of the Old Testament seem to have adopted a complete story from the pagans, making only a few minor changes in adapting it to their purposes. At other times, as in the Genesis accounts of creation, a variety of details were drawn from a variety of sources over many years and centuries before they were finally worked into a harmonious setting for the Good News. However, even when a whole set of details was adopted from pagan sources, a monotheistic core was substituted for the pagan polytheism. These facts have only recently been accepted by biblical scholars and the ordinary Christian in the street.

It has always been difficult for Christians, raised in a western culture and nourished by Hellenic philosophy, to appreciate biblical literature which arose in an oriental, Hebraic tradition. Conceived within the luxuriant symbolisms of the Orient, the story of Eden has been distorted by Christians of the west who forget both its oriental character and its strictly religious intent. Over the centuries Christians have so concentrated on the physical description and details of Genesis that they have missed almost entirely the real message. The result has been a very one-sided, unbalanced explanation of the human situation. The full religious message of Genesis becomes evident only if we recall and appreciate the oriental presentation used by the authors. Within the opulent arabesque of mythic symbolisms the writers and editors of Genesis and the whole of the Old Testament set an irridescent drama of man's situation in this world. This drama, as we will see shortly, is not at all limited to the first man and woman of history. Adam and Eve are rather one facet, one aspect of the human situation. Even so the drama of Eden portrays the human situation with a clarity that speaks to the early Hebrews, the apostles, the medieval serf and modern man equally well provided it is properly understood and explained. The problem of relevance in the story of Eden is not in the text itself, but rather in the readers who must learn to appreciate it.

Psychologically and intellectually it has always been difficult for man to accept his human situation as being directly caused or intended by an all-good God. From a human viewpoint rooted in the fixed world image of Ptolemy and the philosophy of Plato and Aristotle, the logical explanation involves an all-good God who creates a perfect and complete world, placing man in a Garden of happiness and grace. Through perversity and pride, man rebels against his creator. The image of a fallen mankind and a paradise lost is essential in a fixed world image that accepts the Platonic/Aristotelian concept of natures and essences. This explanation is an ideal one for people who accept its basic image and philosophy. In an evolutionary perspective that focuses on becoming rather than on being, that image and philosophy are irrelevant and anachronistic. The problem then becomes one of retaining the essence of the biblical message while replacing its out-of-date setting with an explanation more in accord with our evolutionary image.

To cull the essence from the hull of details requires considerable skill, and two important steps have been made in this direction by modern biblical scholars in their rediscovery of the oriental style of biblical writings. The oriental mind is quite different in its approach to reality, not that this difference makes its approach any less valid or useful than the western view with which we are inculcated. Oriental literature, as we now know, makes use of two literary techniques or genres, both of which we must deal with before we set out the modern biblical image of the human situation.

As an introduction to the literary genre of *corporate personality* we might reconstruct a history of the United States as a Hebrew in the days of Abraham would likely have recorded it. "In the beginning, God created George Washington, the father of all Americans. George lived many, many years and he had many wives, sons and daughters. His first born son, Abraham Lincoln, freed the slaves and led his people through the Civil War. And Abraham had many sons and daughters. His life was long and filled with many years, from 1809 to 1961, when his first-born son, John F. Kennedy, succeeded him as leader of the chosen people. . . ." It was common in the oriental style of history to pass over unimportant details and people, concentrating all our attention on key figures in history. Thus the oriental historian often picks out certain important individuals and lets them represent a whole group or nation. In some cases this person is a historical person. The Old Testament writer, for instance, tells us that God threatened to destroy Achab when he actually meant that God punished Achab's whole family and nation for their sins. In other cases the writer may select a fabled figure of folklore as well known to the Hebrews as Paul Bunyon and Johnny Appleseed are to Americans, King Arthur and the Knights of the Round Table are to the English, or Frederick the Great is to Germans.

Genesis gives us many examples of this literary technique. There are fictional characters like Nemrod, "by God's grace a huntsman bold," "the first great warrior" and founder of the empire of Babylon; Jabel, "the first founder of all those who live in tents and herd sheep;" Jubal, "the founder of all those who play music on the harp or the pipe," and Tubalcain "who became a smith, skilled in every kind of brass and iron work." But there are also more historical figures like Abraham and Noah around whom countless legends developed.

A classic example of corporate personality appears in the story of Cain and Abel. Far from our image of early cave men, Genesis pictures Cain and Abel as the very civilized first sons of Adam and Eve, Cain the vengeful, violent farmer and Abel the God-fearing, peaceful herder of sheep. According to the biblical account, God is pleased with Abel's sacrifice for reasons not mentioned by the authors and displeased with Cain's offerings. Murder follows and Cain is exiled by God into a foreign land—"Then Cain said to the Lord, Guilt like mine is too great to find forgiveness. And now you are robbing me of my land, I shall be cut off from your protection and wander over the earth, a fugitive; anyone I meet will slay me." Who Cain's potential murderers might be did not concern the authors of Genesis even though they say he and Abel were Adam's first sons. "So Cain was banished from God's presence and lived as a fugitive, east of Eden. And now Cain had knowledge of his wife, and she conceived." Again questions of detail like where Cain's wife came from did not bother the biblical authors because they saw both Cain and Abel as figures of something beyond a historical pair.

In its original setting, the story of Cain and Abel presents a well-developed world, populated and highly cultured. Farming and domestication of animals were ways of life totally unknown to mankind until recent times, perhaps some fifteen thousand years ago. When the tribe of Abraham left its homeland near Ur about the year 2,000 b.c., the Israelites continued their semi-nomadic, pastoral life. Somewhere in their repeated and antagonistic contacts with the Canaanites around the Promised Land the folklore legend of Cain and Abel gradually emerged. The earliest version most likely came into being around the campfire as a glorification of the peaceful shepherd and a denunciation of the warlike Canaanite farmers. Through many generations and tellings the story grew, modified and elaborated on.

Much later, perhaps a thousand years later, the editors of Genesis saw in the mythic legend of Cain and Abel a fine illustration of man's relationship with his creator. Such a story could be very useful when incorporated into the prehistory, the first eleven chapters, of Genesis which set the stage for the Covenant Yahweh chose to make with Abraham, Isaac and Jacob. To set the stage for this covenant with the Chosen People and with the human race, the authors traced back to the very beginning of mankind a solidarity in sin that required redemption. Thus just as the infidelity and sin of the Chosen People found a loving response from Yahweh in the Covenant, so the sinfulness of all mankind found a loving response from Yahweh in the promise made the first man in the Garden after the fall.

The other literary technique used by the authors of Genesis and oriental writers in general is that of *historical etiology*. Again we can use Cain and Abel as an example since their story incorporates both genres. The dictionary defines etiology as the "assignment of a cause, as for instance, the etiology of some folkway." Adding the historical dimension, we have a literary device which allows a writer to explain the origins of some custom or reality of life by projecting a present, or future, situation into the distant past. Thus the authors of Genesis projected a very human situation he knew from personal experience into the unknown reaches of the past, to the very origins of mankind. In this way he set the stage for the Covenant and also explained the origins of evil and hatred among all men.

Today more and more theologians and biblical scholars are suggesting that the story of Adam and Eve does not recount the actual history of human origins. As John L. McKenzie, S.J., has noted, "Modern exegesis makes it clear that the vast majority of (biblical) interpretations do not see how these two characters we call Adam and Eve can be historical in the same sense that David and Bethsheba are historical." The story of Adam and Eve, as the story of Cain and Abel, is "an attempt to describe the human condition" rather than give an actual historical record of man's origins.

In setting the stage for the ratification of the Covenant with Abraham, the authors selected *four stories* to illustrate man's solidarity in sin and mankind's need for redemption from sin and hatred. Each of these stories adds its own facet to the human drama and the sequence is quite logical. First the story of separateness and self-independence portrayed by a married couple, Adam and Eve. Then the cruel expression of hatred and jealousy between two brothers, Cain and Abel, and the sinfulness of Noe's neighbors that called down God's wrath in the flood. And finally, the tower of Babel when mankind's pride and egotism ended in the total breakdown of communication and dialogue between men. Each of these four stories has its own unique flavor, to which we might devote a few moments. First, the story of Eden. Traditionally the tree of life symbolizes an access to immortality, divine friendship and eternal life. To eat the fruit of the tree of life would mean that man could live forever in the friendship of God. But man was attracted by the other tree in Eden, the forbidden tree of the knowledge of good and evil. Eat this fruit, "and you will be like God, knowing good and evil" is the perennial temptation experienced by man. Knowledge for the Hebrews was a very practical and experiential reality. Hence we might express this temptation in another way, "Why should you, man, noble lord of this earth, have to depend on God to decide what is good or evil for you? Why not set yourself up as God, capable of determining for yourself what is right and wrong?"

In the ancient eastern languages Adam means "man," "humanity," and also "from earth and to earth," whereas Eve is derived from the Hebrew root meaning "to live." Both names give evidence of an etiological narrative that uses the literary technique of corporate personality also. As Rahner and Vorgrimler point out in their *Theological Dictionary*, the parable of Eve's production from Adam's rib underscores the fact that she is of the same nature as man, different in character but of equal value. This is emphasized by the name she is given in Genesis 2:23, *'ishshah*, the woman, the completeness of man, *'ish*. Eve is pictured as the mother of all living men and through her archetypal marriage with Adam the key to all mankind's participation in the promised redemption.

These images were very meaningful to the Hebrew people in their simplicity. Even today, when we can point to genetics, anthropology and sociology as basis for our claim that all mankind shares the same nature, rights and dignity, these simple images have their value, when properly understood.

In the New Testament, Paul picks up the theme of Adam and adds a new dimension to it. In dealing with mankind's universal and corporate salvation in and through Christ, the new Adam, Paul sets up a contrast in his Letter to the Romans. Mankind can only achieve re-creation by solidarity in Christ, the conqueror of death and the unique source of life, the first-born of all mankind. Adam, the first man, is introduced in a very subordinate role and only as a means of explaining and exalting the saving role of Christ. In extolling the wonders of our new life in Christ, Paul contrasts this condition with mankind's universal misery brought about by our share in the sinful guilt of the first man, Adam. Solidarity in life is thus contrasted with solidarity in sin, but the emphasis is clearly on the former.

The historical reality of a unique couple, Adam and Eve, from whom all men have descended by biological generation is no longer a problem. The key problem, as Pius XII pointed out in his encyclical *Humani generis*, is not Adam and Eve, but the explanation of "original sin." This is fortunate because evolutionary origins occur in populations and not through unique isolated couples. Modern genetics, paleontology and developmental biology present an almost overwhelming convergence of arguments against the descent of mankind from one unique couple, Adam and Eve.

A second story, that of Cain and Abel, complements the story of the human situation we see in the relationship between husband and wife, Adam and Eve. Once the first man rebelled against his creator and rejected his divine vocation to love others by embracing his own finite nature, what better example to show how this initial sinfulness grew and spread than a man murdering his own brother out of hatred and jealousy? Projected from the days of the Hebrew people back into the dim, unknown times of man's origins the legend of Cain and Abel takes on new dimensions and meaning. Mythically, Cain and Abel, like Adam and Eve, become classic symbols of the sinful humans we all know and are.

"Time passed, and the race of men began to spread over the face of the earth, they and the daughters that were born to them. . . . And now God found that the earth was full of men's inequities, and that the whole frame of their thought was set continually on evil; and he repented of having made men on the earth at all. . . . And God wiped out the whole world of earthly creatures, man and beast, creeping things and all that flies through the air, so that they vanished from the earth; only Noe and his companions in the Ark were left." Like a virus, sin spread throughout the human race!

After the flood Noe's descendants again populated the earth. "Hitherto, the world had had only one way of speech, only one language. And now as men travelled westwards, they found a plain in the land of Sennaar, and made themselves a home there. . . . a city, and a tower in it with a top that reaches to heaven. . . . But the Lord broke up their common home, and scattered them over the earth, and the building of the city came to an end. That is why it was called Babel, Confusion, because it was there that the Lord confused the whole world's speech." Not only was the whole of mankind sinful, but now man tried to build a monument to the heavens, a tower that would be testimony to his pride and a defense against any future deluge. The result was the ultimate in the human situation, the most complete and universal expression of the "original sin," the complete breakdown of communication in the human race.

These four myths portray in a perennial way the true human situation. When man proudly tries to play God, the absolute judge of right and wrong, the door to divine grace and life is closed to him. Symbolically he is exiled from the Garden of God's friendship. When man sets himself up as God, he commits the ultimate sin of self-idolatry; he denies his finite human nature and rejects his need for others. In Adam and Eve, Cain and Abel, Noe's neighbors and the builders of the Tower of Babel we can see all mankind and ourselves. The temptation to play God is always there to distort man's God-given goal of becoming more Christlike, a mature Christian. This maturity and its challenge is particularly evident today as the Christian, and particularly those in the Roman Catholic tradition, find themselves challenged to accept the responsibility of mature adults and transcend the silver-spooned, black and white legal morality of Christian childhood.

Up to this point we have used the term myth in describing the story of Adam and Eve as well as the other biblical accounts of our human situation. Before going on any further we should

give some precision to our use of that term. There is a perplexing tension in any serious attempt to interpret biblical prehistory.
As Joseph Blenkinsopp has pointed out, "the story of the Man
and the Woman should be read *neither as history nor as myth*
(my emphasis) but as a dramatic paradigm born of experience,
perhaps the finest and the most sophisticated piece of wisdom
writing in the Old Testament." Strictly speaking a myth deals
with the action of the gods, the intrusion of the sacred into this
profane world. But the story of Adam focuses on the actions
of man in a world which the creator blessed because it is good.
Yet the story of Eden is a form of myth, however modified, for
it expresses, in the words of the Marxist Garaudy, "the invasion
of the transcendent into man's life . . . expressed in the language
of imagination and in the terms of each epoch's conception of
the world." The Eden narrative is a perennial myth in a very
real sense. Following through with Garaudy's view, we might
say that by recounting in imaged and symbolic form how and
why evil appeared in the human race, the myth of Eden bestows
meaning on our human existence as we experience it. It presents us with a *negative* model for human behavior, an example
we should disimitate. The myth of Eden then is immensely important in our developing image of man simply because it makes
present and accessible for every age of human history and every
culture the inexplicable mystery of man's perversity.

The tension inherent in the story of Eden can best be illus-
trated in the two complementary approaches to it taken by
western Christianity over the past four hundred years. Heir of
the Greco-Roman culture with its love for the myth, Roman
Catholicism has consistently tried to tame the transcendent
mystery of evil by encasing it in the literalism of the clear,
concrete images of myth. Protestantism, on the other hand, has
followed its own proclivity for disincarnating and stressing the
transcendent element in the narrative. The Genesis stories were
generally not viewed with the literal seriousness of Catholicism,
at least as the explanation for the origins of evil in mankind.
The preference was to deemphasize much of these accounts
simply in terms of the usual florid Oriental literary styles. Thus,
without resorting to mythic explanations, John Calvin spoke of

the first man's fall perverting the whole order of nature in heaven and on earth while Martin Luther viewed man as simultaneously sinner and saint, a sinner who could achieve salvation by God's grace received through faith alone. In reality the two approaches are complementary and inseparable. The insights obtained from the mythic interpretation complement those garnered from the more abstract theoretical approach.

This interesting dual approach is evident throughout the Old and New Testament, and especially in the writings of John and Paul, the "original sin" is not presented as some isolated action long ago in the dim recesses of unrecorded human history. It is rather presented as the human situation, as mankind's solidarity in the drama of proud rebellion against love and merciful recreation through divine love.

Complex as is the human situation the biblical writers have called "the sin of the world" and we term the "original sin," we should look at the "situation-state" of man in more detail. Every man finds himself in a unique yet universal situation by the very fact that he is born into a human race where sin, rebellion, hatred, egotism and selfishness are rampant. Mankind is so bound together in social relations that one man's selfishness and inhumanity sooner or later affects all men. And this interconnection is increasing with each passing day. Each of us is situated in a sinful mankind. At the same time, however, each of us also contributes to that sinful state. In the "sin of the world" there is both a *passive* element from which we suffer and over which we have no control and an *active* element in which we contribute to the sinful state of a sinning mankind. Whether a human society is limited to a small family or tribe as it was in the days of prehistoric man, or whether that society embraces Watts, South Africa, Detroit, Moscow and Viet Nam as it does for us today, all mankind experiences the reality of the human situation.

We can draw a comparison between the biblical concept of "the sin of the world" and a child born into a family where honesty is not a virtue. (Such a situation has been well documented by social anthropologist Ruth Benedict, though our application here is based on the theologically oriented approach of Piet Schoonenberg, S.J.) Schoonenberg has asked us to picture a society where no one knows how practical and useful honesty might prove to be. They simply have never heard of the virtue. Into this situation a child is born and from the first moment of his existence he experiences the effects of dishonesty, lying, cheating and thievery. No one would blame the child for this situation for he is in the beginning a passive victim of it. Yet, no matter how good this child is, no matter how noble his intentions are and no matter how he strives to do what is right, he will never practice the virtue of honesty. As he grows up and becomes responsible for his actions, he will *inevitably and yet freely ratify this situation.* Thus he not only suffers passively from the situation, he also adds to it in an active way.

Applied to "the sin of the world" the example requires two modifications. First, our example deals with a child who finds it impossible to practice a single virtue because it is unknown in his society. The human situation we have called "original sin" affects the whole of human moral life. Second, our example deals with a single child in a small group while "original sin" afflicts all mankind.

Is there then no hope for an escape from this situation? Is man doomed to frustration, torn between his need for loving union with others and his fear of loving? The answer lies in another similarity between our example of the child and the situation-state of "original sin." The only way this child can learn honesty is for him to encounter someone from the outside world who knows and loves this virtue.

Like love, sin is contagious. Every child born into the human race enters a society where selfishness, hatred and injustice— all the inhumanity and sins of his parents, family and community affect this child's ability to love very deeply and from the first moment of his existence. Coupled with this situation, every child bears the burden of his finite nature, that "ontological defect" which demands that he transcend his own finite shell in a lifelong process of growth and which yet makes him fearful and hesitant of opening up to others in love. Before this reality the child is powerless. His only hope is a mysterious and personal encounter with the source of all love and transcendence, God.

To learn to love, to accept one's vocation to a life of loving union with our fellowman and our creator, each of us must encounter divine love made flesh. Christians have always seen this encounter with divine love as focused in the person of Christ who alone liberates man from the "powers of darkness," ignorance and hatred.

Such an encounter may come as the result of being born into a family and society where Christlike generosity and love of the parents forms a situation-state that in essence counterbalances the more widespread sinful state of the world. Having seen and experienced the selflessness of Christlike love within his family circle, the child can learn to accept his creative role in society as a finite creature. For the Christian family this birth into a new situation-state is ratified and concretized in the sacrament of Baptism. For the Christian, Baptism is an official act of the community of God's people, united in love, by which they adopt a child into that community of love. It is at once *a pledge* on the part of the Christian community to create for that person a true world of love and *a charge* for the child as he grows up to ratify, accept and meet the challenge of living in a community of love. Thus sacramental Baptism ratifies for the whole community the initiation into love first encountered by the child within his family circle. For a child born into a loving (hence Christlike) family outside the Christian tradition, this openness to love can be and is ratified by what we have traditionally but very unhappily called "baptism of desire."

It is easy to recognize now the fact that the term "original sin" is far from satisfactory in conveying the fuller meaning of the human situation presented in the whole of biblical literature. Rooted in a fixed world image and explained in terms of Platonic archetypes and Hellenic philosophy, the term "original sin" limps badly when transferred to an evolutionary context. The translation of terms from a three-dimensional perspective to an evolutionary four-dimension context is, as we emphasized before in talking about body/soul and matter/spirit, ill advised if not completely illegitimate. But what can we offer as an alternative? Again the theologians and philosophers of process thought have not agreed, but the "human situation" and Schoonenberg's "situation-state of mankind" offer good starting points.

Joseph Sitler, a noted theologian at the University of Chicago, has compared the term original sin with a pail from which we have drained all the old literal statements only to refill it with quite new interpretations. The original doctrine, as articulated in the Pelagian controversies and the decrees of the Council of Trent during the Reformation highlighted the gravity, universality and demonic results of man's propensity for evil. This reality has not changed, though our expression of it has naturally taken on a quite new language. For Jesuit Henri Rondet this new expression is best stated as "the ensemble of (the) personal sins of men of all times." For Hulsbosch, the Augustinian theologian who views man as essentially involved in the lifelong task of cooperating with God in his own creation, it represents the temptation and failure to grow. Englebert Gutwenger of Innsbruck puts it in somewhat different terms when he describes man as existing in a divinely willed state of "innate indifference" from which each of us must eventually make a decision for or against Christ, for or against a life which transcends our finite human self, for or against the eschatological life. It can also take on the rather pithy complexion used by Dr. Ray Hart, a theologian at Vanderbilt University who reminds us, in speaking of original sin, "You can count on man to be a bastard!" More often than we like to recall, this is the reality of man's situation: Hiroshima, Buchenwald, Biafra. . . .

The human situation can no longer be viewed as a static reality, as an original sin committed long ago by one man. It has to be seen as something that grows and develops as mankind grows and develops over the centuries. It is somewhat like a parasite which once having infected a seed multiplies to infect every branch, leaf and root of the growing plant. In the enlarged framework of a personal and collective awareness of mankind's sinfulness, "original sin" is no longer an isolated moment at the beginning of man's history. No longer do we have to go into long, circular explanations of why we today must suffer from the sin of one man one or two million years ago.

But more important, in this new dynamic process perspective, "original sin" loses the exaggerated importance it has been given since the high Middle Ages. Herbert Haag, a Catholic biblical scholar at the University of Tubingen, has argued quite convincingly that there is no biblical basis for the doctrine of original sin which did not begin to excite widespread theological interest among early Christians until at least the third century. Not until the fifth century, when it was formulated and named by Augustine, did it really become a formal part of the Christian doctrine. In this deeper appreciation of the biblical message, Adam is returned to his proper role as a symbol of everyman; no longer is he forced to play scapegoat for the human race. "Original sin" is a dynamic reality, the situation each of us experiences when we are born into the state of a sinning mankind, and a dynamic reality that increases in force and intensity every time we ratify and accept that sinful state in our actions. With every passing generation men continue to add to this reality. Each generation makes its own unique contribution with more maturity, consciousness and responsibility as man advances his control of the world and himself, as man and mankind grows to maturity. Consequently, the weight of inherited sinfulness increases as mankind evolves, but so also does man's sense of responsibility for others and his sense of community.

The human situation we have traditionally labelled "original sin" finds many expressions today in man's continued inhumanity to man. Wars, racial tensions and injustices, poverty, ghettos of every kind, nationalisms, colonialisms, exploitations, the arms race and starvation, these and countless other examples from the daily newspapers constitute the many faces of "original sin." As the New Dutch Catechism points out, "Adam is Man. Cain is to be found in the newspapers and may even be seen within our own heart. Noah and the builders of Babel— they are ourselves."

Reinhold Niebuhr has made an interesting and provocative comment on the function of myths in Christianity. He objects to making a myth nothing more than a fairy tale and prefers to view myths such as those found in Genesis symbolic expressions of an objective reality. Some myths express our deepest intuitions more adequately than others. "Great myths have actually been born out of profound experience and are constantly subject to verification by experience." I would suggest that the myth of Adam and Eve expresses a very profound truth, constantly verified in the experience of each man's daily life.

The fantastic realism and perennial relevance of the human situation as portrayed in biblical literature, whether this be the separation of man and woman, the murder of a brother, the corruption of Noe's neighbors and the proud builders of Babel's confusion, will never be replaced as a summary of how man stands before God and his fellow man. "But," as the authors of the New Dutch Catechism suggest, "it can and must be replaced as a description of the beginning of mankind."

Man and the "Supernatural"

Up to this point we have focused on the human situation mainly from its negative aspect. But parallel with man's sinful situation from the very beginning has been a merciful redeeming love. Divine love parallels human hatred and rebellion.

In the classical picture of "original sin" we would describe this redemptive love as "supernatural." But here again we confront terms and conceptions which have a real meaning and relevance only when used within the fixed world image of Dante, Ptolemy and Aquinas. In an evolutionary dimension the distinction between "natural" and "supernatural" levels of existence loses its orientation and meaning. The distinction is based on a certain philosophical conception of man worked out in terms of a fixed concept of creation and human nature. Whereas the thomistic philosopher and theologian speaks of a universal or general reality called "human nature" in terms of typological thought, the evolutionary view speaks of human personality, the dynamic reality which makes a man a person, "I" rather than "it," an object.

A most important and seminal analysis of this question has

been worked out by Eulalio Baltazar in his study of *Teilhard and the Supernatural*. We will rely heavily here on his critical evaluation of the problems entailed by the classic dualism of the natural and supernatural planes of life.

As Christians we have traditionally maintained that divine grace is a completely free gift on the part of God in no way owed to man as part of his nature. In this context divine grace (life) is indeed "supernatural," above and beyond the nature of man. But if this is true, then we can rightly ask why man should be concerned about this "supernatural" gift which is *not essential to his nature*. We insist that grace is supernatural and not owed to man, yet at the same time we claim that man is incomplete without it and must have it to reach his goal. The dilemma is apparent. The solution can only come, as Baltazar suggests, by shifting our understanding of man from a fixed conception of human *nature* as the *objective* basis for grace to an evolutionary conception of man as *person*, the *subjective* or *relational* basis of grace as Love. The classic thomistic approach treats divine grace as related to an objective human nature whereas the evolutionary approach treats the human person in relation to grace.

In the classic distinction between the natural and the supernatural, theologians have been very much concerned with stressing that God's gift of grace is made freely and that man has no direct claim to redemption. In this static view, man (Adam) was created with a full human nature, and immediately raised or "lifted" to the supernatural plane as a friend of God. When man rebelled, he "fell," losing that supernatural friendship with God who nevertheless in his mercy freely promised to send a redeemer. In the process image of man, with Adam symbolic of every man, this distinction between natural and supernatural has no meaning since the creation of man is a life-long work in which God, the source of all transcendence, constantly reminds and calls man to go beyond, to transcend the narrow limits of his finite personality and unite with others in a loving community. In the evolutionary view, man's very personality demands that he open himself to others. Daily he confronts a force within himself that resists and fears this openness, but at the same time he also experiences the grace (love life) of God and the redeeming example of Christ's love.

Since God freely chose to create the universe and man in a lifelong process in which man himself must be in constant dialogue and communion with his creator (Other) as he learns to express his personality in the context of society, God's love is freely given. Having chosen the evolutionary plan, God has then freely obligated himself to giving man the power and grace of transcendence. The on-going character of creation, our understanding of man as personality emerging from and in the necessary *vs* loving dependence on others, God's constant revelation and communion with all mankind and with each human person: each of these conditions our expression of the problem.

Thus God, the source of all transcendence, reveals himself to the pagan in the world of nature which calls to mind the finiteness of his own personality. In human society the person outside the Christian tradition can come to recognize his need for union with others. This "natural" revelation is just as real and effective for the pagan as is the more direct and clear revelation experienced within the Judaeo-Christian tradition. In both worlds the message is the same: no man is an island unto himself. This is the very essence of Christ's message, for the revelation and message of Christ is Christ himself, the perfect effective example of selfless love given the apostles and the world. The essence then of Christianity, of the Protestant, Roman and Orthodox Churches, is not a list of dogmas and commandments, but rather the message of divine love incarnate, of the need for and grace of transcendence.

Returning for a moment to our example of the "outsider" who introduces the child to the practice of honesty we might say that the outsider is in a way "supernatural" because he belongs to a world outside that in which the child lives. But at the same time we must recognize that he is answering a basic need which must be satisfied if the child is to develop fully. By concentrating on divine grace more as love rather than as some nebulous, supernatural force, we can see how important it is to the development of our human personalities. Without the example and grace of Christ's love, we cannot possibly live a full human life, nor develop our personalities to their fullest. This incarnation of Christ's love also takes on flesh in a very effective way in the people we associate with in every day life, particularly in the Christian family. Once again we are replacing a "god of the gaps" with a conception of God working in and through everything in this universe, continually working to create and bring it to the full perfection of participation in Christ, the first-born of all creation. Thus the universe becomes as it was for the Hebrews a true sacrament for those who know how to see. The sacrament of the universe, the sacrament of social communion, the sacrament of sexual communion, each complement and fulfill the seven sacraments.

Traditionally Christians, especially in the Roman area, have emphasized certain great Sacraments: Baptism, Confirmation, the Eucharist, Penance, Marriage, Holy Orders and the Sacrament of the Sick. In some cases this stress has been extreme to the point that we forget that Christ is *the* great sacrament of man's encounter with God. This emphasis on the seven Sacraments in the context of a fixed world image has also placed in the shadows the biblical tradition of the universe as a sacrament, saving symbol and encounter with God, his creation, love and covenant.

Today we might approach a more balanced picture by recalling that every word of man to man, and every interpersonal symbolic action signifies and imparts communion. Likewise, as Schoonenberg points out, every message and every sign of consecration that appears among the people of God signifies, imparts and nourishes the divine human communion, the life of selfless transcending love. In this context Schoonenberg has suggested in *God's World in the Making* that Roman Catholics add something to their traditional definition of the seven Sacraments. He views these as signs that communicate divine life and love, signs in which Christ's bestowal of salvation on His Church is made visible through the dialogue and interplay between the minister as official representative of the people of God, the Christian community, and the individual. To this basic definition he adds a key phrase to highlight the fact that these seven Sacraments mark *pivotal points* in man's creation: birth, adolescence, loving union at the table and repentance, the start of a family, the anointing of a new minister for the community and finally our entrance into the fullness of the beatific life. Marking these pivotal points in every man's life the seven Sacraments resume their proper place in the overall context of Christ, the Sacrament of Encounter, and the Universe, sign of the Great Covenant.

In the evolutionary image it is now possible to go beyond the dualistic concepts of nature and supernature, and deepen our understanding of the key issue at stake here. Considering the all-embracing force of Christ's love as well as the fact that in creating this universe God "saw that it was good," everything in this world becomes sacred. Everything in this world is in reality blessed by God because he is creating it and calling it, with man, to union. To participate in the creative process, man must develop the ability to see things in their proper perspective, to perceive the real meaning of things. In becoming man, the Son of God penetrated into the depths of the universe. Divine love took on flesh. The task of redemption is nothing other than each man learning to recognize and identify with *Christ in his neighbor and in the world*. Thus, instead of moving from a natural to a supernatural life, as we were asked to do in a fixed world image, we are now asked to move from an unconscious, or preconscious living in Christ's love to a fully conscious, personal embracing of our vocation to love all, all things, all men and our creator above all.

The life-long process in which man is created and creates himself is completed only through an ever growing love and communion with others that allows the full maturation of each human person in the image and likeness of Christ. From one angle, God's redemptive love is entirely required and demanded by this process of on-going creation. God must share his love-life with us if we are to achieve the fullness of our "natural" vocation. But from another angle, the gift is entirely free since God freely chose to create man in this context. Once having freely chosen the pattern of creation, the gift of divine love became a necessity.

We find a confirmation of this evolutionary approach in both the Old and New Testament, for there the conception of man is very much rooted in man as a dynamic, ever-changing person, growing towards full maturity. The biblical conception of grace is likewise dynamic. It is hardly limited to the fixed concept of grace and nature, but rather expressed in terms of love, God's personal love for man and our personal response to that love. The image of a marital covenant between man and God dominates the biblical tradition. Hence it would be a disservice to our search should we continue to reduce man's "spiritual," "religious," or "supernatural" life to a dualism concerned only with the individual's relationship with his Creator. The life of divine grace is the life of love, and as such by its very essence, it can only become vibrantly real when the individual is a true member of the community of love we call variously the Mystical Body of Christ, the Church, or the People of God.

The Transition

We can now pick up a question we left hanging in the air during our discussion of man's image in an evolving universe. Some readers may have been puzzled by the problem of integrating our evolutionary image of man as personality emerging out of the structured complexity of the universe and human society with the classic conception of death as "the separation of body and soul." Such an integration is impossible for two reasons. First, it is impossible to integrate an evolutionary view of man's nature with a conception of death drawn from a fixed world image. If we accept an evolutionary expression of man, then we must also find an evolutionary explanation of death. Second, this suggested and hoped for integration is impossible because the common explanation of death as the separation of body and soul is philosophically impossible even in terms of a fixed world image and certainly in terms of the venerable Aristotelian-thomistic explanation of man.

This second reason requires a brief explanation before we delve into exploratory attempts to work out a new theological explanation of the phenomenon of death.

The intimate and necessary relationship that thomistic philosophy attributes to prime matter and substantial form raises the question of whether either can possibly exist without the other. According to the philosophic premises of the hylomorphic theory, substantial form, which in man is the soul, simply cannot exist without some direct informative relationship with prime matter. Thus to say that death is the separation of man's soul from his body and that the soul goes to heaven, hell or a place of purgation while the body ends up in the grave is utter nonsense. Man's soul can never be without some relationship to matter and it is not enough to suggest that after death man's soul is destined to be reunited with his body at the last judgment. If we define man, in thomistic thought, as the substantial unity of prime matter/spiritual substantial form, body/soul, an explanation of death as the separation of body and soul would place man as man in a state of suspended being. From death to the last judgment, man simply would not exist as man.

In an attempt to solve this dilemma, which Aquinas found insoluble, modern theologians have tried several approaches. Among the more traditional, in the sense that it remains within the framework of Thomism and the fixed world image, is that proposed by Karl Rahner in his short essay on *The Theology of Death*.

Retaining the classic view of man as a substantial unity of body-soul, prime matter-substantial form, Rahner maintains that man's soul does not separate entirely from matter after death. He points out that a substantial form must always be in relation to or informing prime matter. This premise must be safeguarded and respected in any explanation of death. Nor can this relation be merely superficial or accidental. Contrary to the Platonic and Cartesian view, a real relationship with prime matter belongs to the very essence of man's soul.

In this context, Rahner suggests that death brings for man not a complete separation from matter, but rather *a shift in the relationship that exists between his soul and prime matter*. He urges us to view death as a final step in man's maturation, a final opening up to the material universe rather than a separation from it. At the moment of death, then, my soul transcends its limited informing relationship with the small parcel of prime matter that together with it makes up my corporeal being, my body, and opens up to embrace the whole universe of all prime matter. Instead of becoming *acosmic* at the moment of death, my soul then becomes *pancosmic*

During my life on this earth, the potentialities of my soul are limited to a great extent by the limitations of my living body, yet at the same time through my senses and my mind I do reach out to embrace the universe. In a true sense, my soul is even now pancosmic, though this relationship has not reached its fullest development. Just what the pancosmic relationship means for man after death is not at all clear. We can, however, be sure that it does not entail the idea that my soul becomes after death present throughout the universe or that the universe replaces, so to speak, my body. Still Rahner suggests that by giving up its limited bodily shape in death, the human soul opens up to the whole universe and in some way influences the totality of the world in both its physical and spiritual characters.

In the Creed we speak of Christ's "descent into hell." In Rahner's theory, this "hell" or better "limbo" is the heart of the universe. In descending into the heart of our universe, Rahner suggests that Christ established a saving relationship between the universe and the God of love. The whole cosmic order is reshaped through the Cross.

This Christological aspect of Rahner's theory brings into sharp focus the long-neglected tradition of the Eastern Churches, that of the Pantocrator, the Cosmic Christ. In death man encounters Christ in the heart of the universe for, as Teilhard de Chardin repeatedly emphasized, cosmogenesis is ultimately Chistogenesis, the birth of the Whole Christ. Death is, then, a birth into a universe transparent and transformed by divine Love.

Some aspects of Rahner's pancosmic theory are very creative and seminal, but my own reaction is that it begins on a very evolutionary tone and then quietly winds its way back to the traditional framework of a fixed world image and theology.

More recently, two other theologians have moved beyond Rahner's view in a way that seems more in keeping with the evolutionary world image, though both continue to speak of man in terms of body-soul.

Roger Troisfontaines, author of *I Do Not Die. . . .*, is a Jesuit philosopher-theologian with a strong psychological bent. Launching off from a biblical analysis of the "gift of immortality" commonly attributed to Adam in the Garden, Troisfontaines suggests that God intended man from the beginning to experience death as a peaceful transformation followed immediately by the visible resurrection of the whole man, body and soul, into the beatific life. This *death-transformation* would have been for all men a joy and consolation because it would involve the immediate and visible entrance of the whole human being into the community of saints. But, as Genesis points out in mythic symbolism, mankind from the very beginning was rebellious and proud. Because mankind and man has tried from the beginning to usurp the place of God, death, the personal encounter with God, changed from the loving meeting of faithful creature and Creator into a fearful and dreaded encounter with the God rejected in sin. Death-transformation then became for man, because of his rebellion, a death-rupture, the violent, agonizing and painful sundering of man's nature, the death of a man who has rejected God and yet must go to meet Him, leaving behind the finite treasures he made his gods.

This contrast between death as a rupture and as a peaceful transformation is evident in the death of Christ. On the cross, Christ assumed personally the burden of all our rebellion, pride and sin. He suffered to excess the death-rupture of a sinner. "My God, my God, why have you forsaken me?" The sinner dies all alone, isolated by his proud hatred and self-exaltation. The death of the saint, death-transformation gained for us by Christ on the cross, is evident in the peaceful, calm deaths of some of the martyrs and the great patriarchs of the Old Covenant who died in the fullness of years, ripe with age, wisdom and progeny. Since Christ stood in our place on the cross and experienced the excess of death-rupture, we can now approach and experience to some extent the peaceful transformation and entrance into the fullness of life God intended for man. We do this by drawing close to Christ, imitating his selfless love and becoming one with him and our fellow men in the community of love. Yet a fully peaceful death is not possible to man because of that reality we call the human situation or "original sin." Our experience of death cannot be fully enjoyed because each of us has added our personal contribution to the sinful-sinning state of mankind.

Keeping in mind our philosophical premise that death cannot be the separation of body and soul, Troisfontaines advises us to make some careful distinctions in the phenomenon of death. He suggests that death actually consists of three phases: the point at which a person suffers apparent death, the stage of clinical death which can more or less be certified by a physician on the basis of brain and heart damage, and finally the point of no return, *absolute death*. In making this distinction, Troisfontaines solves some very serious problems raised by modern medicine in the reviving of patients whose hearts have stopped beating for some time. These people have suffered apparent and clinical death but have not reached that point of no return, absolute death.

With this distinction as a basis for further exploration, Troisfontaines suggests that Christ did not die on the cross. On Good Friday Christ experienced only apparent and clinical death. It was only at the time of the resurrection that, in this theory, Christ experienced the fullness of absolute death. Christ's death coincided with his visible resurrection. To use Christ as a model for all men and suggest that God's intention was to have all men experience an immediate and visible resurrection at the moment of absolute death-transformation into the beatific life, solves a number of problems besides just the so-called separation of body and soul. Christ was sinless, and since he in no way contributed to our sinful state, his resurrection was immediate and visible. For those of us who have made our own contribution to the human situation, death never becomes quite fully what God intended. We may experience death as a transformation to a greater or lesser extent, but our death-resurrection is hidden from our fellow man until the end of this world when the heavens and the earth will be purified of all hatred and sin. Only in the fullness of time will we experience the complete death-transformation as God intends it for man.

A Hungarian Jesuit, Ladislaus Boros, S.J., has carried this one step further towards a more integrated and acceptable evolutionary explanation of death. Boros suggests that Christ's death-resurrection has opened the parousia and given us the possibility of resurrection *now*. In a sense, the parousia and the last day have already begun. Our resurrection is inchoate at the moment of death but incomplete. It is not visible to all mankind because risen man requires a transfigured universe, totally free of sin.

In the development of theology, Christian thinkers pondered the problem of what happens to man from the moment of death until the last judgment at the end of time. This hiatus had to be filled and to fill it theologians worked out the theory of a particular or private judgment at the moment of death which is ratified and made known to all mankind only on the last day. Both Troisfontaines and Boros ask why we should not also bring forward the resurrection of the whole man to the moment of death, just as in the past we brought forward the judgment. However, this raises one serious question even as it solves some others. That question deals with our traditional concept of a state of purgation, purgatory, if we link death and resurrection.*

Boros has proposed a very interesting image of this state of purification that fits well with both defined Christian doctrines

---

* It is interesting to recall that Eastern theologians, both Orthodox and in union with Rome, have always been very reluctant to go along with the classic picture of Purgatory as worked out by theologians in the Latin tradition. Likewise, as Timothy Ware in his history of *The Orthodox Church* and other theologian-historians have pointed out, the Eastern Churches have never accepted the Latin tradition of indulgences though they do believe in a state of purification after death and in praying for the dead. It seems that on this point as on so many others, the Latin Church has gone its own blissful, dogmatic way, elaborating what Peter de Rosa calls "academic make-believe" and then erecting these human constructs into idols of "unchangeable doctrine." One of the most promising notes of the post-Vatican II days is a growing sense of history and of the valid pluralism of views and explanations within the Church of Christ.

and the evolutionary image of man and death. It is quite different from the medieval purgatory of Dante and may, for that reason, prove upsetting to some. But at the same time, even in its tentativeness, it presents a picture and an explanation that is far more relevant and meaningful to modern man than the medieval anthropomorphisms of the Divine Comedy and "forty years and seven quarantines."

Purgatory, Boros suggests, should not be pictured in terms of space and time so much as in terms of existential personal encounter.

In the classic view of purgatory, a man who died without full repentance for his sins and without having satisfied divine justice by acts of penance would spend an appropriate time in Purgatory. In this place of suffering the soul of a man who died in the state of grace and friendship with God would be given the opportunity of making satisfaction for the misdeeds he had confessed but not fully repented and made satisfaction for. All the remains of our secret selfishness and sinfulness, the *reliquia peccati*, are burned away in a spiritual fire similar to the fires of hell but only temporary. The details of this image have been drawn from the medieval world of the serf and lord. A serf might be forgiven some crime by his master provided he was sorry for it, but a just lord would undoubtedly require his rebellious serf to perform some salutory act as reparation for the crime. Generally speaking this might take the form of an added period of indenture, longer hours in the field, a heavier rent or tax on the fields the serf worked. In any event, the penalty was expressed in terms of time, either directly or indirectly. The development of the idea of indulgences and of propitiatory acts and prayers for the dead follows quite naturally out of this culture and tradition.

But modern man left the pastoral world of medieval serfdom some four or five hundred years ago. Its vocabulary and traditions have become foreign and unintelligible to him. In all too many cases they represent not just harmless anachronisms, but more important and serious, they have become irritating encrustations of ages past.

The evolutionary world image offers a new perspective to

this whole problem. It offers, as Boros suggests, the opportunity to replace certain inadequate and unsatisfactory protrayals of purgatory with a conception that is fuller, more penetrating and at the same time more in touch with the twentieth-century way of thinking. Working from the evolutionary view of man as personality emerging out of the structured complexity of necessary dependence on others, man's failure to live up to his vocation and nature as a fully human person in loving union with his fellow man can take on many faces. It can be expressed (in terms of a fixed world image) as the various isolated, sinful acts of pettiness, hatred, murder, theft, dishonesty, selfishness, egotism, etc. Moral theologians today, however, are placing more emphasis on a person's overall openness or resistance to love than on the isolated, individual actions that may be in conflict with the letter of a law. The traditional concept of discrete actions, venial and mortal sins, is gradually being complemented by attention to the development of the whole personality in view of man's eternal vocation to love. The person who fails to mature remains entangled in the self-centered, egotistic world of the "spoiled brat," and the older he is physically the more evident his immaturity and failure to love others becomes. In every man there is to a greater or lesser extent some immaturity, some shortcomings in the development of his personality, some failure to love as a mature person. Some men approach very closely the perfection to which they are called in this life; others actually reach that perfection. For those who fall short of the goal, the moment of death provides the opportunity to make up for the proverbial lost time.

In proposing the hypothesis of an instantaneous but hidden resurrection of the whole man at the moment of absolute death, Boros suggests that it is only at that moment that a person is able to express his capacity for choice in its fullest and most human dimension. The decision for or against selfless love at the moment of absolute death confirms and crowns a man's life-long quest. If a man has accepted with open heart his vocation to love as a human person in union with Christ, death brings the peaceful transformation into the beatific vision. But, as we have already admitted from common sense, some men do not reach their goal even though they have opted for divine love. At the moment of absolute death, according to Boros, man encounters his Creator, personally, "face to face." Picture for yourself, a man who had chosen love as a way of life but who is still immature, adolescent and incomplete in his development as a human being and person. Face to face with his creator, with pure selfless divine Love, this man experiences all the agonies of growing up in a split instant. In a brief agonizing moment this immature person suffers all the growing pains he would have spread out over many years had he accepted more openly his vocation to love. In the personal direct encounter with Christ and God, all immaturity, all egotism, and all selfishness is consumed by divine love. The deeper and more stubborn the layers of selfishness and egotism, the more painful will be the purification of that instant. Here a purgatory of duration is replaced and clarified by a purgation-maturation in depth. Instead of forty years or seven quarantines, man's purification-maturation at death is measured by the intensity of growth pains suffered by a man in a single purifying, maturing instant of death-birth. Purgatory then takes an integral place in the life-long task of creation-growth.

This discussion of death as a final ratification of our vocation to love as human persons incorporated in the mystical body of Christ raises the question of what happens to the man who has rejected this vocation. A man can persist in his self-centeredness and self-idolatry. A man can reject love, and ultimately reject Christ. In this case, a man totally isolates himself as a windowless monad, cut off from his God, his fellow man and from the universe. The unrepentant sinner who refuses to love stands alone, destitute and cut off from all. It is not God or Christ who condemns a man to hell as eternal punishment for some violation of an arbitrary commandment somewhere in his lifetime. Rather a man condemns himself to an eternity of hatred in a world, both now and after death, where his whole being demands loving union and communion with other men and his creator. Hell, here and hereafter, is self-idolatry, the refusal to admit one's finite nature and consequent need for others, the rejection of love, of Christ. In no way does God cease to love his creatures, even those who reject his love (life). In fact, if God were to cease loving the damned, hell would no longer be hell as the pain of hell lies in the consciousness that as incomplete finite creatures our only hope for fulfillment rests in the God, universe and fellow men we have refused to love.

In this hypothesis it is clear that the old anthropomorphisms and geocentric notions of hell as a special place down below bubbling over with fire and brimstone are no longer needed. Hell is indeed still a place but it is the same world in which the blessed also live in their happiness, our world transformed and glorified by love. God cannot, according to Boros, create an evil place any more than he can create anything evil. It is the unrepentant sinner who is out of place, a misfit alienated from all. The damned live hatefully in a universe transparent with love. The final rejection of love places a man in a double alienation. Within himself the sinner is his own enemy and he knows it; but he also knows that he is not at home in the world outside. If the damned could separate themselves from all others and from themselves—which would amount to self-annihilation— then their hell would cease. The damned exist very much like the three characters of Jean Paul Sartre's play *No Exit*. To live in a world of love and to hate it!

There is a very interesting question in this regard that has often been overlooked in our theological manuals and catechisms, though it often turns up in questions from the man in the street. Basically the question is this: granted that a man creates his own hell here and hereafter by his total rejection of love, can we conceive of any human being so depraved, egotistic and self-centered as to reject totally and completely all expressions of love throughout his life and particularly at the moment of death? The answer to this question has always posed problems for the theologians and no satisfactory answer has been or ever will be found until we ourselves pass the final barrier.

The commonly accepted explanation of hell in western Christianity views hell as a place of eternal punishment for the whole man. But interestingly enough for those who are aware of theological development within the Christian orthodox tradition, two other explanations of hell have equal antiquity and in one case more weight than the commonly known explanation of an eternal hell.

The first hypothesis explains the eternity of hell as annihilation, meaning that the damned simply cease to exist. This explanation takes its origin in the opaque reference of the Book of Revelations to "the second death," which some theologians have interpreted as annihilation. Generally speaking, theologians do not give much weight to this hypothesis.

The second theory is much stronger and far more widely accepted especially in the Eastern Churches though it also has a long and strong history in the West. This is the theory of *apokatastasis* or the ultimate reconciliation of the damned with the Creator. This hypothesis suggests that after an appropriate purification or maturation all men will be reconciled with their Creator. Its strongest point is the difficulty many theologians and men in the street find in accepting the possibility that a man might totally and absolutely reject all expressions of love throughout his life. No man can live without love, in some shape or form, no matter how immature or deformed this might be. Integrated with Boros's suggestion of an instantaneous purgatory or maturation of the human person, this theory seems to be gaining more acceptance among modern theologians.

In all this discussion it should not be necessary, though it might be prudent, to recall that the area of eschatology (what happens to man at death and afterwards) is an area of extrapolation that uses our present knowledge of the world as a basis for speculation and projection.

Christ's Role in Evolution

Up to this point we have concerned ourselves with a history of cosmic evolution as it has occurred in the past. When the modern scientist and philosopher looks at this history he sees a vast cosmic process, a dynamic system which has over eons flowered in organisms ever more complex and ever more conscious. When a Christian looks at the good news brought by Christ he sees again a vast process embracing the whole universe in a dynamic growth that flowers in the freedom and love typified so clearly by Christ, the first-born of all creation. The whole of creation, St. Paul tells us, groans and travails together in the labor pains of a birth, even until now, awaiting the redemption and freedom of the sons of God.

Throughout the Old and New Testaments we find this dynamic image of the world stressed. In all the writings of the old and new covenant we find a repeated insistence on time as a characteristic of all things in our world. For the Hebrews, time was linked to the world of nature where every animal came into being and was born only after a long period of gestation and where every plant grew for many days and nights until the time of harvest came. The biblical writers constantly remind us that the Messias would only come in the "fulness of time," when the world and mankind had matured to the point where his coming could bear fruit. Incessantly they speak of a world in gestation, tending towards its fulfillment in a suffering that can only be compared with the labor pains of birth. The end of the world is portrayed as the time of birth for a new humanity and a new earth, the time of harvest when the ripened fruit and grain are gathered into the barn. The emphasis in this biblical image of the world is always on the end and not the beginning, on the long process of maturation through which all things must pass before they attain their fullest being and culmination in God at the end of time.

Over the centuries western Christians have forgotten the oriental literary genres which underly the story of Adam and Eve. Influenced also by a Platonic concept of an archetype existing in some timeless golden age "in the beginning," we have gradually lost the real impact of this story. Overstressing the "realism" of Adam and Eve in the beginning we have forgotten that Adam is every man and the figure of Christ, the perfect man. As a result a limited conception of "original sin" has been exaggerated far out of balance and proportion. The end of all this, in too many cases, is that Christians have failed to appreciate the role of Christ as the "second Adam, the first-born of all creation."

Stephanus Trooster has pointed out that even Genesis does not teach the *actual* existence of a Garden of Eden. He underlines the fact that over the years we have read into the Genesis account a historical actuality that is not required by the author and, in the process, forgotten the eschatological and etiological dimensions of this *"mashal,* an allegory, a parable." Even for the authors of Genesis, the allegory of the Garden of Eden points to the future, to a paradise to be gained rather than a paradise lost.

It is really Christ and not Adam who is the model of all creation, and particularly of man. The essence of the true Christian life is not a return to some lost paradise, but rather the daily, lifelong journey into the future, towards a fully human, open life patterned on the selfless love of Christ. In this perspective, our aim is to mature and finally die imitating the example of Christ.

The man God creates is, as Ansfried Hulsbosch emphasized, man as he shall be at the end of time. While Genesis seems to look more to the past, Paul and other New Testament writers look to the future, to Christ, the perfect Man (Adam). Yet even in Genesis there is an eschatological or futuristic note in the story of Adam.

This point deserves a brief exploration. In trying to explain and picture the first man, Adam, theologians of the early Christian church turned to a principle of Greek philosophy. Philo Judaeus, for instance, argued that an ancestor had to possess all the perfection and knowledge of all his descendants. Working from this philosophical premise, many theologians subsequently suggested that Adam had a special "preternatural gift" of infused knowledge.

During the middle ages, other theologians went even further in their attempts to make the first man a vivid concrete reality. They suggested that, before the fall, Adam had enjoyed three other preternatural gifts, freedom from pain and suffering, freedom from death and freedom from the tyranny of unbridled passions. In a fixed world image where the emphasis is on the beginning, these explanations were very useful in pointing out to men the life of perfection and happiness God intended for man. Since man had rejected this perfect life in the Garden, every man faced the challenge of regaining paradise.

In an evolutionary image a new meaning appears in these theological speculations of the past. Since our emphasis is now on Christ and on the end (rather than the beginning), let us insert the so-called preternatural gifts into this evolutionary framework and see what happens.

Certainly with the advances man has and is making in technology, in communications, in electronic computers, we are quickly moving into an age of "infused knowledge." In recent years psychologists have been exploring the very controversial but also very promising field of extrasensory perception, man's ability to communicate directly person to person without any reliance on the vocal medium. The legendary "intuition" that a husband and wife who have been married some time often claim to experience is another facet of this. It has been suggested by some scholars that as mankind matures and becomes more human, his need to depend on intermediaries like the written and spoken word may lessen. Thomas Aquinas long ago suggested that direct communication exists among the angels.* Certainly as mankind advances we are achieving

* Schoonenberg has raised the question of the actual existence of angels and devils as pure spiritual (personal) beings, a concept almost universally maintained in Roman Catholic circles. In *God's World in the Making,* he points out that the classic explanation of angels and devils received its greatest impetus in the middle ages, that the biblical revelation is very unclear on the actual existence of personal, purely spiritual beings, and finally that while many theological definitions in the Roman Catholic Church speak of angels and devils their existence is presumed rather than defined. He also suggests, and rightly so, that much of our angelology arose from an Aristotelian philosophical principle commonly known among biologists as the "Great Scale of Being."

In this light and recalling the context of Elkin's explanation of "original sin," it is interesting to raise a further question about the possible archetypal significance of our traditional conception of angels and devils. Namely, what is the *real* meaning behind the names given by tradition and biblical thought to the archangels and Satan: Michael—"Who is *like* God," Raphael—"Who heals *like* God," Gabriel—"Who speaks *for God*" and Satan—who proudly claims to be "The Bearer of Light." Could it be more and more freedom from pain, suffering and ignorance. In doubling the expected human life span in the past fifty years we are still some distance from the potential limit. Biologists have found that the average life span of all the mammals studied thus far indicates that this is roughly six times the growth and development period for a particular species. Since man's growth continues for at least twenty years, his life expectancy should be roughly one hundred and twenty years. We are still some distance from this potential limit, but in terms of Neanderthal and Peking Men we have already achieved some limited "immortality."

It may well be that in trying to picture and explain the nature and creation of man as God intended it in terms of the Garden and a fixed world image, theologians of the past were expressing in a confused, superficial way something we who live in an evolutionary universe now take for granted.

We have already seen how deeply rooted in man's nature is the need to unite with other men in love. This need extends beyond the family and tribe to embrace all the people within a society. But today, with communication, travel, television and newspapers binding the whole world into a global village, mankind is experiencing the tremendous forces of convergence that will eventually unite all mankind in one family.

For all mankind to unite in a loving and personal society requires not just the good will of individual men everywhere. It also requires a focal point around which all men can unite. On each of the earlier stages of evolution, unions only lead to the emergence of a new species or form of life when the components can center or converge around some point of focus in which the union is structured and made possible. If we extrapolate from these earlier stages of cosmic evolution on the as-

---

that Michael and Lucifer symbolize the drama of "original sin," the temptation to self-idolatry, in a pre-cosmic stage? As a result of pride, Lucifer becomes in truth "the Father of Lies," the perfect symbol of all self-deception and self-idolatry. This satanic, demonic urge every human being experiences might then be symbolized by the pre-cosmic myth of Michael and Satan, much as it is symbolized in a cosmic setting by the myth of Adam and Eve.

sumption that evolution is consistent, then we can discern certain characteristics that seem to apply to a focal point around which mankind can unite and converge. In order to achieve a differentiated union that will preserve what is essential to the integrity of the components even while binding them together, any true union of man must preserve and nourish the personalities of the men uniting. Hence the focus of human convergence must be *personal*. Mankind cannot and will not unite in an impersonal union. To attract all men who have an indestructible will to life, this point must also be *eternal*. It must offer men an effective hope for an everlasting life. At one and the same time, this focus must function within each man, and yet stand totally beyond them all. It must be *immanent* and yet *transcendent*. Love, as we have noted, is the only force that can unite men without destroying or weakening the integrity of their personalities. Thus viewed, the focus of all human and cosmic convergence must be personal, eternal, immanent and yet transcendent LOVE.

It should be quite obvious to any one within the Christian tradition that Jesus Christ, the God-Man, fulfills these requirements magnificently. Christ is the very essence of divine love become flesh, immanent and personally touching every man through the sacraments and yet completely transcending all creation, a pure and infinite person. Christ is indeed the Great Pantocrator of the Eastern liturgies, the Alpha and Omega of all creation, the beginning and end of all. He is the first born of all creation, the real Adam and the goal of all men, the Omega.

6

the road traversed
and the road ahead

So laboriously slow were the early stages of cosmic evolution it is hardly fair to the proverbial snail to use him as a basis for comparison. For countless eons, the universe practically stood still, and yet progress was made. Imperceptible in our terms of hundreds or thousands of years, evolution within the primeval oceans nevertheless did occur and from the rich mixture of protenoids and other materials the living cell eventually organized. From our evidence today it seems to have taken more than half the history of our world for this first step to become a reality. Another full quarter of our earth's history passed before plants and animals finally invaded the land. A snail's pace might be more appropriate at this point for comparison.

Some three hundred million years passed before the first mammals made their appearance on the scene. The pace quickened to a leisurely stroll as man evolved a million or two years ago. Then with the neolithic revolution some ten thousand years ago mankind experienced the "march of history." More recent times, and particularly the past two or three generations of man, have seen evolution match the speed of the "iron horse," the "horseless carriage," and then the "flying machine." Today, with its activity centered in man's socio-cultural convergence, cosmic evolution has accelerated with frightening and fantastic speed to hurtle mankind into an uncharted future, not in some distant time generations away but tomorrow. After a very slow start human knowledge, for instance, has recently reached an explosive pace. It took but a half a century for man to double all the knowledge gained by mankind from the beginning to the mid-eighteenth century. Today our accumulation of knowledge doubles with each passing decade!

The road already traversed by cosmic evolution has been tediously slow. But that is in the past and today we face the equally inconceivable fact of a fantastic acceleration. What lies ahead? Where are we headed? To attempt an answer to such questions, natural as they are, is to cast oneself in the role of prophet, and that is always a dangerous role. Yet if we look at our past history and if we look into scientific developments that are not yet common knowledge, certain concrete indications are evident.

Until the appearance of the prehominids just before the birth of man, evolution *on the general plane* can best be described as constantly diverging into countless new species and forms. Some of these managed to survive and mutate, thus adding to the variety of living organisms. Countless others suffered extinction, only to form a bridge of corpses over which the stream of evolution could pass. On each level of cosmic evolution, an initial and often lengthy phase of divergence produced an opulent diversity. On the subatomic plane, over two hundred particles; on the atomic level, ninety-two natural elements and their many isotopes; on the molecular plane, the plethora of organic and inorganic compounds; and in the world of the cell, the vastness of the animal and plant kingdoms. Many forms of life and prelife remain today only in fossil traces. Others have found a relatively stable ecological niche where they can survive and multiply for ages on end: the shark, the crocodile, coelocanthe, the one-celled animals, the invertebrates, sequoia and others. Only a minute few, blessed with a certain creative instability and lack of adaptedness, form a water gap through which new forms have arisen. *On the general plane*, and despite the occasional convergence of a group to form a new species, evolution prior to man is divergent. Very much like longitudinal meridians as they leave the pole of a globe and diverge.

With early man we notice the first hints of a shift in the pattern. In its earliest stages mankind still pursued the dialectics of divergence at least on the biological and geographical planes. As primitive man migrated across the face of the earth from his birthplace somewhere in Africa, geographic isolation and subsequent mutations brought about the formation of races and subraces. Distinct cultures and ethnic patterns appeared. But unlike the earlier stages of evolution, human divergence has not led to a full splintering of the species into new and distinct forms. Mankind has remained a single species, unique in the fact that the forces of convergence had their effect from the very earliest days of man's emergence. Fragmentation of the human species has been at most superficial, concerned only with the secondary and accidental characteristics of race. From the first moments of mankind's birth, the psychosocial forces rooted in communication and self-consciousness, in tribal and familiar instincts, overpowered the biological tendency towards divergence. However preconscious or instinctual this social cohesion might have been in those earliest days of our history, it was this convergent force and energy which allowed mankind to remain a single biological species. No matter how far into the wilderness the explorers ventured, they always retained some contact with their homeland. Geographical isolation never became complete enough to permit the evolution of a new species of man. And even if the geographic isolation were complete in some cases, it never lasted long enough for the slow forces of genetic mutation and natural selection to form reproductive incompatibility and thus a new species.

As ages passed and the human population grew within the confines of the Old World, social contact and communication between men also improved and grew in strength. The simple factor of geometric increases in the population brought men into closer physical contact with one another, sometimes friendly, sometimes in war and conquest. In either case, the effect was heightened by growing pressures of convergence on the psycho-social level and the evolution of new complexes within human life. Before 6000 B.C. the total population of the human race was under twenty million. It reached a hundred million somewhere around 300 B.C. and five hundred million by the end of the seventeenth century. In less than two hundred years more, by the middle of the eighteenth century, mankind had doubled its number to one thousand million. Early in the twentieth century, in less than a hundred years, mankind had again doubled and this will be again repeated by 1980.

Along the path of this exponential curve, some very interesting and instructive developments have occurred in man's social patterns. Tribes and tribal units replaced the smaller family and clan groupings. In the neolithic period, small city states emerged and the whole current of human evolution took on a convergent character. Mankind matured as it experienced more and more the growing tensions of urban and national communities. Despite the tensions and problems accompanying this growing convergence, the trend does not seem to be sloping off at all. Instead, even as men rebel or break down under the strain of social convergence, the pace continues to draw the network of man ever tighter. Today one quarter of the near two hundred million Americans are packed into the small coastal strip of land embracing megapolis: Boston, New York, Philadelphia, Baltimore, and Washington, D.C.

As Teilhard de Chardin and others have pointed out, mankind has now reached a point of convergence where the Age of Nations lies behind us. Mankind has entered a planetary age where all men dwell in a single village so to speak, global in scale and embrace and yet as tightly knit as any tribal society of primitive man. The task ahead involves nothing more than the creation of a new earth in which all mankind is effectively and personally joined in the human endeavor.

We have already pointed out a basic fact of the Judaeo-Christian tradition: *the coming of the Kingdom of God cannot be separated from the full evolution of man as man.* Every human being, and particularly those in the Judaeo-Christian tradition where the mystery of the divine incarnation is basic, must learn to throw himself into the task of building the earth. Man must immerse himself in the scientific endeavor, in planning, controlling, directing and perfecting his own evolution. Man, as we emphasized in our explanation of creation, cooperates with God in his own creation and in the creation of mankind. Scientific research, art, love, social and economic pursuits, all play an essential role in the fulfillment of man and the coming of the Kingdom of God.

In this context, it is interesting to note the definite relationship between the eschatological hopes of the early Christian community and the gradual shift of these hopes into the more concrete and effective area of technological development and scientific advancement of later centuries. Ernst Benz, a leading Lutheran theologian and historian, has traced this relationship in some detail, pointing out the continuity between the early Christian hopes for salvation, the Kingdom of God, the technological utopias of Thomas More, Thomas Campanella, Samuel Colt, Francis Bacon, and Johann Valentin Andreae, the social utopias of the nineteenth century, and our modern scientific culture.

If mankind is to unite in the task of building a planetary civilization, certain requirements are imposed on us by the very nature of the human person and by the past history of cosmic evolution. Perhaps we can avoid the role of prophet and stick to the more restrained ground of biological philosophy or analysis by searching our past evolution for keys to future developments. Throughout the history of evolution, convergence has led to the union of component elements and the formation or emergence of new and higher levels of existence. Yet in none of these unions is synthesis ever achieved at the expense of the individual integrity of the combining elements. No *real union* ever occurs in nature which does not differentiate and preserve the elements it unites at the very same moment it lifts them up to a higher plane of being. Thus on the human level, any union of men that destroys or weakens their personalities is actually an abortion of evolution, a miscarriage. This is a vital principle since the main axis of evolution runs through the atom, molecule, megamolecule, cell and organisms of ever increasing complexity/consciousness with little time wasted on the deadly anonymity of "unions" such as the crystal and the ant hill.

On the human level, only a union based on personal love

can preserve and nourish the human personality. Applied to human society and the conditions of mankind today, this principle reveals several important guidelines. Mankind as a whole is engrossed in a global convergence. Nations are becoming more and more interdependent as the walls of national pride and isolation crumble. We are fast approaching a world community, a crucial step in planetisation or socialisation in which men are more and more bound together in a common life. In this process it is vital that individual men become more human and more personal.

Hence the question arises, a question that causes all sorts of anxiety and concern today: does this growing convergence of mankind bring us to the monotony and anonymity of a classless society? In terms of our past history, this fate would obviously be a denial of our cosmic roots and a miscarriage of the age-old process of evolution. In the emergence of a planetary society, one nation cannot smother another just as one man cannot truly unite with another if he destroys the other's personal integrity. Even though political and economic differences must be breached to achieve an effective union of action and love, it would be a serious mistake for any nation to feel that it has everything or nothing to contribute to the task of human convergence. It would be seriously wrong for those in the western world where industry and technology are well advanced, to look on the newly emerged nations of Africa and Asia or the less technologically oriented nations of the Far East as having nothing to contribute to the advancement of society and mankind. It would be contrary to all available evidence to claim that all races and all nationalities are equal in every respect. True, in their human dignity as unique and indispensable members of mankind, all races are equal, but the basis for this dignity varies from one race to another and among the many different nationalities. Each race and nationality possesses specific traits invaluable for the whole human race. Each race and nationality has something unique and irreplaceable to contribute to the new community of man. It would be a distinct disaster if in the course of human convergence any of these treasured marks and features of individual races and cultures were lost. For the local customs and color of the French countryside, the Ukraine, the Sudan, Tibet or the Eskimo to disappear in the shadow of western technology and American efficiency would be a tremendous loss to mankind. For the folklore and native art of any people to be engulfed in an enforced imposition of western culture would likewise be an irreparable loss. Human convergence is to be achieved only through the differentiated union of components which retain their integrity and dignity in the union. The West has just as much to learn from the Afro-Asian world as those peoples have to learn from the American-European civilization. One has only to recall the sad demise of true missionary efforts by the Jesuits deNobili and Ricci in India and China three hundred years ago and the subsequent rise of pseudo-gothic and pseudo-baroque churches exported to the Orient by less perceptive Christians.

The dramatic shift in emphasis from the biological to the psycho-social has brought many important changes in human evolution. In the future these changes will become even more important as man extends his control over the biological factors of his environment. Human evolution has escaped the direct, full control exercised in the past by natural biological causes. Organic evolution operates on the raw material of hereditary characteristics within a given population in which individuals reproduce at varying rates and with varying success. Certain individuals are "selected by nature" because their hereditary make-up increases survival and, more important, reproduction. Others are eliminated because their hereditary constitution reduces viability and/or fertility. In the situation of man today we often create and control the very environment we live in. In the past animals evolved as they adapted to a changing environment; today man adapts and changes the environment to suit his needs and desires. In effect, civilization and human technology have decreased and weakened the forces of natural selection based on biological adaptation. By weakening, or even eliminating the forces of natural selection in the biological realm, human civilization has permitted many mutations to persist in the human gene pool which otherwise would have been eliminated or maintained at the minimum level produced by occasional mutations. Man today, consciously or unconsciously, selects his hereditary constitution on the basis of social fitness rather than biological adaptability.

In this context, it is easy to see how as human convergence continues, more and more emphasis will be placed on the role of social structures, particularly the state and government. Faced with the overwhelming complexities of modern urban society, individual citizens will rely more and more on government programs to assist and advance human evolution. This is already evident in the many state-wide and federal programs aimed at alleviating or controlling poverty, ghettos, air and water pollution, the care of the aged and other social problems resulting from urbanization and mechanization. In the process, inevitably and yet gradually, the classic distinctions of European and colonial American social castes will disappear. As our means of communication, travel and advanced education continue to expand, the hereditary privileged classes will dissolve in a new social structure. The equality of opportunity demanded by men around the world will itself reinforce this shift in our social patterns. Industrial and scientific research teams will replace the lonely scientist of ages past who single-handedly wrung secrets from the world of nature.

In this technological society it will soon be imperative for men and women in almost every position of life around the world to have some acquaintance with technology and science if they are to survive. In this new world the ability to survive will place a premium not on a person's family position or background, but rather on his ability to adapt to an ever changing and ever more technological way of life. In this society there will be much more room for personal variability, despite our first impression that automation, mechanization and urbanization are destroying personal and individual expression. True, these advances do hold that possibility, but one must contrast the toleration we find in the large urban areas for nonconformity and individual expression against the intolerance found in much smaller, tightly knit rural communities and towns.

One of the more important changes occurring with the appearance of man was the shift from biological to cultural evolution and the impact this has had on values within the human community. Among the prehominids, or among the higher primates today (excluding man), leadership falls to the strongest individual. In human society leadership is based more on wisdom, a characteristic rooted in the learning processes wherein time is a crucial element. With man leadership then falls to the aged. Coupled with man's growing control over disease this shift carries some important considerations for our future. Neanderthal man considered twenty-five or thirty years a ripe old age. In 1900 man's average lifespan was forty years. Today, in western Europe and North America, the average lifespan is almost double that. In America the rise has been steady, though far from spectacular, climbing 6.7 years from 1943 to 1964. In other countries, particularly those of the orient where life expectancy was quite low at the turn of the century, the shift is more dramatic. From 1945 to 1967, the life expectancy of a Japanese baby girl has doubled, from 37 to 73 years. While not as spectacular a change, the life expectancy for Americans has likewise doubled though this has taken almost seventy years from 1900 to the present.

This trend in human evolution is likely to continue in the future. In terms of man's rapidly increasing storehouse of knowledge it might be a valuable trend. However, for the present, we seem only to have extended man's life expectancy without overcoming the deterioration that accompanies life beyond the 70–80 turning point. Man today can expect to live beyond three score and ten, but he must also face the inevitability, for the present, of biological and mental deterioration beyond that point. In man's future evolution medicine will undoubtedly place more and more emphasis on the control of this deterioration in the science of gerontology.

Already some promising, though quite controverted, work is in progress testing the relationship between memory and tRNA, transfer ribonucleic acid, one of the key links in the chain between the genes of the chromosomes and the final production of proteins and enzymes. A number of recent experiments indicate that it may be possible to improve memory in older animals (whose protein and enzyme production is on the downgrade) by injected tRNA extracted from the brains of younger trained animals. It has been suggested, for instance, that there may be a definite connection or relationship between old age and the loss of memory that accompanies it. As a person ages, his body seems to lose the ability to synthesize new proteins for repair. Since memory also seems to be associated with protein synthesis, it may be that injections of RNA, the template for protein synthesis, may prove to be a remedy for both the physical deterioration and failure of memory in old age.

More recent experiments seem to indicate the clue to long term memory may rest in the millions of information bits encoded in the DNA molecules of the brain cells.

In 1957 Dr. Arthur Kornberg, of Stanford University, made the first of two important breakthroughs in this line by isolating an enzyme that will "transcribe" or duplicate the information contained in a DNA chain. Working with a cell-free, apparently lifeless system, this crucial enzyme and the proper subunits or building blocks, new synthetic DNA chains or polymers, can be produced provided natural DNA is available as a model or template. With this enzyme an unlimited number of copies can be made of almost any DNA chain, with each newly synthesized chain containing all the hereditary information of the original template or model. For this work Kornberg received the Nobel Prize in 1959.

In 1967 Kornberg carried this process one step further in the first synthesis of a biologically active DNA molecule. After eleven years of work, Kornberg produced in a test tube a totally artificial copy of an infectious DNA virus. Though the virus used contained only five or six genes this achievement has laid the foundations for the eventual synthesis of the more complex DNA found in human cells. In December of 1969 a Harvard University research team isolated for the first time a single gene, the lactase complex in a common intestinal bacterium, thus opening the last door separating man from the age of genetic engineering. If today we can isolate a specific gene which is responsible for producing a definite enzyme or protein, if with Kornberg's techniques we can then duplicate that gene in the test tube and inject it into human cells where it then functions, as has already been accomplished with mouse viruses in humans, then we stand at the threshold of manipulating man's very genetic foundation.

At a 1967 symposium commemorating the 200th anniversary of Columbia University's College of Physicians and Surgeons, Nobel-prize-winning geneticist Joshua Lederberg suggested that man may soon be able to change his characteristics and cure diseases by introducing new genes into the body. Pointing out that we already use live virus in vaccines in mass immunization programs, Dr. Lederberg suggested that genetic engineering with artificially produced DNA is simply the next logical step.

A good example of genetic engineering which, according to Lederberg, may be "technically possible" within "a few years" is the disease phenylketonuria. A child afflicted with this disease suffers brain damage and severe mental retardation because his body lacks the genes needed to convert phenylalanine to tyrosine. Normally phenylalanine is used by our cells to make new proteins, melanin pigment from the intermediate tyrosine, and in other metabolic processes. In a child suffering from PKU (phenylketonuria), certain gene(s) are missing and cannot produce the essential enzyme(s). The result is a buildup of phenylalanine, resulting in brain damage and mental retardation. A possible cure would be the artificial synthesis of these missing genes and their injection into the child's body where they would be incorporated into the cells and function as normal genes producing the needed enzyme. Such hybrid cells have already been produced with natural DNA material from mice being incorporated into living human cells. Similar treatment might remedy the enzyme-protein in balances of mental disturbances such as schizophrenia.

On a more exotic scale, and returning for a moment to our discussion of the human brain, there is an extension of the now famous heart, liver and kidney transplant operations. In some experiments with the brains of monkeys and dogs, Dr. Robert J. White, director of the neurosurgery department, Case Western Reserve University School of Medicine in Cleveland, and his colleagues, have succeeded in isolating a brain completely from the donor's body and providing it with artificial support. In some cases blood has been supplied through a small heart-lung machine while in others the blood supply came from another monkey or dog sitting in a nearby chair. Both the isolated and the transplanted brains gave normal reactions to stimulations of the visual and auditory nerves. While a brain has been transplanted or rather grafted onto another animal of the same species with temporary success both in the United States and Russia, no attempt has yet been made to replace an animal's brain with the brain from another individual. The possibilities however are undeniable, and the questions raised quite provocative.

More down-to-earth and less spectacular from our viewpoint today is the long path of technological advances that have led rapidly to the present possibility of genetic engineering and brain transplants.

To live man must eat. For the Neanderthal man who had to gnaw and tear raw meat from bones teeth were essential for survival. This is still true for the Eskimo who frequently lack wood for cooking and for their women who knead animal hides into soft clothing with their teeth. Adapting the environment to his own deficiencies and creating artificial replacements to overcome these deficiencies, modern man has taken charge of his own survival in ever greater degrees. The wooden dentures worn by George Washington and the crude eyeglasses worn by Benjamin Franklin are not very far removed in time from our modern dentures and contact lenses. In technology there is quite a gap, but the same gap exists in our mind as we look to the future. The gap is in techniques, not in time, and with the technological revolution spurred on by electronic computers the time gap may fall into an exponential curve.

Some native tribes of the South Pacific manage to eke out a precarious living by hunting sharks whose fins they sell as medicine to the wealthy Chinese of Hong Kong. In this dangerous living many individuals lose a limb or two and must then depend on the charity of others for survival. The handicap is obvious. And for countless centuries man has been almost helpless in dealing with this handicap. Babies born with a hereditary trait known as phocomelia (undeveloped arms and legs) had little if any chance of surviving. Today such children, and those with a similar condition produced by drugs like thalidomide, face a new world of opportunity despite their handicap. In the past twenty years, stimulated by medical advances during the first and second World Wars, the situation has changed drastically.

Modern bio-engineers have developed orthopedic marvels of great sophistication. Artificial arms can now be controlled by the patient himself. Impulses from tiny electrodes embedded in the eye-brow muscles or infra-red beams from a tiny source mounted in a pair of eyeglasses can trigger a properly programmed miniature computer which then activates the artificial arm to carry out a variety of movements and actions. Power for these activities can come from carbon dioxide cartridges attached to the arm-aid. A further refinement involves the embedding of electrodes in the muscles that lead to the missing arm. Thus when a person thinks about moving his missing arm the minute electrical changes, myopotentials, occurring in those same muscles can be picked up by sensitive receptors and fed into the programmed computer which then instructs the arm-aid to pick up an egg or hammer.

A wide variety of "artificial aids" are being developed by scientists who combine all the skills of doctors with the technological know-how of engineers.

Several types of electronic larynxes are now available which enable a dumb person to actually speak. In 1941 the first artificial kidney was developed. The heart-lung machine as well as a wide range of artificial hearts, from simple plastic valve replacements to electronic "pace-makers" and complete pumps, are in various stages of development and use. Nylon and dacron replacements for blood vessels, plastic bone replacements and other "miracles" of modern science no longer amaze us. What was startlingly new yesterday is old hat today. Ten years from now men may consider it quite ordinary for a blind man to "see" because a miniature television camera has been successfully attached to his optic nerve tracks.

Laser beams are now being used to "spot weld" a detached retina back in place. They can also be used in microsurgery to eliminate any need for cutting into the body to reach the diseased organ. Converging laser beams, harmless when taken separately, can cauterize and destroy a diseased part of an organ deep within a patient's body without the skin being even touched by the doctor. Aneurysms, those very dangerous balloons that sometimes form in the weakened wall of a blood vessel, can now be controlled by coating with latex, or by shooting horse hairs into them with a special microgun (pilojection) or by inserting a tiny magnet in the region and allowing metal filings to gather around it. In the latter two cases blood clots around the foreign material and reduces the danger of a rupture in the weakened wall. Blood vessels can be stapled, and FM sensor-transmittors the size of a shirt button can be maneuvered into almost any region or organ of the body to report on conditions there. Liquid crystals, which change color in response to different temperatures in the tissue they are applied to, can indicate a deep-seated malignancy or poor circulation with the doctor hardly touching the patient. Using ultrasonics a doctor may diagnose the fat content of his patient's liver or discover a hydrocephalic fetus in the uterus without touching his patient.

Fetology, the science and control of human development in the uterus, is a newly named branch of medicine and experimental biology. It brings together many different disciplines and experts from widely varied fields to focus on a crucial aspect of man's future.

Today a doctor can check on the progress of a human fetus in a number of ways. He can, for instance, take a sample of the amniotic fluid which bathes the baby in the uterus. Then, by checking skin cells found floating in that fluid, cells sloughed off by the fetus, he can tell the sex of the child. More important he may find an extra chromosome indicating an abnormal situation. At the 1967 European Cup women's track and field competition, Miss Ewa Klobukowska, co-holder of the world 100-meter dash record, was ruled ineligible because an examination of chromosomes found in cells scraped from her cheek skin revealed "one chromosome too many." A possible explanation is that the twenty-one-year-old miss is a genetic mosaic: instead of the normal XX female chromosome complement, geneticists have suggested Miss Klobukowska has two types of cells, one type containing a single X chromosome in addition to the normal complement of autosomes or body chromosomes, and the other containing one X or female chromosome and two Y or male-determining chromosomes. Such a condition produces a person who appears to be a sexually immature female, often quite tall and with underdeveloped breasts. Genetic engineering in early pregnancy might control such a distortion. If the doctor finds that a specific autosome, one of the twenty-first pair controlling general body characteristics, is duplicated so that the individual has three instead of the normal two chromosomes of this set, he knows certain enzymes will be overproduced and result in mongoloid idiocy unless corrected by medication.

A modification of this technique of sampling the amniotic fluid, known as amniocentesis, can be used to analyse the blood of the fetus. If the sample of blood indicates an Rh complication, a complete transfusion of blood can be given the fetus inside the uterus as early as the 22nd week of pregnancy. A much simpler solution is being developed which relies on immunizing the mother with injections of anti-Rh gamma globulin. Once immunized with these foreign anti-bodies, the mother's Rh negative blood will no longer respond to the antigenic effect of the fetus' Rh positive blood leaking through the placenta.

Intrauterine color television, a new development from Japanese scientists, can be coupled today with amniocentesis and other techniques to monitor completely the development of a human fetus in the womb. As a result, doctors may be able to confirm and perhaps even correct certain abnormalities like muscular dystrophy, sex-linked hereditary traits like hemophilia and delayed or ambiguous genital development in male fetuses, and the congenital blindness and severe mental deficiency associated with pseudoglioma.

Experiments in semidelivery have proven successful with a

variety of animals: lambs, dogs, and monkeys. Here a surgeon can draw the arm or leg of a fetus through an incision in the mother's abdomen and uterus. He can then operate on the limb to correct any malformation such as polydactyly (six instead of five digits). In the case of severe anemia or enzyme difficiencies he might insert a catheter which would then remain attached to the embryo during its whole embryonic life and through which the doctor could continually monitor and adjust the enzyme levels, etc. In the past five years Dr. Asensio has used semi-delivery with human fetuses at least a half dozen times at Columbia-Presbyterian Hospital in New York City. It has been suggested rather seriously that this technique opens the door to drastic manipulation of the fetus. Fantastic operations are possible on the fetus which present almost insuperable obstacles after birth, among these would be grafting or new and additional sets of limbs or even the transplanting of a whole head.

But man's newly acquired ability to modify radically his embryonic development extends, as we have already pointed out, down to the bedrock of the gene. Dr. Rollin Hotchkiss, a molecular biologist at the Rockefeller University, told the 1965 meeting of the American Institute of Biological Sciences that we can expect important breakthroughs in the area of genetic engineering before 1970. Nanosurgery, a technique using the electron microscope and laser beam, he suggested, will allow operations ten thousand times more delicate than those now possible with the microsurgery of pediatricians. Hotchkiss has already modified genes in bacteria by administering altered DNA to replot the genetic codes by which the bacteria reproduce progeny like themselves. On the basis of his own and other experiments, he is convinced that man will, in the not too distant future, be able to inject viruses bearing specific hereditary information into a pregnant woman where it would be incorporated into the information system of the embryo's cells. Much, of course, remains to be done before we reach that stage of technology.

On a more practical and real plane other possibilities are just around the corner. Scientists have already made important advances in developing a practical "artificial womb." With such a machine it would be possible to induce a very premature delivery in a mother prone to miscarriage. Her child, born perhaps only one or two months after conception, might then be placed in an artificial womb to develop to full term without any danger of miscarriage. The psychological effects of this procedure have yet to be explored both for the mother and child. What effect will the "cold" artificial womb have on the emotional life of the child when it is decanted?

A minor but interesting sidelight to this whole question of fetology has come to light at the University of the Witwatersrand, Johannesburg, South Africa. In the mid-1950s Professor Ockert S. Heyns was searching for a means of relaxing and stretching the abdominal muscles during labor to reduce the pains of childbirth. The possibility of reducing atmospheric pressure outside the abdomen by means of a small decompression chamber seemed to be an answer. A dramatic shortening of the labor period was the first result, but the use of decompression sessions from about the eighteenth week on now appears also to reduce toxemia and other dangerous conditions of pregnancy. For the child some intriguing side effects have been noted—though these deserve more detailed study before they are fully accepted as facts. Children born after a series of decompression treatments during pregnancy appear to develop faster, both physically and mentally. This may possibly be linked with improved circulation of blood in the embryo and in the uterine region produced by the relaxing decompression. Studies on South African babies indicate an 18% higher average for decompressed babies on the tests developed by child psychologist Arnold Gesell. Six "decompressed" children observed at their first birthday appeared as developed physically and behaviorally as normal two-year-olds. Since 1955 over five thousand South African births have been preceded by decompression treatments. But while thirty-six national health hospitals in Great Britain are using this technique it remains very much in the experimental realm.

The fact that man is a mammal and walks erect has had serious implications for human embryology long ignored, mainly perhaps because until recent years there was nothing man could do about the situation. An erect posture brings with it considerable alterations in our anatomy. Our spinal column is S-shaped rather than arched as in the other mammals, including the primates. Our pelvis has become massive enough to support the whole weight of our body and internal organs. At the same time our internal organs have shifted around in the abdominal cavity. These changes may well account for the fact that the human female is the only mammal to bear her offspring in intense pain and suffering. Birth is a very important biological function and for life to continue it must be as safe and functional as possible. Yet in the human, the process of childbirth opens both mother and child to the serious dangers of infection, disease and the definite risk of death. In the seventeenth and eighteenth centuries nearly twenty percent of the mothers giving birth in English hospitals died of infections. The rate of infant and maternal mortality among primitive people is very high. Granted all this, and the fact that man will likely remain an erect mobile creature, is it illogical to conceive of a solution to the problem of birth in terms of the artificial womb? May not the time come when men will consider decantation from an artificial womb as the ordinary course of affairs in the life of man?

Embryologists have known for some time that the head of the sperm bearing an X (female) chromosome is oval shaped in humans and reacts differently in an electrical field than the round-headed Y-bearing sperm. When an X-bearing sperm fertilizes an egg which in man can only carry an X chromosome, the child will be a girl; when the sperm carries a Y chromosome, it will be a boy. The chances should be fifty-fifty, and they are—in the long run. Initially, however, since the Y-bearing sperm is far more vulnerable to the acidic conditions of the female reproductive tract, and since for reasons unknown almost a third of the males conceived die during pregnancy, the father must produce far more Y-bearing than X-bearing sperm. For every one hundred girls conceived between 150 and 160 boys are conceived. At birth, however, the proportions have balanced out somewhat so that 106 males are born for every hundred girls. For over twenty years Russian cattlemen have placed seminal fluid of prize bulls in U-shaped tubes to which they applied a mild electrical current. The sperm migrate to the positive or negative pole, depending on their chromosome content. The segregated sperm can then be drawn off and used in artificial insemination of prize cows to produce offspring almost entirely male or female. If one is raising cattle for beef, an all male herd is definitely desirable. A dairyman, of course, would prefer all female offspring. Dr. Manuel Gordon, at Michigan State University, has found that with rabbits the Y-bearing sperm migrate to the negative pole and the X-bearing sperm to the positive. In using this segregated sperm, Dr. Gordon has obtained offspring that were 64% males, or 71% females, instead of the usual 50/50.

Countless experiments have been performed with success in the area of artificial insemination and fertilization. Frozen human sperm has been used successfully for insemination and in 1960 three healthy children in Iowa were fathered this way. Given an effective artificial womb, it may be possible in the near future for a child to be conceived and carried full term without any biological connection or dependence on father or mother. (And what happens to our definition of "father" or "mother" in this context?) Or an egg donated by a fertile woman might be fertilized by sperm from a sterile woman's husband and the developing zygote implanted in the sterile woman's womb to be carried full term. Working at Harvard University, Dr. Hector Castellanos and Dr. Somers Sturgis have explored another interesting avenue. After removing small pieces of ovarian tissue from healthy women and mincing them with corneas rejected by eye banks as unfit for corneal transplants, the doctors transplanted the mixture into the ovaries of barren young women in an attempt to relieve symptoms similar to menopause. A side result of some of the transplants has been that the barren women begin to ovulate in a normal way, and could thus have children of their own.

It is now a common practice for animal breeders to stimulate a champion ewe with hormone injections so that she releases a hundred or more eggs at a time rather than the usual one or two produced. These eggs can then be fertilized with frozen or fresh sperm from a prize ram, the zygotes implanted in a doe rabbit that has been tricked via hormone injections into thinking she has mated and is pregnant. After shipping the pseudo—now really—pregnant doe rabbit via air freight to some distant land, a team of veterinarians will remove the developing sheep embryos from the rabbit "incubator" and transplant them into the wombs of ordinary ewes who have also been tricked into pseudo-pregnancy by hormone injections. The end result is a prize flock of sheep produced in a single breeding season!

Even more exotic in the field of experimental embryology is the now classic work of Briggs and King. These scientists have been able to remove the nucleus from a frog or salamander egg and transplant into that ennucleated egg the nucleus extracted from a cell of a much older embryo. Depending on the age and condition of the donor cell, these eggs developed quite normally, some of them reaching the adult stage, despite the fact the the nucleus implanted in the egg came from another animal.

The ultimate in esoteric embryology is reached with certain experiments in hybrid fertilization. In this case, an egg may be fertilized by the sperm of an animal from another species altogether. Cases are known where eggs have been "fertilized" by sperm from animals in a different class or even a different phylum: thus an egg of the sea urchin *Sphaerechinus* has been "fertilized" by the sperm of the *Antedon* sea lily, and the egg of the sea urchin *Strongylocentrotus* by the sperm of the mollusc *Mytilus*.

Where Briggs and King have used nuclei from older embryos for transplantation into ennucleated eggs of frogs, Dr. John Gurdon, of Oxford University, has recently confirmed a major extension of this technique. Dr. Gurdon has successfully transplanted nuclei taken from the intestinal cells of adult frogs. Over 30% of such transplants developed into tadpoles; though, due to subtle damage with yet imperfect techniques, only 1-2% reached the adult stage and reproduced. This advance brings the possible "cloning of people" one step closer to reality. We may in the future be able to reproduce human populations asexually, by-passing completely the egg and sperm.

In somewhat the same vein is the work of Dr. Stewart of Cornell University. Working with isolated single cells taken from a mature carrot plant leaf or stem, Dr. Stewart has grown full plants. In the future it may be possible for scientists to take a single cell from the skin of some genius, artist, or writer, place it in the proper medium and end up nine months later with a fully-developed human baby identical in its hereditary constitution with the donor.

All of these varied experiments raise some very serious legal and moral questions, but the fact that they are possible and in some cases already a reality in the laboratory makes it imperative that we face now the questions and discuss them rationally.

As our science advances and our medical technology extends its control over disease, the selection pressures against certain biological handicaps is bound to decrease more and more. In ages past a child with phenylketonuria had no chance of surviving more than a few weeks. And few people with diabetes mellitus survived to have children of their own. Both of these diseases were then kept at a minimum by natural selection. Today, however, with insulin shots, special phenylalanine-free diets, etc. the person with diabetes or PKU can lead an almost normal life. The frequency of both diseases has correspondingly risen quite drastically in recent years, and seems to be pointed towards even higher frequencies in future populations of man.

Medical control of disease is one thing, but it seems increasingly evident that as our knowledge of heredity advances man will have to practice some form of genetic control. One area in which this has already been suggested focuses on the problem of sickle cell anemia. This disease affects members of the negro race exclusively, though similar anemias affect Italians, Turks, Greeks, Sicilians, Asiatic Indians and Africans who come from areas where malaria is common. The gene for normal hemoglobin occasionally mutates in such a way that the red blood cells become rigid and quite fragile. Such abnormal cells easily break down and form dangerous clots. When oxygen is scarce, these abnormal cells assume a sickle-shape, characteristic of the disease. Under ordinary conditions natural selection would eliminate this harmful mutation from the population as most children so afflicted die before reproducing. Yet in malaria-infested regions, the gene is quite common. The reason is that while sickle-cell anemia is harmful, and when a person has two mutated genes also lethal, the malarial parasites seem to have little effect on a person who has normal blood but is a "carrier" with one normal gene and one recessive gene for sickle cell anemia. Thus Negroes with two normal genes die because of malaria, those with two sickle genes die because of the anemia, but those with one of each gene live. Blessed with a "hybrid vigor" these "carriers" of sickle cell anemia survive and increase in number with each generation, despite the fact that a quarter of their children die of malaria or are subject to it and another quarter suffer from the fatal anemia.

Recently Dr. Charles F. Whitten, on the medical faculty of Detroit Children's Hospital, suggested that we could control or abolish sickle cell anemia among the American Negro if individuals were informed that they are carriers of the disease and discouraged from marrying another carrier. (In the United States where malaria is rare, Negroes with two normal genes survive and thrive whereas in Africa they would be subject to malaria.) Since the disease is recessive and only shows up when the genes from both parents are defective, a child born of the marriage of a normal person and a carrier would be either normal or a carrier. When two carriers marry, one half of their children on an average will be carriers and one quarter will have the fatal disease. Dr. Whitten has suggested that a program of genetic counseling be introduced in the high schools to inform the teenagers of this problem and to let each student know his genetic background and chances for children in marriage. We already have civil laws requiring blood tests before marriage, chest X-rays for teachers and food handlers, etc. It is possible that our preventive medicine will be extended even further in the days to come. In the case cited here however a complicating factor is the limitation of the disease to one segment of the population so that racial and minority emotions are triggered by any discussion of the problem.

Another area of great promise in man's future evolution is

the biochemistry of the human mind. Psychologists, biochemists and pharmacologists are only beginning to explore the problem of modifying the human personality, its expression and mental activities with drugs. We have very little information on how the tranquillizers, pep pills and psychogenic or psychedelic drugs work. Yet we use countless drugs today in the hopes of controlling, correcting or improving man's personality. There are some good indications that certain psychoses—schizophrenic and manic-depressive among the more important ones —may be due to faulty biochemistry in the brain which can be restored to normal by proper enzyme or drug treatment. If drugs can be used to correct a psychosis or neurosis, it may be that in the near future we will use them to improve a normal condition. We already seem to be much further along this road than most of us care to admit. Again questions about the advisability, morality and value of such steps abound on every side.

The possibilities for man's future evolution, a few of which we have explored here, are almost beyond imagination. Though we have left untouched the very important field of electronic computers, the communications media and advances in transportation, the possibilities mentioned here may sound like biological fantasies or nightmares, depending on one's vantage point. Yet we have not played the role of prophet, preferring to remain on the more solid ground of scientific prognosis rooted in the experiments going on today in the laboratories and hospitals around the world.

Confronted with these prospects many men today feel compelled to echo the words of the French poet mathematician, Pascal (1623-1662):

"When I consider the short duration of my life, swallowed up in the eternity before and after, the little space which I fill, and even can see, engulfed in the infinite immensity of spaces of which I am ignorant, and which know me not, I am frightened, and astonished at being here rather than there; for there is no reason why here rather than there, why now rather than then. . . . The eternal silence of these infinite spaces frightens me."

There is much truth in Pascal's view, and yet there is something missing in it. Pascal's world image, drawn from the ancient fixed cosmologies we examined in our first chapter, was an image shaken and uncertain. Galileo and Copernicus, the German philosophers of nature, Descartes, Francis Bacon, the young Leibnitz, and even Pascal himself were gently nudging man's thinking into evolutionary patterns and molds. Small wonder, in that revolution, that Pascal lacked an act of faith which sees in the vast process of cosmic evolution something more that a senseless, meaningless drama in which man is lost. Without falling into a naive supernaturalism or rosyglassed optimism, it is possible to see in cosmic evolution a true place for man. If man has been dethroned as the center of the Ptolemaic fixed world image, he can now take his place as the tip of evolution's arrow. Evolution can be viewed as God's way of creating the universe with man.

Viewing the world in these terms we can repeat the words of Pierre Teilhard de Chardin (1881-1955):

"The world is a-building. This is the basic truth which must first be understood so thoroughly that it becomes an habitual and as it were natural springboard for our thinking. At first sight, beings and their destinies might seem to us to be scattered haphazard or at least in an arbitrary fashion over the face of the earth; we could very easily suppose that each of us might *equally well* have been born earlier or later, at this place or that, happier or more ill-starred, as though the universe from the beginning to the end of its history formed in space-time a sort of vast flower-bed in which the flowers could be changed about at the whim of the gardener. But this idea is surely untenable. The more one reflects, with the help of all that science, philosophy and religion can teach us, each in its own field, the more one comes to realize that the world should be likened not to a bundle of elements artificially held together but rather to some organic system animated by a broad movement of development which is proper to itself. As the centuries go by it seems that a comprehensive plan is at work in the universe, an issue is at stake, which can best be compared to the processes of gestation and birth; the birth of that spiritual reality which is formed by souls and by such material reality as their existence involves. Laboriously, through and thanks to the activity of mankind, the new earth is being formed and purified and is taking on clarity and definition. Now, we are not like the cut flowers that make up a bouquet; we are like the leaves and buds of a great tree on which everything appears at its proper time and place as required and determined by the good of the whole."

a selected annotated bibliography

Alszeghy, Z. and M. Flick (1966) "Il peccato originale in prospettiva evoluzionistica," GREGORIANUM (Rome), 47:2, pp. 201-225. Summarized as "Original Sin and Evolution," THE TABLET (London), (September 17, 1966), pp. 1039-1041.

Amaldi, Ginestra (1961). THE NATURE OF MATTER: PHYSICAL THEORY FROM THALES TO FERMI. University of Chicago Press.
A technical analysis of man's understanding of matter with an emphasis on modern theories.

Anshen, Ruth Nanda, ed. (1961) ALFRED NORTH WHITEHEAD: HIS REFLECTIONS ON MAN AND NATURE. Harper & Row (New York).
Excerpts from his writings.

Baltazar, Eulalio R. (1966) TEILHARD AND THE SUPERNATURAL. Helicon (Baltimore).
A masterpiece. Details the transition necessary on the crucial question of nature/supernature. The last two chapters are vital to any understanding of process theology in the Christian framework.

Barbour, Ian G. (1966) ISSUES IN SCIENCE AND RELIGION. Prentice Hall (Englewood Cliffs, N.J.).
A scholarly analysis of many problems linking both theological and scientific insights. The Catholic views presented are generally quite traditional and do not represent more

modern Roman thought on such problems as original sin, monogenism, and matter-spirit which in liberal Roman thought often parallel the neo-Protestant views advocated by Barbour.

Barbour, Ian (1969) "Teilhard's Process Metaphysics." JOURNAL OF RELIGION (Chicago), 49:2, pp. 136-159.

Barrett, Paul (1965) "A theology of death." NEW BLACK-FRIARS (Cambridge, Eng.) 46:266-73.
A brief review of some new Roman Catholic insights.

Benz, Ernst (1966) EVOLUTION AND CHRISTIAN HOPE. MAN'S CONCEPT OF THE FUTURE, FROM THE EARLY FATHERS TO TEILHARD DE CHARDIN. Doubleday (Garden City, N.Y.).
A Lutheran historian and theologian, Benz presents an important insight into the writings of American protestant theologians of the 19th and early 20th centuries where evolutionary ideas quite similar to Teilhard were offered. Besides a brief chapter on Sri Aurobindo, this work is valuable for its history of Christian eschatological hopes and the development of technology.

Berdyaev, Nicolai (1965) CHRISTIAN EXISTENTIALISM. Donald A. Lowrie, ed. Harper & Row (New York).
A useful anthology.

Berdyaev, Nicolas (1955, 1960) THE DESTINY OF MAN. Geoffrey Bles (London), Harper & Row (New York).
A key summary of Berdyaev's thought on man, the origin of good and evil, human society and man's future.

Berdyaev, Nicolas (1954, 1962) THE MEANING OF THE CREATIVE ACT. Harper & Row (New York), Crowell-Collier (New York).
Completed in 1914, this work offers some of Berdyaev's most fruitful thoughts on creativity in terms of human sexuality, individualism, love, art, society, etc.

Bertalanffy, Ludwig von (1933, 1962). MODERN THEORIES OF DEVELOPMENT. Oxford University Press, Harper & Row. (New York).
The first statement of the "organismic biology" synthesis.

Bertalanffy, Ludwig von (1952, 1960) PROBLEMS OF LIFE. C. A. Watts (London), Harper & Row. (New York).
A classic summary and exposition of "organismic biology."
Bertalanffy, Ludwig von (1967) ROBOTS, MEN AND MINDS: PSYCHOLOGY IN THE MODERN WORLD. Braziller (New York).
Bertalanffy, Ludwig von (1968) ORGANISMIC PSYCHOLOGY AND SYSTEMS THEORY.
Volume one of the Heinz Werner Lecture Series. Barre (Mass.).
Bertalanffy, Ludwig von (1969) GENERAL SYSTEM THEORY: ESSAYS ON ITS FOUNDATION AND DEVELOPMENT. Braziller (New York).
Bertalanffy's latest three works attempt to find in the systems theory a solution to the mechanistic/vitalist dilemma.
Bonhoeffer, Dietrich (1959) CREATION AND FALL. TEMPTATION. Macmillan (New York).
Some very unusual and provocative interpretations of Genesis 1-3.
Boros, Ladislaus (1965) THE MYSTERY OF DEATH. Herder & Herder (New York).
An evolutionary interpretation of death and the afterlife despite a basically fixed conception of man and original sin. Very good on a new interpretation of Purgatory.
Burke, Carl F. (1966) GOD IS FOR REAL, MAN. Association Press (New York).
Youngsters from a city ghetto reveal their insights into biblical stories, translating these into their own language.
Chauchard, Paul (1965) MAN AND COSMOS. Herder & Herder (New York).
A very useful study of Teilhard's methodology, scientific phenomenology, by a neurophysiologist. Quite traditional on original sin and other doctrinal points.
Comfort, Alex (1966) THE NATURE OF HUMAN NATURE. Harper & Row. (New York).
The chapter on human sexuality is very helpful along with the concluding two chapters on man's future.

Cullmann, Oscar (1950) CHRIST AND TIME. THE PRIMI-
TIVE CHRISTIAN CONCEPTION OF TIME AND
HISTORY. Westminster Press (Philadelphia).
The classic study of the early Christian conception of time,
both cyclic and linear.

Daly, Mary (1968) "Dispensing with trivia." COMMONWEAL
(New York), 88:11, pp. 322-325.
A succinct comment on the meaning of Christian faith.

Defraine, Jean (1965) ADAM AND THE FAMILY OF MAN.
Alba House (New York).
The master study of "corporate personality" as a literary
genre in the Old and New Testament. Very scholarly and
technical in approach.

DeRosa, Peter (1967) CHRIST AND ORIGINAL SIN. Bruce
(Milwaukee).
A valuable integration of various aspects of original sin
with Christology. A very useful work, particularly in the
area of the expressions of original sin in modern society.

Dobzhansky, Theodosius (1956) THE BIOLOGICAL BASIS
OF HUMAN FREEDOM. Columbia University Press
(New York).
An interesting view of man's cosmic roots and the relation-
ship of human consciousness to the inorganic and sub-
human worlds.

Dobzhansky, Theodosius (1967) THE BIOLOGY OF ULTI-
MATE CONCERN. New American Library (New York).
A fine review of the vitalist-mechanist controversy, the
various theologies of a God of the gaps, evolution and
transcendence.

Donceel, Joseph F. (1967) PHILOSOPHICAL ANTHRO-
POLOGY. Sheed and Ward (New York).
Third revised edition of PHILOSOPHICAL PSYCHOL-
OGY. Extremely useful for a historical analysis and pic-
ture of developments in the Thomistic-aristotelian view of
man and nature.

Donceel, Joseph (1965) "Teilhard de Chardin and the Body-
Soul Relation." THOUGHT (New York City) 40:158,
pp. 371-389.

A traditional neo-thomistic approach, yet very creative in its use of views proposed by Barthelemy-Madaule, Schoonenberg, Rahner, Troisfontaines and Boros. The conception of death is the real focus of the article.

Donceel, Joseph (1968) "A pangalactic Christ?" CONTINUUM (Chicago, Ill.), 6:1, pp. 115-18.

A brilliant speculation on the theological implications of life on other planets and the Christology this demands.

Dourley, John (1968) "Teilhard on Creation." THE CORD (St. Bonaventure, N.Y.) 18:6-9.

This four-part article is a masterpiece, giving a detailed analysis of Teilhard's major statements on creation, and in the last part a scholarly and very profound, open evaluation and comment. The best on the topic.

Dubarle, Andre-Marie (1964) THE BIBLICAL DOCTRINE OF ORIGINAL SIN. Herder & Herder (New York).

A pioneering work by a Roman Catholic theologian; quite useful on the question of corporate personality and historical etiology.

Dyer, George J. (1967) "Theology of Death," CHICAGO STUDIES. 6:3, pp. 275-96.

A brief but good summary of new explanations of what happens to man at death. Scholarly but easily understood.

Eiseley, Loren (1960) THE FIRMAMENT OF TIME. Athenaeum (N.Y.).

A flowing, vivid portrayal of man's changing vision of nature and himself. Solid and very readable.

Eliade, Mircea (1954, 1959) COSMOS AND HISTORY. THE MYTH OF THE ETERNAL RETURN. Pantheon (New York), Harper & Row (New York).

Basic study of cyclic thought in primitive cultures.

Eliade, Mircea (1963) MYTH AND REALITY. Harper & Row (New York).

Further insights into the cyclic pattern of thought.

Elkin, Henry (1958–1959) "On the origin of the self." PSYCHOANALYSIS AND THE PSYCHOANALYTICAL REVIEW (New York), 45:4, pp. 57-76.

The basic statement of Elkin's approach to original sin in

terms of the emergence of personality in the new-born child.

Ewing, Ann (1967) "Antimatter and Creation." SCIENCE NEWS. 91:64-69.
Detailed summary of Dr. Alfen's integration of the "big bang" theory and the world of antimatter. Nontechnical.

Fannon, Patrick (1967) "The Changing Face of Theology: XI. The Last Things." CLERGY REVIEW (London) n.s. 52:12, pp. 922-928.
A summary of new views proposed by English theologians; Boros is also dealt with.

Flew, Antony, ed. (1964, 1966) BODY, MIND, AND DEATH. Collier-Macmillan (New York).
A selection of readings ranging from Hippocrates to Gilbert Ryle on the question of consciousness.

Francoeur, Robert T. (1967) "Antediluvians and the search for Adam." THE CRITIC (Chicago), 25:4, pp. 27-34.
A careful and detailed analysis of the special conference called by Paul VI to discuss new approaches to the doctrine of original sin in July of 1966.

Francoeur, Robert T. (1964) "Cacti, mushrooms and the mystical life." SPIRITUAL LIFE (Milwaukee), 10, pp. 255-62.
An early study of the relationship between psychogenic drugs and the mystical life. A more detailed and very helpful study is that by Masters and Huston.

Francoeur, Robert T. (1966) CHANGING IDEAS ABOUT MARRIAGE. Abbey Press (St. Meinrad, Ind.).
Should be read against a more detailed background provided by Daniel Sullivan's article on psychosexuality.

Francoeur, Robert T. (1966) "Death . . . and a question of growth." THE LAMP (Poughkeepsie, N.Y.), 64:11, pp. 10-11, 23-24.
Review of Boros' theory of purgatory.

Francoeur, Robert T. (1966) "The emergence of personality and 'the original sin'." DARSHANA INTERNATIONAL (Meribadad, India), 6, pp. 21-31.
Summary and critique of Henry Elkin's interpretation of

original sin as part of man's development as a person; comments on angels.

Francoeur, Robert T. (1966) "Evolution of man and the universe." CATHOLIC SCHOOL JOURNAL (Milwaukee). 66:10, pp. 24-26.
A brief statement of the present position of Catholic theology on evolution and the origin of man. Rebuttals and a reply appear in the May 1967 issue.

Francoeur, Robert T. (1966) "The influence of Teilhard de Chardin." HOMILETIC AND PASTORAL REVIEW (New York), 67, pp. 109-16.
A review of the impact of Teilhard de Chardin's evolution-, ary synthesis on Catholic thought.

Francoeur, Robert T. (1965) "The nature of self in a philosophy of being and a philosophy of becoming." RESEARCH JOURNAL OF PHILOSOPHY AND SOCIAL SCIENCES (Meerut, India), 2:2, pp. 16-29.
Analysis of Teilhard's conception of man; somewhat dated.

Francoeur, Robert T. (1965) PERSPECTIVES IN EVOLUTION. Helicon (Baltimore).
A summary of the contrasting theologies of the fixed and evolutionary world images with emphasis on the transition necessary in the area of Adam and Eve, original sin, the preternatural gifts, etc. Some points in the scientific material on human evolution dated.

Francoeur, Robert T. ed. (1961) THE WORLD OF TEILHARD DE CHARDIN. Helicon (Baltimore).
Refers particularly to James Reilly's essay on Teilhard's phenomenology and its relationship to Plato's myth in the Timaeus.

Francoeur, Robert T. (1969) "Utopian Motherhood—Window of the Future." MARRIAGE (St. Meinrad, Ind.), 51:4, pp. 4-9 and 63-68.
Survey of new developments in human reproduction with some comment on ethical implications.

Francoeur, Robert T. (1969) "Nouvelles orientations sur la reproduction humaine." IDOC INTERNATIONAL (Paris), No. 2, pp. 68-82.

Francoeur, Robert T. (1969) "And Baby Makes One: The new embryology." THE CRITIC (Chicago), 28:1, pp. 34-41.
Summary of five new developments in human reproduction.

Francoeur, Robert T. (1970) UTOPIAN MOTHERHOOD: NEW TRENDS IN HUMAN REPRODUCTION. Doubleday (New York).
A detailed analysis of man's growing technological control over reproduction and its ethical impact.

Garaudy, Roger (1966) FROM ANATHEMA TO DIALOGUE: A MARXIST CHALLENGE TO THE CHRISTIAN CHURCHES. Herder and Herder (New York).
Contains a very valuable discussion of "original sin" within the Marxist context of an evolving world image of man.

Greene, John C. (1961, 1963) DARWIN AND THE MODERN WORLD VIEW. Louisiana State University Press (Baton Rouge) and New American Library (N.Y.).
An exploration of the impact of Darwin's evolutionary biology on the religious and intellectual thought of the past one hundred years.

Haag, Herbert (1969) IS ORIGINAL SIN IN SCRIPTURE? Sheed & Ward (New York).
A Catholic biblical scholar at the University of Tubingen, Haag argues that there is no scriptural basis for the Christian doctrine of original sin.

Hamilton, William (1967) "New Thinking on Original Sin." HERDER CORRESPONDENCE 4:5, pp. 135-140.
A broad, fairly deep survey article, exposing the problems of reinterpretation and outlining new views.

Hefner, Philip (1967) "Toward a new doctrine of man: The relationship of man and nature." ZYGON (University of Chicago), 2, pp. 127-51.
A provocative, somewhat conservative approach to an evolutionary conception of man. The author presents certain basic requirements for this new view.

Hulsbosch, Ansfried (1965) GOD IN CREATION AND EVOLUTION. Sheed & Ward (New York).

A wide ranging study of the impact of evolution and biblical thought on various dogmas, especially valuable in his insights into man's nature, original sin and creation.

Huxley, Julian (1964) EVOLUTION: THE MODERN SYNTHESIS. Wiley & Sons (New York).

The basic statement of "synthetic evolution," the evolutionary synthesis that has resolved many, if not all, the problems posed by neo-Darwinism and neo-Lamarckism. Essential for any intelligent understanding of biological evolution.

Jaki, Stanley (1967) THE RELEVANCE OF PHYSICS. University of Chicago Press.

This work fills an important gap in our attempt to work out an evolutionary cosmology. Though the author is not favorable to the organismic approach of Teilhard, Bertalanffy and Whitehead, his insights offer some fruitful and stimulating parallels.

Jeanniere, Abel (1967) THE ANTHROPOLOGY OF SEX. Harper & Row (New York).

The 20-page foreword by Daniel Sullivan is a masterpiece outlining an evolutionary approach to human nature and human sexuality. The first book by a Catholic theologian to venture into the area of a fully evolutionary Christian anthropology.

Kahn, Herman and Anthony J. Wiener (1967) THE YEAR 2000. A FRAMEWORK FOR SPECULATION ON THE NEXT THIRTY-THREE YEARS. Macmillan (New York).

This 430 page encyclopedia of information is the best available at present. The data covers a wide range of topics, from international politics, cultural anthropology, urbanization, industrial and technological revolutions, economic and populational problems, war, research and social changes. Indispensable.

La Fay, Georges (1964) LA MONTÉE DE CONSCIENCE. ESSAI DE SYNTHÉSE. SYNTHÉSE DE LA PENSÉE DE TEILHARD DE CHARDIN. Les Éditions Ouvrieres (Paris).

This short work, in two parts, offers one of the best summaries of Teilhard's thought on the evolution of consciousness. The second part contains diagrammatic presentations that are very helpful.

Landers, Richard R. (1966) MAN'S PLACE IN THE DYBO-SPHERE. Prentice-Hall (Englewood Cliffs, N.J.).
A very readable account of the relationship between man, human society and a computer technology, the emerging world where machineman and manmachine come close to being identical.

Läpple, Alfred (1967) KEY PROBLEMS OF GENESIS Paulist Press (Glen Rock, N.J.)
Biblical interpretation, with some very interesting discussions of various problems of Genesis, chronologies, numbers, and symbolism.

Lohfink, Norbert (1965) "Genesis 2-3 as 'historical etiology'." THEOLOGY DIGEST (St. Louis, Mo.), 13, pp. 11-17.
Summary of the evidence for viewing this crucial section of Genesis as an example of the historical etiology literary genre.

McDermott, Timothy (1968) "Original Sin, I & II." NEW BLACK-FRIARS (London) 49:572 and 49:573.
An excellent brief summary of the traditional explanation of original sin and a review of some new interpretations.

McMullin, Ernan, ed. (1963) THE CONCEPT OF MATTER. Notre Dame University Press (Notre Dame, Ind.).
A scholarly and thorough study by 20 authors and experts. Heavy and detailed, but useful, for the expert.

Matson, Floyd W. (1964, 1966) THE BROKEN IMAGE: MAN, SCIENCE AND SOCIETY. Braziller (New York), Doubleday (Garden City, N.Y.).
A provocative interdisciplinary approach to a new image of man and his place in society.

Meilach, Michael D. (1968) THERE SHALL BE ONE CHRIST. The Franciscan Institute (St. Bonaventure, N.Y.).
A valuable collection with two outstanding essays, Ewart

Cousins' comparison of Teilhard and Franciscan Christology, and John Dourley's detailed analysis of Teilhard's
conception of creation.
North, Robert (1967) TEILHARD AND THE CREATION
OF THE SOUL. Bruce (Milwaukee).
A difficult but very fruitful study of the nature of matter-
spirit, creation of the soul, and related problems. His critical
comments and distinctions on the relation of matter and
spirit are extremely useful.
O'Manique, John (1969) ENERGY IN EVOLUTION. Garn-
stone Press (London).
Volume 3 in the Teilhard Study Library, this is a careful
and valuable treatment of the dynamics of molecular evolu-
tion with integrations with the evolution of higher forms
of reality.
Overman, Richard H. (1967) EVOLUTION AND THE
CHRISTIAN DOCTRINE OF CREATION. Westminster
Press (Philadelphia).
An excellent analysis of Whitehead's conception of evolu-
tion and creation in terms of Alfred North Whitehead's
ideas. Invaluable in this regard for a comparison and com-
plementing of the insights of Teihard.
Platt, John R. (1966) THE STEP TO MAN. John Wiley & Sons
(New York).
An interesting venture into the accelerating evolution of
man's social and intellectual nature.
Poulet, Georges (1956) STUDIES IN HUMAN TIME. The
Johns Hopkins University Press (Baltimore).
A basic study of cyclic and linear time in modern litera-
ture.
Rahner, Karl (1961) ON THE THEOLOGY OF DEATH.
Herder & Herder (New York).
An exposition of his theory of "pancosmicity" of the sub-
stantial form or human soul.
Rahner, Karl (1965) HOMINIZATION: THE EVOLUTION-
ARY ORIGIN OF MAN AS A THEOLOGICAL
PROBLEM. Herder & Herder (New York).

Interesting insights into the question of matter–spirit,
though still within the traditional fixed world image. His
metaphysical defense of monogenism has been rejected by
Schoonenberg and others as inconclusive and even invalid
as a philosophical argument.

Reese, James M. (1967) "Current Thinking on Original Sin."
AMERICAN ECCLESIASTICAL REVIEW (Washing-
ton, D.C.), 67, pp. 92-100.

A too-terse survey of a complex problem. Pope Paul VI's
private talk on original sin on July 11, 1966 is approached
completely outside the context of what happened subsequent to the pope's opening address to the 12 experts.
Reese claims that all attempts to synthesize the new theories
and explanations are "not devoid of concordism" and
states clearly that my own essays in this direction involve
the "danger of a popular approach." He obviously takes
my tentative essays as definitive solutions.

Reiser, Oliver L. (1966) COSMIC HUMANISM. A THEORY
OF THE EIGHT-DIMENSIONAL COSMOS BASED
ON INTEGRATIVE PRINCIPLES FROM SCIENCE,
RELIGION, AND ART. Schenkman (Cambridge, Mass.).

A very provocative, if controversial, attempt at a new
cosmology, based on evolution but integrating many aspects
of our modern knowledge.

Rideau, Emile (1968) THE THOUGHT OF TEILHARD DE
CHARDIN. Collins (London), Harper & Row (New
York).

The only detailed and analytic exegesis available of
Teilhard's cosmology and anthropology. Though the author
fails to take the step into a fully evolutionary cosmology
and anthropology in his commentary on Teilhard's ideas,
he nevertheless prepares the essential groundwork to a
fuller exploration of the Teilhardian venture.

Rosenfeld, Albert (1968) THE SECOND GENESIS: THE
COMING CONTROL OF LIFE. Prentice Hall (Englewood Cliffs, N.J.).

A Masterful tour of the biological revolution as applied

to control of the mind, reproduction and the make-up of the human body.

Rosnay, Joel de (1966) LES ORIGINES DE LA VIE DE L'ATOME A LA CELLULE. Les Editions du Seuil (Paris).
The finest and most lucid explanation of modern theories on the emergence of living organisms available.

Scholes, William A. (1968) "A Stride in Solar Astronomy." SCIENCE NEWS. 93:336-337.
A summary of the new radioheliography studies made with the Culgoora Australian radio disks.

Russell, John L. (1962–1963) "The principle of finality in the philosophy of Aristotle and Teilhard de Chardin, I & II." HEYTHROP JOURNAL (Oxon, England), 3:347-57; 4:32-41.
An important classic approach to the ultimate nature of things.

Russell, John L. (1960–1961) "Teilhard de Chardin, THE PHENOMENON OF MAN, I & II." HEYTHROP JOURNAL (Oxon, Eng.). 1:271-84; 2:3-13.
A very creative approach in terms of neo-thomism.

Schoonenberg, Piet (1964) GOD'S WORLD IN THE MAK-ING. Duquesne University Press (Pittsburgh).
A very important work, pioneering the new evolutionary anthropology. Schoonenberg was the first Roman Catholic theologian to really tackle the problem of expressing man's nature in terms of evolutionary monism. His insights into original sin are also important.

Schoonenberg, Piet. (1965) MAN AND SIN: A THEO-LOGICAL VIEW. Notre Dame University Press, (Notre Dame, Ind.).
A very scholarly and thorough examination of the theological development of our views on original sin. The concluding chapter gives a fine summary of the new biblical views.

Schoonenberg, Piet (1967) "Some Remarks on the present discussion of Original Sin." IDO-C (Information Document-

The latest review of Schoonenberg's views and interpretations.

Smulders, Piet (1967) THE DESIGN OF TEILHARD DE CHARDIN. AN ESSAY IN THEOLOGICAL REFLECTION. Newman (Westminster, Md.).
Quite traditional in approach, but very creative in his approach to the preternatural gifts of Eden.

Stebbins, G. Ledyard (1969) THE BASIS OF PROGRESSIVE EVOLUTION. The University of North Carolina Press (Chapel Hill).
Develops in broad outline a philosophy of nature and evolution based on recent molecular biology and current fossil evidence.

Stover, Leon E. and Harry Harrison (1968) APEMAN, SPACEMAN. Doubleday (N.Y.).
Though primarily a science fiction anthology, this collection contains some very provocative scientific prognoses, particularly in the area of cultural and applied anthropology.

Sylvia Mary, Sister. (1965) NOSTALGIA FOR PARADISE. Desclee (New York).
A provocative study of pagan and Christian myths and legends of man's creation, fall and redemption. Very helpful in appreciating the broad scope of the biblical accounts and their various interpretations.

Taschdjian, Edgar (1966) ORGANIC COMMUNICATIONS. Brown (Dubuque, Iowa).
A stimulating new approach to biology based on the General Systems Theory. Introductory comments on the origins of science give some helpful background on the relationship between science, philosophy and religion.

Taylor, Gordon Rattray (1968) THE BIOLOGICAL TIME BOMB. New American Library (New York).
Somewhat dated but still useful and interesting introduction to the whole gamut of the biological revolution in which man takes control of his own evolution.

Thomsen, Dietrick E. (1969) "The Universe's Missing Anti-matter." SCIENCE NEWS. 96:562-63.
A terse and solid summary of the conflicts between particle physics and cosmology.

Trooster, Stephanus (1968) EVOLUTION AND THE DOCTRINE OF ORIGINAL SIN. Newman (Glen Rock).

Whyte, Lancelot Law (1948) THE NEXT DEVELOPMENT IN MAN. New American Library (New York).
A penetrating analysis of the society and civilization modern man must construct if he is to survive.

Zaehner, R. C. (1963) MATTER AND SPIRIT. THEIR CONVERGENCE IN EASTERN RELIGIONS, MARX, AND TEILHARD DE CHARDIN. Harper & Row (New York).
An extremely difficult, but very provocative tour de force on oriental thought regarding the nature of man and the universe. Weak on Teilhard, but well worth the effort needed to penetrate the author's message.

Teilhard de Chardin, Pierre
(Note: Unless noted otherwise, the following books are all published by Harper and Row (New York) and Collins (London).)
(1965) THE APPEARANCE OF MAN. "The singularities of the human species" (chapter 17) is one of Teilhard's last attempts to articulate his synthetic view of man's primacy as the arrowhead of evolution.
(1960, 1965) THE DIVINE MILIEU. His classic essay on the interior life and spirituality.
(1964) THE FUTURE OF MAN. A wide ranging collection of very readable essays, touching on education, political systems, atomic power, and man's future.
(1969) HUMAN ENERGY. Contains the very important "Essay on a personal universe."
(1966) MAN'S PLACE IN NATURE. Written ten years after *The Phenomenon of Man,* this 120 page essay presents the scientific side of Teilhard's synthesis.
(1959) THE PHENOMENON OF MAN. The most de-

tailed and longest of Teilhard's writings. The classic expression of his synthesis.

(1968) SCIENCE AND CHRIST. This collection of some of Teilhard's theological writings contains the very important essay on "Super-Humanity."

(1968) WRITINGS FROM THE TIME OF WAR. Undoubtedly one of the most seminal collections in the collected works, this volume contains, among other writings, "The Cosmic Life," "Christ in Matter," "Battle against the Multitude," "The Great Monad," "The Names of Matter," "My Universe," "The Creative Union," and "The Eternal Feminine."

(1969) COMMENT JE CROIS. Contains some of the most important theological essays of Teilhard: the 1922 and 1947 essays on original sin, a 1950 discussion of monogenism, a 1920 essay on the Fall and redemption among others. Not available as yet in English. Editions du Seuil (Paris).

(1970) HUMAN ENERGY. Six major essays including "Spirit of the Earth," "Sketch of a Personalistic Universe," "The Phenomenon of Spirituality" and "Human Energy."

Unless noted otherwise, the above works by Teilhard are all published by Harper and Row (N.Y.) and Collins (London).

index